SANTAYANA

The Arguments of
the Philosophers

EDITOR: TED HONDERICH

Reader in Philosophy, University College, London

The group of books of which this is one will include an
analytic and critical account of essentially each of the
considerable number of the great and the influential
philosophers. Each book will provide an ordered
exposition and an examination of the contentions and
doctrines of the philosopher in question. The group of
books taken together will comprise a contemporary
assessment and history of the entire course of
philosophical thought.

Already published in the series

Plato J. C. B. Gosling

Forthcoming

Meinong Reinhardt Grossman

SANTAYANA

An Examination of his Philosophy

Timothy L. S. Sprigge

Routledge & Kegan Paul
London and Boston

First published in 1974
by Routledge & Kegan Paul Ltd
Broadway House, 68–74 Carter Lane,
London EC4V 5EL and
9 Park Street,
Boston, Mass. 02108, U.S.A.
Printed in Great Britain by
The Camelot Press Ltd, London and Southampton
© *Timothy L. S. Sprigge 1974*

ISBN 0 7100 7721 1

Library of Congress Catalog Card Number 73–91038

Contents

Preface	*page*	vii
Acknowledgments		ix
Abbreviations of Santayana's Works		x
Notes on the Text		xii

I Introduction — 1
1 *The importance of Santayana's philosophy* — 1
2 *Outline of Santayana's philosophical development* — 11
3 *Outline of Santayana's life* — 21

II Scepticism — 30
1 *Introduction* — 30
2 *Solipsism of the present moment* — 31
3 *Doubting the existence of an experiential flux* — 36
4 *The possibility that nothing exists* — 39
5 *Essences as the sceptic's resting point* — 42
6 *Does the given guarantee its own existence?* — 44

III Animal Faith — 47
1 *The return from scepticism* — 47
2 *Animal faith* — 52
3 *Substance* — 54
4 *The uniformity and animation in nature* — 58
5 *Santayana's epistemology in general* — 62

IV The Doctrine of Essence — 65
1 *Essences as the given* — 65
2 *Different sorts of exemplification* — 69
3 *The generic and the indeterminate* — 72

4 *Complex essences*   74
5 *Pure Being*   78
6 *Do essences have natures?*   81
7 *Internal and external relations*   82
8 *Beauty as a liberator of essences*   86
9 *The doctrine of essence*   92

V   Spirit and Psyche   95
1 *The psyche*   95
2 *Santayana and behaviourism*   102
3 *The glory and the impotence of spirit*   107
4 *Intuition and intent*   116
5 *Determination of the intended object*   121

VI   The Material World   125
1 *Treatment of matter in* The Life of Reason   125
2 *Santayana's aims as philosopher of nature*   132
3 *Indispensable and presumable properties of substance*   134
4 *Space*   138
5 *Spirit's vision of the physical world*   143

VII   Substance   148

VIII   Truth   163

IX   Truth and Time   176

X   Santayana's Ethical Theory   188
1 *The scope of Santayana's ethics*   188
2 *Value qualities*   189
3 *Reason*   197

XI   Spiritual Life   209

XII   Concluding Remarks   218

Notes   221

Index   241

Preface

In working on Santayana I have derived great benefit from discussion with various philosophical persons, to whom I should like to express thanks. First among those to whom I owe thanks is Santayana's close friend and assistant Daniel Cory, author of the splendid *Santayana: The Later Years*, the news of whose death at just about the time that my manuscript was despatched to the publishers has been a bad blow. The various conversations I had with him in Bexhill in the autumn of 1967 were especially inspiring, informative, and enjoyable. It was a rare privilege to discuss Santayana with one who had been so close to him. I had intended to thank him here also for his signal generosity in presenting me with a variety of Santayana's major books which, sad to say, are out of print. I had hoped that he would not find my book too unworthy of its subject, now that it at last sees the light. It is a sad disappointment that he is not here to see the work completed.

During the year 1968–9 when I was at the University of Cincinnati I had the opportunity to discuss Santayana with various people especially interested in him. I am particularly grateful for the long discussions I enjoyed in Cincinnati and Nashville with that outstanding Santayana expert John Lachs, which were peculiarly exciting and rewarding. Next I must thank Henny Wenkart both for showing me the Santayana sights of Harvard and Boston (our Stoic walk down Beacon Street in pouring rain while we sought to identify the home of Oliver Alden and of Santayana himself showed signal devotion to the cause on both our parts) and for our valuable discussions at that time in connection with her excellent dissertation on Santayana's thought and my own work thereon. (I should like, at the same time, to thank Mrs Todd and her sister for my delightful stay at their house while I was visiting Boston.) I also recall with pleasure discussing Santayana, in the course of that year, with two distinguished American philosophers who had known him personally, Van Meter Ames and Corliss Lamont.

I have presented Santayana's ideas to various of my colleagues at the University of Sussex and have derived great benefit from the ensuing discussion, unfamiliar as Santayana's thought otherwise was to them, for which I am grateful. This applies especially to Bernard Harrison whose comments on an early version of this work were very helpful. I should also like to thank John Watling of University College London for his comments on this early version and for all that I have learnt from him in discussion over the years. I am grateful also to Ted Honderich for the encouragement he has given me in my work on Santayana and for the stimulus provided by our somewhat opposed philosophic viewpoints. I thank also my wife, Giglia, for help of various kinds, and for having substantially supplied the biographical section of Chapter I.

I dedicate this work to my brother Robert, my earliest philosophical guide, from whose exposition I first heard, with the nominalistic indignation of a fifteen-year-old, the doctrine that there are not only the many tables on earth but also Tableness Itself in Heaven.

Acknowledgments

Quotations from the following works of Santayana are made by permission of Mrs Daniel Cory and the publishers: *The Life of Reason*; *Character and Opinion in the United States*; *Soliloquies in England*; *Poems* (1923); *Scepticism and Animal Faith*; *The Realm of Essence*; *The Realm of Matter*; *The Last Puritan*; *The Realm of Truth*; *Persons and Places*; *The Idea of Christ in the Gospels* (all first published by Charles Scribner's Sons in the USA and by Constable Publishers in the UK); from 'Bishop Berkeley' in *From Anne to Victoria: Essays by Various Hands* edited by Bonamy Dobrée (Cassell and Company Ltd); *Three Philosophical Poets* (Harvard University Press); *Winds of Doctrine* (J. M. Dent and Sons Ltd). The quotation from *Metaphysics and Common Sense* by A. J. Ayer is made by permission of the author and publishers (Macmillan, London and Basingstoke).

I should like to thank the librarians of the Houghton Library, Harvard University, and the Butler Library of Columbia University for allowing me to consult the Santayana manuscripts and books there. The quotation from a holograph note by Santayana in his own copy of *Philosophical Essays* by Bertrand Russell, now in the Houghton Library, is used by permission of the Harvard College Library.

Abbreviations of Santayana's Works

AFSL   *Animal Faith and Spiritual Life*, ed. John Lachs
BR   *The Birth of Reason and Other Essays*, ed. Daniel Cory
COUS   *Character and Opinion in the United States*
DL   *Dialogues in Limbo*
DP   *Dominations and Powers*
EGP   *Egotism in German Philosophy*
HW   *My Host the World: Vol. III Persons and Places*
ICG   *The Idea of Christ in the Gospels*
IPR   *Interpretations of Poetry and Religion*
Letters   *The Letters of George Santayana*, ed. Daniel Cory
LR   *The Life of Reason, or The Phases of Human Progress*
LRI   Vol. 1: *Reason in Common Sense*
LRII   Vol. 2: *Reason in Society*
LRIII   Vol. 3: *Reason in Religion*
LRIV   Vol. 4: *Reason in Art*
LRV   Vol. 5: *Reason in Science*
MS   *The Middle Span: Vol. II Persons and Places*
OS   *Obiter Scripta, Essays and Reviews*, eds J. Buchler and B. Schwartz
PGS   *The Philosophy of George Santayana*, ed. P. A. Schilpp
POML   *Physical Order and Moral Liberty*, eds John and Shirley Lachs
PP   *Persons and Places: The Background to My Life*
PSL   *Platonism and the Spiritual Life*
RB   *Realms of Being*
RE   *The Realm of Essence: Book First of Realms of Being*
RM   *The Realm of Matter: Book Second of Realms of Being*
RS   *The Realm of Spirit: Book Fourth of Realms of Being*
RT   *The Realm of Truth: Book Third of Realms of Being*
SAF   *Scepticism and Animal Faith*

SB   *The Sense of Beauty*
SE   *Soliloquies in England and Later Soliloquies*
STTMP   *Some Turns of Thought in Modern Philosophy: Five Essays*
'System' 'System in lectures'
TPP   *Three Philosophical Poets*
WD   *Winds of Doctrine*

Notes on the Text

References are to the original editions of the works in question. The abbreviations of titles are explained in Chapter I, pp. 11–13, and in the list on p. x.

The references to RB (*Realms of Being* – one volume edition) may be converted into references to the original four separate volumes thus:

Pages xxv–xxxiii of RB are peculiar thereto, consisting in an additional introduction.

Pages v–xix and 1–180 correspond to the same pages of RE (*The Realm of Essence*).

Pages 183–92 of RB correspond to pages v–xiv of RM (*The Realm of Matter*).

From page numbers 193–398 of RB subtract 192 to find corresponding pages of RM.

Pages 401–6 correspond to pages v–x of RT (*The Realm of Truth*).

From page numbers 407–546 of RB subtract 406 to find corresponding pages of RT.

Pages 549–54 of RB correspond to pages vii–xii of RS (*The Realm of Spirit*).

From page numbers 555–854 of RB subtract 554 to find corresponding pages of RS.

It should be observed that my account of Santayana's position is derived from a thorough study of Santayana's work as a whole and that the references usually draw attention to only a few of the relevant passages. So scattered are Santayana's remarks on a given topic that it would be a life's labour to assemble all the passages on which one's interpretation is based.

I

Introduction

1 The importance of Santayana's philosophy

Although it is generally recognized that George Santayana is an important figure in the history of American philosophy, academic philosophers, especially in Britain, tend to pay little attention to his work today. There is a tendency to suggest that he is in truth a literary figure rather than a philosophical one, and more justice has been done to his importance as a thinker by those who, in our specialized world, take literary or cultural criticism as their field rather than philosophy. But though Santayana's literary criticism, his novel, and his poetry, certainly deserve attention, his importance as a philosopher is greater. Not only was he at one stage an influential figure in American philosophy, more by way of his earlier than his later writings, but, and this is far more important, his writings, especially his later ones, elaborate a philosophical system of great intrinsic value, from the study of which our contemporary philosophers could learn a great deal. Such, at least, is the opinion which inspires the present book, and I hope that my reader will come to see its justice. What I am offering is something between an introduction to, and a commentary on, his philosophy, that is, his ontology, his epistemology, and his moral philosophy. (I shall only deal in passing with his aesthetic theory, and shall virtually omit consideration of his political philosophy.) It can be called an introduction inasmuch as I shall not assume any prior familiarity with Santayana's work, but in other respects it is a rather more thorough and ambitious enterprise than that term suggests. The aim is to expound and discuss in some detail Santayana's treatment of a wide range of issues of concern to philosophical minds, both in the narrow sense in which 'philosophy' is usually now understood in universities and in a wider sense.

The first thing which must strike one who opens a philosophical work of Santayana's is the style, rich in poetic resonance and alert with epigram. According to his nature, he will either be attracted or repelled thereby. No admirer of Santayana can really wish that he had written otherwise, but this beautiful style does have its disadvantages. First, it frequently suggests to philosophers of the dustier kind that his work belongs solely to the world of *belles lettres* or, still worse, is of the 'uplifting thoughts' genre and this prejudices them against paying it serious attention.[1] Second, for those in whom beauty does not rouse this kind of prejudice, there is a danger of being lulled by the hypnotic cadences into a state where critical faculties and thorough understanding are at a low ebb. In truth, Santayana's philosophical books are much tougher and more difficult in their content than they may appear at first, and are not likely to be understood properly without the kind of hard work which everyone expects to undertake in reading such philosophers as, for example, Russell or Whitehead.

Actually Santayana's style, in spite of its rhetorical and poetical character, is at the same time a highly concentrated, economical and effective mode of communication for those attuned to it and who do not demand a legalistic inflexibility in a philosopher's language. Points which would each take a chapter or more to develop in more academic philosophical writings, follow upon each other so thick and fast that they are easily missed. It is true that this economy is a consequence of his not dotting every i and crossing every t in the manner of a G. E. Moore. Not every consequence one might think of, or every conceivable alternative, or every unintended interpretation which a reader who has missed the main line of his thought might foist upon the words, is followed up or dismissed in detail; yet it is often evident from subsequent passages or from other writings, that Santayana had thought the matter out in more detail than at first appears. Since it is not every reader who has the time or the appropriate sympathy to grasp all this, a commentary which will unpack some of his highly concentrated theses and arguments is most desirable, and this, together with some exhibition of the relevance of his philosophy in the present intellectual scene, and some critical comment, is what the present work is intended to provide.[2]

Lately some of Santayana's manuscripts not prepared by him for publication have been published.[3] It is interesting to note that many of these develop in pedestrian detail points tossed off in the published works in a brief epigram, and show that he had quite clearly articulated in his own mind consequences and connections which the reader of his finished works is left to draw for himself.

Nothing can be more untrue than that Santayana was a thinker of various undeveloped separate insights.[4] His later philosophy has the merits, if also some of the demerits, of that of a thorough systematizer (in spite of the fact that, as a supporter of what he regards as the orthodoxy of common sense, he sometimes presents himself as an opponent of philosophical systems in general). Every position is developed with an eye to its place in the whole system. It is curious that anyone should have failed to recognize this (and indeed those few who have seriously studied his works always have realized this, but he is sometimes thus dismissed by those who have been put off by some impression which a casual glance at his pages has given them), but perhaps there is this much excuse. Though Santayana developed in his own mind, after meditations lasting many years, one of those total philosophical systems which has a place for everything, a system remarkably clear, cogent and complete, the actual presentation of it is in some ways unsystematic. One can seldom find a single place where all the essential features of his treatment of some single issue are gathered together. His best remarks on a topic are often found in a chapter, or in a book dealing, on the face of it, with some quite other matter.

Sometimes this manifests rather an unconventional categorization of issues than a failure in systematic presentation. Philosophers have increasingly tended to think in terms of a set list of philosophical topics: perception, other minds, induction, universals . . . and expect a philosophical work in a certain area of philosophy to treat of them one by one. Santayana's discussions of these stock topics are scattered among chapters each of which has a unity arising from some less stereo-typed set of conceptual connections. This makes a difficulty, incident-ally, for a teacher of philosophy who wishes to introduce readings from Santayana into the reading lists provided for his students, since one cannot point to some single chapter or essay which gives his treatment of some recognized topic on which students work. This may contribute to the neglect of Santayana among academic philosophers.

The conventional categorizations of philosophic issues have their value and one thing I seek to do in this book is precisely to offer a presentation of Santayana's theories divided up in these more familiar ways, thereby facilitating a comparison with other, and especially current, theories on these topics.

But I am not writing only for the academic philosopher or student. Santayana is a writer of interest to a far wider range of thoughtful people than this, especially to many of mainly literary interests. While this book is concerned with Santayana rather as a philosopher than as a literary or social critic, novelist, or poet, I hope that such readers may find this book of value as a study of this side of his genius, even if they are not well acquainted with the history or present tendencies of philosophy.

Santayana is, in my opinion, a major philosopher. His epistemology – quite misrepresented by common reference to him as merely an example of radical scepticism – offers a solution to many disputes in this field which is relevant to current philosophic controversy. Still more important is his ontology. It is regrettable that discussion of the status of what are often called Platonic entities should be carried on (much of it at Harvard of all places)[5] in complete ignorance (one presumes) of the most sustained attempt in modern times to present a kind of demythologized Platonism.

Most important of all for us today is Santayana's treatment of mind, and of moral and spiritual values, from the point of view of a philosophy which is, in one important sense of the word, materialist. Santayana held that man is a physical thing among other physical things and that all those movements and speech acts which constitute his behaviour are ultimately explicable (in ways certainly as yet unknown) in terms of laws of a basically physical kind. Now this is a view which more and more people are adopting today, both professional philosophers, psychologists, and others. They adopt it, moreover, not with the kind of regret with which some moved towards it in the nineteenth century but with a sort of fierce joy in it as putting paid to any notion of an inner source within us of imaginative and spiritual creativity. Such thinkers are faced, on the other hand, by others who, sensitive to the spiritual and aesthetic values which seem to be given no place within this scheme, try to show that man is not simply an object among other objects for the natural sciences to study, and the burden of whose thought is therefore in a manner obscurantist. In fact debate over the nature of the mind and imagination of man, and of the status of so-called private experiences, has in a manner taken the place of the debate over God and the Bible in the nineteenth century, with the computer designer and the artificial intelligence unit taking the place of the geology and evolutionary biology which were developing in those days. In all this I think that Santayana has an especially valuable message for us, for his is an out-and-out materialism (in the sense that for him all proper explanation is by reference to physical laws) which actually provides a grounding for an essentially religious or spiritual view of life and a recognition of an aspect of man which though physically determined is not itself physical. The same thing has, of course, been attempted by others but not with the same clarity of mind and depth of insight.

Santayana, as I have indicated, has been largely neglected by philosophers in recent decades, though there is certainly quite a revival of interest in him as a literary and social critic, especially in the USA.[6] At one time, however, he was recognized, at least in the USA and to some extent, it seems, in France and Italy, as a major philosopher, and

4

there have, of course, always remained those who have recognized his worth.

As a Professor at Harvard (from 1889 to 1912) he had the somewhat disturbed respect of such elder colleagues as Josiah Royce and William James as the skilled and charming propounder of a somewhat sinister type of thought. His first publication was a volume of poems, but his *The Sense of Beauty* (published in 1896) when he was thirty-three soon gained him some respect as a philosopher. The work which really put him on the map of American philosophy, however, was the five volumes of *The Life of Reason* (1904–5). These had a great influence in the USA, especially in the development of the philosophic movement known as *naturalism*. At that stage philosophers in the USA were still concerned with the discussion of substantial questions of value, while the movement towards a narrowly academic discipline remote from any attempt to come to terms with the basic problems of human existence, which really only overcame American philosophy after the Second World War, was already in gradual growth in Britain. That the volumes attracted less interest in Britain is understandable considering that, on the one hand, they were not the sort of work greatly to interest those concerned like Russell (who was himself, however, on the whole, an admirer of Santayana)[7] to see philosophy develop into a somewhat recondite specialist science or calculus[8] of no special interest to the general affairs of men (for though Russell was, as we all know, a man of deep and active social concern there is little organic link between this and his philosophy, and he was a main herald of the somewhat dessicated analytical philosophy which followed) while, on the other hand, their frankly naturalist or materialist outlook was hardly designed to appeal to the surviving metaphysicians, who shared Santayana's more humane conception of the role of the philosopher, as one primarily concerned to deepen our sense of life's basic values.

Santayana's earlier reputation as a writer on broadly humanistic and cultural themes has stood in the way of his acceptance by philosophers as a serious writer on the more abstract themes of epistemology and ontology. His mature treatment of these latter is first exhibited at some length in *Scepticism and Animal Faith*, published in 1923 when he was close on sixty years old, and it appears to have commanded a fair amount of interest when it first came out. Whitehead, in particular, considered it a work of first rate importance.[9] However, the various volumes of *Realms of Being* which followed seem to have had a rather small readership, especially among professional philosophers. A contributory factor was his complete retirement for many years past from the academic world. Influential philosophers, for some time past, have tended to be those whose pupils at some 'top' university have carried their message abroad.

One must bear in mind the heady excitement caused by various new winds of thought which were beginning to blow at that time, mostly either connected with technical developments in logic or with developments in psychology. Philosophical revolution was in the air, and metaphysical systems were under attack. Santayana was neither a traditional metaphysician still there as a dragon to be slain, nor was he a fellow fighter in the modernist cause, while his philosophy was quite remote from any developments in logic. That it was not quite so remote from developments in psychology was not noted. He was simply 'out of key with his time' (far more so, it would seem, than the author of these words, his fellow resident in Rome, Ezra Pound) quietly pursuing his own preoccupations in detachment from all contemporary controversy. Remote, also, these books may have seemed to those caught up more strongly in the international politics of the late 'thirties, so that Santayana may have found fewer readers among the general intelligentsia than he had done in earlier years.

It appears, then, that Santayana's ontology was published at a time when an ontology undertaken without an elaborate logical apparatus was least likely to catch attention, and thus never got caught up into the main stream of the philosophic community's consciousness, impressive as it has always seemed to some, especially in America.

The time is now, I believe, propitious for doing greater justice to Santayana's ontology. Many would now acknowledge that the basic issues of philosophy were much less altered by developments in symbolic logic than at first seemed to be the case. It is true that there is still a general devotion to the 'linguistic turn' in philosophy, but at least ontology is beginning to be recognized in some quarters once more as at the heart of philosophy.

I have already suggested one curious prejudice which the English-speaking philosophic reader must surmount if he is to give Santayana the attention which his philosophy deserves, a prejudice which, I believe, has stood in Santayana's way since the 'twenties, namely the belief that a beautiful literary prose, ornamented with many playful metaphors, cannot be the vehicle of serious thought on first principles.

Bertrand Russell taught the lesson that philosophy should be concerned like science with a dry search for truth, and not with picturing the world in some emotionally pleasing fashion. Thus any impression of rhapsodic uplift has been enough to condemn a work to remain unread beyond a casual glance.

'Rhapsodic uplift' would be a most incorrect description of Santayana's writing. Not only is his view of things not particularly optimistic but his style, full of metaphors as it may be, is, as I said, a fine vehicle for the concentrated expression of complicated abstract thought. Still, a preliminary glance at his writings might give those, anyway unsympathetic to his doctrines, a sense that some description of this sort is applicable.

It is, indeed, true that Santayana's writings do offer a poetic celebration of a certain view of things, and do invite one to the adoption of certain emotional attitudes. In some ways he is reminiscent of Lucretius, whom he much admired. Claims are made, and arguments given for them, but the view of things thus proposed becomes also a vision of the world to be poetically celebrated and communicated by appropriate literary devices.

To my mind the poetic celebration of a well supported view of things is something to be grateful for, provided the strictest reasoning and intellectual clarity are there also. Perhaps the former has sometimes tended to dull the latter, and this may give some excuse for the suspicion with which philosophers are wont to look at beauty in philosophic writings, but no such dulling is to be found in Santayana. The emotional resonance of his language goes with a highly concentrated presentation of subtle intellectual discriminations. It would be silly to think that Santayana's style requires apology. I only note that as a matter of fact it does seem to put off some people who would surely find the actual intellectual content of Santayana's thought highly instructive.

In any case, sharp reasoner though he was, Santayana held a different view of the place of argumentation in philosophy from that of most 'professional' philosophers. Reasoning, he held, is a preparation for vision rather than an end in itself. Consider his remarks upon philosophical poetry as exemplified by Lucretius, Dante, and Goethe:

If we think of philosophy as an investigation into truth, or as reasoning upon truths supposed to be discovered, there is nothing in philosophy akin to poetry. There is nothing poetic about the works of Epicurus, or St Thomas Aquinas, or Kant; they are leafless forests. . . . The reasonings and investigations of philosophy are arduous, and if poetry is to be linked with them, it can be artificially only, and with a bad grace. But the vision of philosophy is sublime. The order it reveals in the world is something beautiful, tragic, sympathetic to the mind, and just what every poet, on a small or on a large scale, is always trying to catch.

In philosophy itself investigation and reasoning are only preparatory and servile parts, means to an end. They terminate in insight, or what in the noblest sense of the word may be called *theory*, Θεωρία – a steady contemplation of all things in their order and worth. Such contemplation is imaginative. No one can reach it who has not enlarged his mind and tamed his heart. A philosopher who attains it is, for the moment, a poet; and a poet who turns his practised and passionate imagination on the order of all things, or on anything in the light of the whole, is for that moment a philosopher. (*Three Philosophical Poets,* pp. 8–11)

Santayana diverges still further from the dominant note of Anglo-American philosophy in recent years when he denies that it is the special role of the philosopher to be in a state of puzzlement about things. In the Preface to a collection of his poems he says:

For as to the subject of these poems, it is simply my philosophy in the making. I should not give the title of philosopher to every logican or psychologist who, in his official and studious moments, may weigh argument against argument or may devise expedients for solving theoretical puzzles. I see no reason why a philosopher should be puzzled. What he sees he sees; of the rest he is ignorant; and his sense of this vast ignorance (which is his natural and inevitable condition) is a chief part of his knowledge and of his emotion. Philosophy is not an optional theme that may occupy him on occasion. It is his only possible life, his daily response to everything. He lives by thinking, and his one perpetual emotion is that this world, with himself in it, should be the strange world which it is. Everything he thinks or utters will accordingly be an integral part of his philosophy, whether it be called poetry or science or criticism. (*Poems* (1923), pp. xii–xiii)

The divergence of such opinions on the nature and scope of philosophy from those current in the universities of the English speaking world today scarcely requires emphasizing. Such a statement as the following is, I think, representative of the current view that philosophy has no particular connection with the discovery of a satisfactory way of living:

That the philosopher is indifferent to everyday concerns, because his gaze is fixed on higher things, and that he therefore is able to bear misfortunes calmly, is a doctrine which was made popular by the Stoics. It is, indeed, one of the curiosities of history that although the Stoics contributed nothing of interest to philosophical theory, their image of a philosopher is still the predominant one. It is enshrined in our language, 'To take things philosophically' means to react like a Stoic. I need hardly say that this image nowadays bears little relation to the facts. No doubt academic persons still tend to lead cloistered lives, but philosophers are not more cloistered than the rest, rather the reverse: neither, as a class, do they seem to be any less nervous and irritable than the general run of scholars. There is indeed no good reason why they should be. (*Metaphysics and Common Sense,* A. J. Ayer, p. 1)

Such a tone of voice is far from that of Santayana, for whom the ultimate purpose of philosophical dialectics is to arrive at a synthetic vision of the world and of one's own place in it, at once intellectual and aesthetic, which may inform the character of one's life and thought as a whole. Here surely Santayana is at one with Plato, Aristotle, Spinoza, Schopenhauer, Bradley and Whitehead, to mention only a few who could hardly be jettisoned from the philosophical pantheon even by the driest of conceptual analysts.

I do not wish, at this point, to engage in debate on the proper scope of philosophy. There is no doubt that in the case of Santayana an imaginative vision of the world, a way of life, and a set of opinions on matters which the most academic of academic contemporary philosophers would admit as belonging to his specialism, are found in close connection with one another, but whether this is a good thing or a bad thing does not affect one point which I am especially anxious to make: namely that Santayana's views are important and relevant to the settling of the problems of philosophy viewed in the narrowest manner, and that the current feeling, right or wrong, that philosophy of life is one thing, and philosophy as a specialist intellectual discipline is another, has prevented recognition of this fact, by creating a sense that Santayana's work is not worth the serious attention of the professional or academic philosopher.

The main purpose of the present work, therefore, is to offer a detailed account of Santayana's mature epistemology and ontology, with some treatment in the final chapters of his ethics and his analysis of spirituality. The main sources for this are *Scepticism and Animal Faith* (SAF) and the four volumes of *Realms of Being* (RB), but there are many other writings which are essential for any full grasp of his position.

Santayana's final system of philosophy was firmly settled in all its main details by the time that SAF was published, when he was almost sixty. I shall not be much concerned with tracing the stages through which his thought developed prior to this time, though I shall on occasion consider contrasts and affinities between the earlier and the later work. Moreover, there are a number of cases where positions on which he did not substantially change his mind are developed in more detail in the earlier writings (especially in *The Life of Reason*) so that a concentrated later statement of the point can only easily be grasped by reference back to an earlier presentation of the point. I shall, in any case, be closing this chapter with a brief survey of his philosophical output, followed by a brief outline of his life.

Santayana was steeped in the history of philosophy, and he did not so much strive for originality as for a total balanced view incorporating what was sensible in each of the main traditional philosophies. It is not so much for any single theory that Santayana is to be admired, as for the total system in which the positive insights of so many different philosophies are shown to be complementary when properly qualified. [10] But although his separate positions can often be said to be simply that of X or Y or Z presented afresh, his system is not merely eclectic, but rather an original synthesis of the insights of many philosophers usually thought to be divergent. Moreover, just as, according to Santayana, an essence is in a certain sense not the same essence when taken in isolation as when it figures as an element in some more complex essence, so are these various insights not quite the same insights when figuring in Santayana's unique synthesis as when they figured in different and less balanced systems. (In fact, this is an example of, rather than merely analogous to, Santayana's thesis regarding complex essences.)

If I hesitate to use the word 'synthesis' here, it is on account of its Hegelian associations which are somewhat inappropriate in this connection. I mean only that Santayana's system grants truth to a great many positions, when once purged of their dross, advanced by philosophers who are normally thought of as antagonists in their outlook, e.g. Democritus, Plato, Aristotle, Descartes, Locke, Hume, Fichte, Schopenhauer, and William James. There is no question of Santayana thinking of every philosophical theory as a moment in the final truth of things. Many familiar doctrines are given quite flat and quite undialectical denials, e.g. any such view as that *spirit* is the basic power in the world.

Sometimes in reading Santayana, I have thought: 'But really most of what Santayana is saying is just Locke refurbished' or 'just Descartes refurbished'. But then I have found another earnest reader of Santayana (in this case John Lachs) who has at times thought: 'Well, really most of Santayana is just Aristotle presented in a modern guise'. Bertrand Russell appears once to have said that Santayana's philosophy all came from Leibniz, [11] while I have found others who see in his work mainly a restatement of Hume. One might see him also as a modern Platonist (rather than an Aristotelian). Well, if Santayana's philosophy were somehow the systems of Plato, Aristotle, Locke, Leibniz and Hume rolled into one consistent whole that would surely make it something rather remarkable. Besides, what philosopher presenting a total system by the twentieth century could really expect it both to be substantially true and totally original in all its main positions? Those who get too excited about a revolution in philosophy run the risk of jettisoning the accumulated wisdom of the ages by presenting some modest technical advance as the very heart beat of a true philosophy. In fact, the one field in which humanity definitely does advance, exact scientific knowledge, seems to leave the main philosophic issues fairly much where they were. With some important exceptions, one cannot isolate some single proposition in Santayana's treatment of a given philosophic issue and say that he was the first to think of it or argue for its truth, but one can say that a highly original and creative mind is shown in the total philosophic system which he constructed, and that it is a system which deserves and will repay close scrutiny.

The connection of Santayana's thought with such a particularly wide range of philosophers of the past,[12] so that he does not belong simply to one tradition but is in a manner the heir of so many, does pose his expositor with something of a problem as to the extent to which he shall enter into comparisons and source indications. I have not set out to do this in any systematic way. It will take me time enough to present and discuss Santayana's system, without continually pointing out just where it coincides and where it departs from that of earlier thinkers who took something like the same point of view on some issue, though there are occasions where it seemed especially worth while to do this. For the same reason I have not spent much time on detailed comparisons of Santayana's positions with that of philosophers of the present day, though I have often had such in mind.

2 Outline of Santayana's philosophical development

The chief writings from Santayana's pen, especially, but not only, from a philosophical point of view are as follows:

1889   *Lotze's System of Philosophy* (doctoral dissertation posthumously
       published for the first time in 1971).
1894   *Sonnets and Other Verse.*
1896   *The Sense of Beauty* (SB).
1899   *Lucifer: A Theological Tragedy.*
1900   *Interpretations of Poetry and Religion* (IPR).
1901   *A Hermit of Carmel, and other poems.*
1905   *The Life of Reason, or, The Phases of Human Progress* (LR).
       Vol. I: *Reason in Common Sense* (LRI).
       Vol. II: *Reason in Society* (LRII).
       Vol. III: *Reason in Religion* (LRIII).
       Vol. VI: *Reason in Art* (LRIV).
1906   Vol. V: *Reason in Science* (LRV).
1909–
1910   'System in lectures' ('System').
       (These are notes for lectures given in these years, which were
       first and posthumously published in *Review of Metaphysics*,
       Vol. X, no. 4, June 1957. They were edited for publication by
       Daniel Cory.)
1910   *Three Philosophical Poets* (TPP).
1911   'The Genteel Tradition in American Philosophy.'

(Address delivered before the Philosophical Union of the University of California, 25 August 1911. Published in the *University of California Chronicle*, Vol. 13, no. 4 (11 October 1911) and reprinted in revised form in *Winds of Doctrine* (see below).)

1913   *Winds of Doctrine* (WD).

1915   'Some Meanings of the Word Is', *Journal of Philosophy, Psychology and Scientific Methods,* Vol. 12, no. 5, 4 March. (An early version of the 1924 article.)

1916   *Egotism in German Philosophy* (EGP).

1918   'Literal and Symbolic Knowledge', *Journal of Philosophy, Psychology and Scientific Methods*, Vol. 15, no. 16, 1 August.

1920   *Character and Opinion in the United States* (COUS).
         'Three Proofs of Realism', *Essays in Critical Realism* by Durant Drake *et al.*

1922   *Soliloquies in England and Later Soliloquies* (SE).

1923   *Scepticism and Animal Faith* (SAF).
         The Unknowable; The Herbert Spencer Lecture Delivered at Oxford, 24 October 1923. Published by the Clarendon Press, and reprinted in *Obiter Scripta* (1936).

1924   'Some Meanings of the Word "Is"', *Journal of Philosophy*, Vol. 21, no. 13, 3 July. (Reprinted in *Obiter Scripta*.)

1926   *Dialogues in Limbo* (DL).

1927   *The Realm of Essence: Book First of Realms of Being* (RE).
         Platonism and the Spiritual Life (PSL).

1930   *The Realm of Matter: Book Second of Realms of Being* (RM).
         'A brief history of my opinions' in *Contemporary American Philosophy*, eds. G. P. Adams and W. Montague.

1931   *The Genteel Tradition at Bay.*

1933   *Some Turns of Thought in Modern Philosophy: Five Essays* (STTMP).

1936   *The Last Puritan: A Memoir in the Form of a Novel.*
         (Lest this title mislead it may be pointed out that it is more truly a novel in the form of a memoir.)
         Obiter Scripta, Essays and Reviews, eds. J. Buchler and B. Schwartz (OS).

1938   *The Realm of Truth: Book Third of Realms of Being* (RT).

1940   *The Philosophy of George Santayana,* ed. P. A. Schilpp (containing 'A General Confession' and 'Apologia pro Mente Sua' by Santayana himself (PGS).)

1940   *The Realm of Spirit: Book Fourth of Realms of Being* (RS).

1942   *Realms of Being* (One volume edition. This is complete, and not, as is sometimes stated in print, a shortened version. It contains an additional Introduction of some importance (RB).)

1943   *Persons and Places: The Background to My Life* (Autobiography vol. 1) (PP).

1945   *The Middle Span: Vol. II Persons and Places* (Autobiography
       vol. 2) (MS).
1946   *The Idea of Christ in the Gospels* (ICG).
1951   *Dominations and Powers* (DP).
1952   (Santayana's death.)
1953   *My Host the World: Vol. III Persons and Places* (Autobiography
       vol. 3 (HW).)
1954   *The Life of Reason* (shortened version prepared by Santayana and
       Daniel Cory).

This list is not a bibliography.[13] It merely gives the date of first
publication of each of Santayana's books, prepared as such by himself,
and also a very few of those of his articles and so on which seem to be of
outstanding philosophical importance, and in some cases indicates in
brackets the abbreviation of their title which will often be used throughout this book. The following five collections of writings by Santayana
should also be listed, each of which contains important material either
not previously published or not previously published in book form:

1955   *The Letters of George Santayana*, ed. Daniel Cory (*Letters*).
1957   *The Idler and His Works*, ed. Daniel Cory.
1967   *Animal Faith and Spiritual Life*, ed. John Lachs.
       (This also collects together essays by various hands on Santayana
       (AFSL).)
1968   *The Birth of Reason and Other Essays*, ed. Daniel Cory (BR).
1969   *Physical Order and Moral Liberty*, eds John and Shirley Lachs
       (POML).

Santayana's poetry is mostly of a philosophical character, though
some of it tended to mislead readers as to his actual outlook. Perhaps
the most important work in this connection is *Lucifer*.

It was with *The Sense of Beauty* that Santayana first appeared as a
philosopher in print (apart from some early pieces in Harvard periodi-
cals). This work was based on a lecture course in aesthetics which he had
been giving at Harvard. Writing of it in later years, he dismissed it as
pretty well a potboiler, demanded from him as an American academic.[14]
Ironically, it is the work of his which seems to have been subjected to
far the most discussion. Its central thesis is that beauty is the feeling of
pleasure taken in contemplating an object, projected on to it so as to
seem a quality of the object itself and not simply of our reaction to it.
It also discusses the psychological and physiological explanation of the
fact that certain objects do and others do not seem beautiful. Santayana
did not wish to disparage beauty by thus analysing it. Indeed he urged
that the experience of beauty was the highest value in man's life.

The work made an impression because it combined a thoroughly naturalistic and down-to-earth account of aesthetic experience, pointing out, for instance, its sexual basis in many cases, without being in any way iconclastic or 'debunking'. Here is a familiar Santayanian theme hinted at, that the roots of good are humble and naturalistic, but that the unearthly flower is not therefore to be valued the less.

Santayana gave a rather different account of beauty in his later works, grounded in a sounder analysis of the perceptual situation,[15] and it is a pity that so many readers are familiar with this alone among Santayana's works.

Interpretations of Poetry and Religion, a collection of essays, gives more explicit expression to many characteristic views of Santayana's, such as later take their place, somewhat transformed, as parts of his total mature system of philosophy. One can sum up the main themes briefly as follows: Religion is poetry applied to life, and poetry is a kind of religion existing in a certain sort of detachment from practice. At their best the two would coincide. The conceptions of Christianity are literally false, but they provide a poetical statement of many truths about human life and a way of looking at things such as induces emotions appropriate to man's actual condition. This is the book, incidentally, which William James described as 'the perfection of rotteness'.[16] The thesis to which James particularly objected was that the aesthetic contemplation of ideal forms of life is a good in itself, which rather gives value to action than derives its own value from the action to which it prompts.

Thus far Santayana appears to have been admired for the beauty of his writing and the precision of his thought, but regarded as somehow sinful and un-American, one who would lure youth away from the world of deeds and enterprise for which a decent educationalist should prepare it, to a dream world of poetic reverie, without even having the decency to pretend (as would the usual sort of metaphysician) that it had a real existence in some transcendent realm. The quarrel between idealist and pragmatist, united as they were on the need to infuse a spirit of optimistic endeavour into their pupils, was a mere family quarrel between protestant reformers beside the debilitating temptations to lotus eating held out by the sinister Spaniard with his strange relation to the Roman church.[17]

In the years 1905–6 Santayana published the five volumes of *The Life of Reason* and was at last considered to have gained some sort of respectability.[18] On the whole this work could be regarded as morally robust (almost 'manly' – James's word of highest praise) and reforming in spirit. Even the sub-title 'The Phases of Human Progress' was encouraging. Santyana now seemed to preach the need for vigorous action inspired by the vision of ideal goods, and to condemn inactive contemplation. Moreover, the period in which 'the philosophy of naturalism' was to become an inspiring slogan for the young academic was beginning,[19] and Santayana was accepted as one of the leaders in this movement, almost worthy to rank beside the ever brightening light of John Dewey.

How far had there been a change in Santayana's standpoint?

Such classifications as 'poetic quietism' and 'idealistic activism' are really very crude terms in which to think of a philosophy so rich, complex, many sided and balanced, as that of Santayana. It has been said that the sanity of Santayana is more frightening than the madness of others,[20] and if there is truth in this remark, it is precisely because he always refused to be pushed into any conventional classification of thinkers such as automatically carries with it some set of conventional allegiances. His aim was to recognize the element of validity in all points of view and to show how they relate to one another; not to become a partisan of any conventional party viewpoint, nor, in Hegelian fashion, to see each one as intrinsically pointing on to the next, but rather as each containing separable aspects of truth and error. Having so many sided a total philosophy, it was bound to happen that the different works give different degrees of emphasis to its various aspects.[21]

Insofar as the central thesis of *The Life of Reason* may be summed up in a paragraph, it might be somewhat as follows.

Every impulse of a conscious being carries with it a sense of the goodness of its object, and that object may truly be said to be a good for that impulse, so that if that impulse stood alone, that good would be a good as absolute as good could be. However, both within the single individual, and still more within society, there are many opposing impulses, setting up rival goods and condemning each other's goods as evils. There is, however, one impulse which has arisen in human life, with this special character, that it is an impulse to have as many other impulses satisfied as possible in a manner harmonious one with another. The name of this higher order impulse is Reason. Reason itself has no heaven-sent right to control other impulses, it is simply an impulse which has its own vision of the good life. So far as men share this vision they can co-operate in bringing about its aims. Reason never condemns any impulse as evil in itself, it simply seeks to integrate rival impulses together, and to check, without distaste, such impulses as cannot be thus integrated. *The Life of Reason* sketches the extent to which the main branches of human thought and activity, common sense concepts, social organization, religious beliefs and institutions, art, and science, have been or might become instruments of the life of reason thus conceived.

It is easy to see that such a conception would appeal, to those who had thought of his earlier work as the perfection of rottenness, as a far more inspiring and healthy minded affair, and that they would welcome him as an ally in the pragmatist or instrumentalist cause. Religion, art, etc., were now judged for their use, it seemed, and not simply as satisfying indulgences for the scholarly hermit. (Indeed the hostility to Santayana's later writings on the part of many American intellectuals sprang from a feeling that he had returned to the cult of aesthetic self-indulgence and away from the inspiring ideals of *The Life of Reason*.) [22]

Doubtless, Santayana's viewpoint had developed, and in a direction which one may even agree was more healthy minded. However, there were vital differences between him and his admirers, or so at least it later seemed to Santayana, [23] which tended to go unobserved at the time, and which supplied the thread of connection with his earlier thought.

One of the things which Santayana found most alien in the ideology suggested in the works of James and Dewey, was the valuing of everything for what it might lead on to. [24] Knowledge was valued not because the having a sense of how things are is in itself a satisfaction, or a value, but because it produces effective activity, while that activity and its results is itself only valued for its further effects. Santayana had a strong sense that value must ultimately lie in something which can be rested in with satisfaction for its own sake, and not for its results. It is this theme which inspires much of the quietism of the earlier and later writings; restless busy-ness or distraction is the evil Santayana is most concerned to attack. It is one element of the puritanism he condemns in his novel.

Connected with this antipathy to busy-ness is the fatalistic element in Santanyana's thought, with its implication that though one should enjoy ideal states of society to the extent that they come, and enjoy the thought of them when absent, there is little that can be done in the way of deliberately realizing these aims, seeing that the course of history is determined at a much deeper level than that of the fluctuating visions of the good in any individual consciousness. [25]

These themes are not absent in *The Life of Reason*, but they are less prominent than are other seemingly more activist trains of thought. He tends here rather to take the view that for Reason, impulses which simply end in their own satisfaction are of little importance beside those which contribute to the satisfaction of many other impulses as well. [26] This comes out particularly in his treatment of Art. (It is also to be found in his treatment of poetry in *Interpretations*, but *The Sense of Beauty* has a rather contrasting tone.) Emphasis is laid on the superiority of art which is at once practical and aesthetic in its values (and thus part of, rather than a rest from, daily life) over merely 'fine' art.

One cannot describe Santayana's view of art as a utilitarian one in the usual sense of that term. His position is rather that satisfaction in what is immediately given to consciousness is too important to be left to periods of so-called leisure, and that in a really civilized community everything in the daily round is both an immediate satisfaction and an instrument to some remoter good. Everything will then be both good in itself and good as a means.

Actually, there is much here that is common to Santayana and Dewey, and also to James. Yet somehow there is a difference in total impact. For Dewey and James the immediate satisfactions of which they some- times talk seem to be rather elementary sensational processes, whereas for Santayana the most memorable satisfactions, and therefore the ones susceptible of the most deliberate pursuit, take the form of intelligence in act rather than of some dumb swoon. [27] Separation of the aesthetic and the intellectual leaves only an impoverished version of each for Santayana, and their junction in philosophical poetry is the highest form of each. Santayana's idea that the free mind will not value ideas solely for their truth-value may sometimes seem to bring him near to the I. A. Richards who taught that, since in poetry and informational prose quite different ends were in question, emotional adjustment and grasp of facts, it would be to the benefit of each were they kept more sharply distinct than has usually been the case. But there is really a large difference. Even when the incubus of *fact-finding* is laid aside, the light which the spirit casts upon the possibly non-existent forms it contem- plates is essentially *intellectual* for Santayana. [28]

It is, perhaps, his fatalism and pessimism which most separates Santayana from the general American intellectual milieu of his time. But what shall be said in that case of the sub-title of *The Life of Reason*, 'The Phases of Human Progress'? 'Of all words in the modern lexicon,' Santayana once wrote, 'to me the most odious was Progress.'[29] A surprising remark for one who had thus sub-titled his most ambitious work.

What Santayana detested was any notion that there is some general tendency for chronological and moral progression to coincide, and still more did he detest any notion that a period of culture, an artist, a thinker, was to be valued chiefly for the addition he made towards some great human progression towards some fabulous future ideal or to the development of his art across time. One finds this theme again and again in Santayana. It was his principal objection to the Hegelian philosophy. The following two illustrations of his feelings in this matter may amuse:[30]

It is usual to regard Berkeley, in the history of philosophy, as a stepping-stone between Locke and Hume; but this seems to me a grave injustice, convenient for compiling text-books, but born of the mania for seeing evolution everywhere and, what is worse, evolution in single file. . . . To call Berkeley a stepping-stone between Locke and Hume is like calling an upright obelisk a stepping-stone between two sphinxes that may be crouching to the right and to the left of it. No doubt the three are in perfect alignment along one particular path, and this may be the most interesting fact about them to a person hurrying by them towards something else. Yet even that subjective analysis of ideas which was begun by Locke and completed in Hume, figured in Berkeley only as a cathartic, or an argument *ad hominem,* calculated to clear the mind of proud scientific illusions and to bring it in all humility face to face with God. His intuition pointed steadily, like an obelisk, to the zenith; whilst his more contorted and pregnant neighbours, like sphinxes, digested their inward contradictions.

The other more profound example comes in his dismissal of any attempt to justify the essential goodness of the universe or its creator by seeing all evil as contributing to some far-off divine event to which the whole creation moves. He agrees with James that even the dissatisfaction of the humblest of individuals at the end of things would invalidate such a theodicy, but he goes further in charging that even the perfect happiness of all in the future cannot justify evil now, for the point of a present is not simply to bring forth a future:[31]

> As William James put it, in his picturesque manner, if at the last day all creation was shouting hallelujah and there remained one cockroach with an unrequited love, *that* would spoil the universal harmony; it would spoil it, he meant, in truth and for the tender philosopher, but probably not for those excited saints. James was thinking chiefly of the present and future, but the same scrupulous charity has its application to the past. To remove an evil is not to remove the fact that it has existed. The tears that have been shed were shed in bitterness, even if a remorseful hand afterwards wipes them away. To be patted on the back and given a sugar-plum does not reconcile even a child to a past injustice. And the case is much worse if we are expected to make our heaven out of the foolish and cruel pleasures of contrast, or out of the pathetic obfuscation produced by a great relief. Such a heaven would be a lie, like the sardonic heavens of Calvin and Hegel. The existence of any evil anywhere at any time absolutely ruins a total optimism.

To return from our digression: If Santayana so detested the term 'progress', with all its associations at that time with a determined optimism, why did he use it in that title?

One reason, perhaps, may have been precisely a wish to do justice to a side of things to which he knew he had some personal antipathy. This,

I suspect, is true of various aspects of *The Life of Reason*. More important, however, was a wish to enlist this laudatory word in the service of an outlook different from that it usually went with. Progress, in *The Life of Reason*, is not some general pattern to which the history of the species mostly conforms. He was quite ready to believe that in the future the general path of things might be downward. What he did hold was that every now and then some human community has made some steps towards a rational way of life, and it was these various temporary episodes of progress which he wished to study, not as historical phenomena, but as filling out the ideal which a man who loves reason will cherish, whether he sees much present hope of its fulfilment or not. Thus Santayana was not drawing up a blue-print for social reform, but articulating a system of values such as distinguishes what is most truly worthy of love among those things which have, and those things which have not, occurred. The activity of articulating the heart's ideal is carried on for its own sake, as perhaps in the end being the highest satisfaction. There is, perhaps, an element of paradox here, but it is one central to Santayana's thought. Those admirers of *The Life of Reason* who felt that his later writings were a falling off from its noble activism did not appreciate how far this contemplation of ideal forms of life was even then regarded as a good in itself. Not, of course, that Santayana did not think the ideal better realized than unrealized, and would have done what he could towards its realization, but that perhaps even then it would be the satisfaction taken in contemplation of its harmonious workings which would be the highest good in an ideal society.

One unfamiliar with his thought may get a quite false impression, from what I have said, of Santayana as a kind of absolutist in morals, who thought of societies as orderable in merit according to their degree of approximation to some one and only valid ideal.

Nothing could be further from the truth, as we shall see. No philosopher has held to a more extreme moral relativism. For Santayana any genuine moral judgement expresses, adequately or otherwise, what some impulse within the thinker is striving towards, or would strive towards if possible. Reason is one such impulse and in *The Life of Reason* it is the values of that impulse which Santayana strives to articulate. This is in no way a denial that other incompatible ideals expressing other impulses have an equal validity. Moreover, reason itself in different concrete situations forms different ideals according to the kinds of impulses it is concerned to harmonize. Thus Santayana recognizes that various alternative ideals of reason, which share only a certain formal property, may be of equal validity one with another. The philosopher who is, if one may so speak, inspired by reason as such, will be able to participate imaginatively in various different ideals of reason, even though no actual society could actualize them all.

This is an account of practical rather than theoretical reason, but Santayana tends to identify the latter with the former insofar as its operation is rendered more efficient by experience and reflection. An alternative way in which he sometimes tends to assimilate them conceives of reason in general as a process of harmonizing ideas, whether these ideas be ideal ends of action or representations of the way things are, which gradually transforms an initial chaos of impulsive aspiration and spasmodic sensation into the conception of a unitary world of some reliability offering calculable opportunities of good and threats of evil. [32] (The transition is conceived of as occurring both ontogenetically and phylogenetically.) The original mutual involvement and possible separation of practical and theoretical reason, or intelligence, is a theme on which Santayana develops various intriguing variations. [33]

The discussion in *The Life of Reason* (mainly in *Reason in Common Sense* and *Reason in Science*) of the more theoretical side of *reason* constitutes Santayana's first sustained treatment of epistemological issues. What seems best in it is found in a more developed form in his later writings, though some topics were more fully treated then than later. I shall discuss it only insofar as some of its aspects may throw light on the later theories, either by way of contrast or by suggesting how some positions advanced in very summary form in the later writings are to be interpreted.

A certain ambiguity in point of view characterizes the earlier epistemology. There seems to be an oscillation between some kind of subjective idealism and a representative realism. Santayana later insisted that he had never meant to imply that the material world existed in idea only, and that the impression arises, on occasion, only from the fact that he is concerned in this book with the development of *the idea* of external things and not with the external things themselves. [34] This is doubtless true, but the terminology invites confusion on the point. Rather the same sort of ambiguity attaches to the status allotted to universals. [35]

The main outlines of his later philosophical system seem to have developed themselves in his mind quite shortly after publication of *The Life of Reason* as emerges especially from notes which survive to lectures given in 1909–10 ('System in Lectures'). The first published expression of some of his main ontological contentions seems to have been in a discussion of Bertrand Russell's philosophy published in *Journal of Philosophy* for 1911 and reprinted in *Winds of Doctrine* (1913). Thereafter it was developed in a series of writings of which the chief are included in the list above. So far as epistemology and ontology go it will be mainly with this later system that our concern in this book will lie, for it is this which represents Santayana's really significant contribution to these subjects. When we discuss ethical issues, however, we will be taking the earlier work much more fully into account, for here the later writings do not so much supersede as complement the earlier work.

3   Outline of Santayana's life[36]

George Santayana was born in Madrid in 1863 of Spanish parents. At the age of nine he left Spain to live for many years in the USA. He retained Spanish nationality all his life, and so far as he felt that he belonged to a nation at all, he continued to feel himself a Spaniard. He felt that Avila, that 'barren town of obsolete dignity', remained in some sense the vantage point from which he viewed the world. It was there that he had lived till then with his father, his mother having left Spain when he was five in order to take her older children by her first, and American, husband to be brought up in Boston. But in spite of his sense of his Spanishness he admits, in his autobiography, that after having lived so long in America his 'Yankee ways' made him feel a foreigner when he returned to Spain, and apart from quite frequent references to Don Quixote, there is very little discussion of things Spanish in his voluminous and widely ranging writings.

The early life of Santayana's mother has a somewhat romantic and even exotic quality. She travelled widely in her childhood, as her father changed his postings in the Spanish colonial service. Her mother died when she was sixteen, and four years later her father, then Governor of Batan, in the Philippines, died also, leaving her the only white woman on the island. The resourceful young woman continued to live there in these circumstances until a young man named Augustin Santayana arrived as the new governor, at which point, or so at least runs the story in George Santayana's autobiography, her sense of the proprieties induced her to depart for Manila, where she met and married George Sturgis, a young New England Protestant and merchant, who was there on behalf of his large family business. It was not till many years later that the Señor Santayana became her second husband.

The young couple returned to Boston and had five children. There she was welcomed by, though it seems that she hardly became one of, the distinguished and rich family of the Sturgises. The firstborn child, a boy called Pepin, died at the age of three, and George later interpreted the withdrawnness of his mother's character as her response to this death, which, he thought, provoked the strongest emotion of her life. In George's opinion, at least, she had had no deep love for either of her husbands, who did not perhaps live up to the ideal set for her by her father.

Strangely enough, it was in Manila that her husband died, at the age of forty, when there with his family on an unsuccessful commercial venture, leaving her once again in a position calling for great resources, for she had four young children and little money. She returned to Boston, and lived quietly there with assistance from her husband's rich relations. However, on a visit to relatives in Spain she remet Augustin Santayana in Madrid, and embarked on what the one child of this union describes as 'so ill advised a marriage without either passion or reason'. They set up house in Avila, shortly after the birth of George in Madrid in 1863. Spanish was the main family language, though one imagines that the elder children must have continued to speak English much of the time. To two of these at least, George and Susana, Santayana was deeply attached, and it must have been a shock for him, when he was five years old, that his mother returned to Boston to fulfil a commitment to her first husband, to bring up his children in America, leaving George, for the next four years, to be brought up by his father.

On the departure of the Sturgises an uncle and aunt, and their daughter, a young woman called Anita, came to live with the Santayana father and son in their house in Avila, thus forming an unhappy family group that remained for Santayana 'the type of what family life really is'. His aunt, 'a woman of the people, was most at home in the kitchen', while Antonita was preoccupied with suitors. She finally married a widower with two daughters of around Santayana's own age, who all moved in, little to the boy's satisfaction. Soon Antonita's own child was born, still-born, in the house and the horror and tragedy of the event made a deep impression on Santayana. The screams of agony, the glimpse of the dead child like green alabaster looking to the young Santayana (or so he reported as an old man) 'too beautiful to be alive', and Antonita's own death shortly after, following on what must have seemed, and indeed was, his strange desertion by his mother, must have given the boy a discouraging view of life from the start. After this things became increasingly difficult. Antonita's father took to drink and became demented, while her mother fussed obsessively over the two young girls. At last Santayana *père* detached himself from this group of relatives, and decided to take George over to his mother in Boston to be brought up there, returning himself to solitude in Spain. Santayana's descriptions of his first impressions of America are amusing; the sordidness of the pier and the beauty of design in the buggy in which brother Robert met them exhibiting at once that general ugliness of the environment and that charm of well designed mechanical contrivances which was always to characterize the USA in his mind.[37]

Soon Susana had taught George to speak English, in which he quickly became word perfect, having an excellent ear. Much later, when he had tea with Lady Stanley of Alderley, grandmother of Santayana's friend Lord John Francis Stanley Russell, and of Bertrand, she commented with surprise that he spoke English in an accent just like Queen

Victoria. (I myself have put the question of Santayana's accent to several people who knew him, and have received the remarkable reply – which perhaps casts an interesting light on the dispute between Locke and Berkeley on general ideas – that Santayana spoke English *with no accent whatever*.) Few would doubt that Santayana grew up to become one of the great masters of English prose, but it is interesting that Santayana himself thought that his limitations as a poet arose partly from the fact that English 'was not my mother tongue' so that 'its roots do not quite reach to my centre. I never drank in in childhood the homely cadences and ditties which in pure spontaneous poetry set the essential key' (Preface to *Poems*, 1923).

Santayana did not see his father again until he visited Spain in 1883 when he was twenty, but they corresponded, certainly to begin with, regularly, and there is now a large collection of the letters between them at the library of Columbia University. They are in Spanish, but a translation available at the library in typescript was arranged by Professor Corliss Lamont, who presented the letters to the library. On a visit there, I only had a chance to read a few of them, but I gained an impression that they are of great interest, as showing that the father's ideas may have had quite an influence on the son. We find, for instance, Augustin expressing the view to his young son that religious accounts of the world are to be regarded as a kind of poetry. Santayana, of course, had been baptized a Catholic, and his sister Susana, who had become a passionate Catholic herself, did her best to see him grow up as one, but neither of the parents can be described as believers.

Augustin Santayana had started his career as a lawyer, but made his career in the Spanish colonial service, ending up as financial secretary in the Philippines. He had retired before his marriage, cherishing a few remaining contacts with important persons. His chief pleasure was in painting which he undertook rather as a craft than as a fine art. He was a mild and diffident man, according to his son, cut off more and more by increasing deafness, who spoke seldom but then to good effect. He was a staunch liberal, who looked upon England, of which he only had the briefest personal experience, as the best of countries. Upon the whole Santayana appears to have respected and liked his father, and to have had a happy relationship with him when he visited Spain again as a young man. Augustin Santayana died in 1893. His mother he seems to have found unloving and as for himself, he says: 'I only loved her enough to suffer from her hostility.'

Two nice stories may, however, be quoted regarding his father and his mother respectively:

On one of the many occasions when he thought, or dreaded, that he might be on his deathbed, he felt a sudden desire for some

boiled chicken, without in the least giving up his asseveration that
he was dying; and as his deafness prevented him from properly
modulating his voice, he cried out with a shout that resounded
through the whole house: *¡La Unción y la gallina!* 'Extreme
Unction and a chicken!' Extreme Unction only, be it observed.
That is the last Sacrament, to be received passively, without
saying a word. It would put him to no inconvenience. To have
asked for confession and communion would have implied much
talking; he was too far gone for that. Extreme Unction would do
perfectly to avoid all unpleasantness regarding his funeral and
burial in holy ground. Nobody would need to be distressed about
his soul. And meantime, since these were his last moments, and
the consequences of any imprudence would make no difference,
why not boldly indulge himself one last time, and have some
boiled chicken? That, I am confident, was his thought. And he
had the chicken. The last Sacrament, this time, was not required.
(PP, pp. 28–9)

In the 1880's, when we lived in Roxbury (a decayed old suburb of
Boston) a rich widow who lingered in a large house round the
corner, and had intellectual pretensions, came to call and to invite
my mother to join the Plato Club – all the very nicest ladies of the
place – which met at her house once a fortnight in winter. My
mother thanked her, and excused herself. The president and host
of the Roxbury Plato Club would not take no for an answer.
Might not my mother *develop* an interest in Plato? Would she not
be interested in *meeting* all those superior ladies? In what then *was*
she interested? What did she *do*? To this my mother, driven back
to her fundamental Philippine habits, replied without smiling: 'In
winter I try to keep warm, and in summer I try to keep cool.'
Diogenes could not have sent the President of the Plato Club
more curtly about her business. (PP, p. 33)

Santayana's strongest affection within the family, and perhaps
throughout his life, was for his half-sister Susana. She was ten years
older than him, and was very much the leader in the family. In her teens
she became a devout, if not fanatical, Catholic, and this caused tension
with her Protestant brothers, and with her religiously easy-going
mother. She it was who taught Santayana his catechism and saw to it
that in some degree he grew up a Catholic, though he sometimes
attended Protestant services also. What Santayana soon came to cherish
as morally significant imaginative ideas were for Susana literal truths
productive of a good deal of personal anguish. The family was not well
off and this limited its participation in local social life, so that as a young
woman Susana looked more and more to her religion as a substitute for

the social life which she should have been enjoying. It was a hard blow for her when her attempt to enter a convent failed after six months when it was decided that she was not suited to become a nun. She had a small personal inheritance from her father, and she eventually used this to return to Spain, there to live with her stepfather. In middle age she married a crusty old Spanish widower with six children, and Santayana used often to stay with them, not without some disappointment at the rather fat and ordinary middle-aged woman which she had become. She used to worry that he was moving further from God, and he was sad that her religion instead of being a source of joy was an unnecessary worry.

Looking back on family life in 302 Beacon Street, where he lived from his ninth to his seventeenth year, Santayana felt how disunited a family they had been. They could not afford to entertain in any case, and Santayana had no close friends till he was fifteen or so. There was little communal family life, and each member lived his own life in his own room. To begin with he went to the poor boys' free school, but subsequently moved to the Boston Latin School, where he stayed eight years, and seems to have been a success. That he was not without physical heartiness is suggested by the fact that he became Lieutenant-Colonel of the Boston School Regiment. His chief interests about this time would seem to have been in architecture, and light versification.

In 1882 Santayana went up to Harvard as an undergraduate. The freshmen all did the same prescribed courses, and sat in alphabetical order, a fact which brought about a friendship between Santayana and a young man called Thomas Parker Sanborn. Together with some other friends they started the comic magazine *Lampoon*, which survives to this day, Santayana's main contribution being a series of cartoons, rather in the manner of George du Maurier, to judge from the only one I have seen. They also served together on the original editorial board for the *Harvard Monthly* and were at the centre of a group of literary young men. It was a grave shock for Santayana when Sanborn gave way to melancholia and, in 1889, cut his throat in his bath. The fact that rather a number of young men from Harvard came to such early death seemed to Santayana a symptom and a symbol of the failure of American life to offer any adequate life goal to young men of culture and sensitivity. Sanborn is one of the models for Oliver in *The Last Puritan*, which deals with the problem of spiritual aspiration in a void.

Santayana was very poor compared with most of his friends, and was forced into some austerity in his way of living, though he could borrow respectable clothes from his half-brother for smart visits. However, at the end of his freshman year his mother was able to provide him with money for his first return visit to Spain, where he struck up very friendly relations with his increasingly deaf old father once more. He also visited other relatives in Spain, resisting various attempts to get him married, and toured Spain and France in pursuit of architectural beauty. From then until his final departure from America in 1912 he visited Europe almost every year. His next visit seems to have been with his rich young Jewish friend, Charles Loeser, who was somewhat cut off from the main current of Harvard life, and who largely financed the trip.

Santayana's studies were, of course, soon centred on philosophy, his love of Spinoza's Ethics being perhaps the main magnet thereto. The two teachers who meant most to him in philosophy were Josiah Royce and William James, with neither of whose philosophies he had much sympathy but by both of whom he would seem to have been a good deal influenced. His social and intellectual relations with James, in particular, were sometimes rather prickly, but in spite of the vigorous criticisms they at times passed on each other, they had a good deal of respect for each other's personalities and philosophical abilities.[38] James took some trouble to persuade the business-like President Eliot that, even if the detached Spaniard was not likely to be a good committee man and was somewhat lacking in the healthy optimism which was thought desirable in those instructing youth, he was too good a philosopher not to have upon the faculty.

Before becoming a Professor at Harvard, Santayana had shared the Walker Fellowship, for graduate students, with Charles Strong, and they had used the money to study for two years in Berlin together. Strong became quite a well-known philosopher, and when in 1920 a volume of *Essays in Critical Realism* was issued as a joint effort by various American philosophers, Strong and Santayana were picked out as the joint founders of the movement (itself a response to the movement heralded by *The New Realism* of 1912 by various hands, of whom perhaps E. B. Holt is the best known, which was more in the line of James). Strong was liberated from vulgar material necessities by his marriage to the daughter of John D. Rockefeller. He was soon a rich widower and his grand establishment in Paris was for many years as much of a real home for Santayana as he ever had. The friendship was a curious one, marred it would seem by a good deal of bitterness. Strong seems to have envied Santayana's greater success, but to have needed his visits as a refreshment to his own somewhat isolated philosophizings. Though not the deepest, it was the longest, in terms of time actually spent together, of Santayana's friendships.

In 1888 Santayana returned to Harvard to finish his graduate studies under Royce and completed his doctoral dissertation on a subject which he seems to have adopted with little enthusiasm, 'Lotze's System of Philosophy'. He then became an assistant and, not long after, a full Professor at Harvard.

In 1896 he spent a year's sabbatical leave in England as an 'advanced student' at King's College, Cambridge. He had already visited England several times and developed a great affection for the country, and at that point he was even quite sympathetic to some of the new developments in philosophy there, having a good deal of contact with Bertrand Russell, and also, it seems, some less happy encounters with G. E. Moore. (The early Platonic realism of these two encouraged him in his own movement in a kindred direction.) He also enjoyed discussions with McTaggart, with whom he became good friends, though they were poles apart in outlook.

Santayana's first contacts with Bertrand Russell came about through his friendship with Bertrand's older brother, John Francis Stanley, then Lord Russell, with whom he had a much closer friendship. This Russell seems to have been the first Englishman whom Santayana ever met, for when, after having been sent down from Oxford, Russell visited America in 1886 and came for a few days to Harvard, someone brought him to visit Santayana, who was entranced by him and seems to have made some impression on Russell in return, even if only as a good listener, as Santayana puts it, for Russell had regaled him with readings from Swinburne in his appealing aristocratic voice. Though Russell seems to have treated Santayana in a somewhat lordly manner, as a convenient fellow to have around for company in the quieter moments of his somewhat frenetic life, they continued good friends until Russell's death. Russell appears as Jim Darnley in *The Last Puritan*; the nickname, Lord Jim, given him in the novel, though so far as the characters are concerned deriving from Conrad, is perhaps in part the author's hint at the aristocratic status of the original for this humble clergyman's son. Santayana's approach to all his friends was highly Platonic, I do not mean just in the vulgar sense of this phrase, but in the sense that he valued them above all as exemplifications of some essence which had a particular significance for him. The appeal of Lord Russell seems to have lain in the prominence of the natural man within him, with a tendency to get into somewhat sordid entanglements, combined with a certain background sense of his transcendental status, behind all these troubles, as a pure spirit. It may be noted that Santayana made some trouble for himself in the prim society of Harvard by appearing as a witness to Russell's good character in one of his celebrated divorce cases.

The dates of Santayana's main publications have been listed. He was acquiring celebrity first as a poet, then as a philosopher, and was a much sought after figure in the smart salons of Cambridge, Mass.,[39] but he kept himself at a certain distance from his academic colleagues, living, so long as he could, a life closer to that of a student. His dislike of American life seems to have increased, and when his mother died in 1911, and his literary success and his careful savings made it financially possible, he retired from Harvard and left America never to return at all. His departure seems to have caused extreme amazement in academic

America, and feelings were hurt. [40] This contributed to producing a certain hostility towards him which is notable in references to him thereafter by some of the American philosophers who had once thought of him as among their leaders.

The remainder of his life was spent living mainly in hotels or on visits to Strong or his sister. He was caught in England during the 1914 war. Among his friends was Robert Bridges (whose *The Testament of Beauty* was believed by the author, but not by Santayana, to relate to the latter's philosophy) who tried to persuade him to accept a non-teaching fellowship at one or other of his two colleges at Oxford, Corpus or New. However, in 1920 at the age of fifty-seven, Santayana settled down to hotel life in Rome, 'Rome where nature and art are most beautiful and mankind least disturbed', where he stayed, for the most part, for the rest of his life. Although not an ascetic in his habits, he was a most unpossessive man, a lover of beauty but quite without the collector's impulse, and he was content to have nothing more than a temporary hotel room to call his own. Thus were the winters spent at the Hotel Bristol, Rome, while the summers were diversified by visits to various places and friends, such as Russell, Strong, Bernard Berenson (his Harvard contemporary now living magnificently just outside Florence) and to his relatives in Spain whom he seems to have helped a good deal in various crises. It was in these years of meditative retirement that the great works of his later period were written, such as shall form the main basis for the discussions of this present book. He mixed little in Italian or cosmopolitan society, but he was visited from time to time by friends and admirers from the USA. A fine description of this long phase in Santayana's life is contained in *Santayana: The Later Years* by Daniel Cory, a poet and philosopher who, besides being a close friend, acted as secretary, or philosophical assistant, to both Santayana and Strong for many years.

When war came in 1939 Santayana, then aged seventy-seven, moved to a nursing home, largely it seems because life in a hotel was becoming too expensive, but also because an old man would be better looked after there during the austerities of war. Thus he moved to the Blue Sisters' Nursing Home, in a quiet street near St John the Lateran. Doubtless Santayana would not have moved there unless he had had a certain emotional sympathy with religious orders (though presumably in Rome there would not be any comparable secular institution) but any idea that this move, in any case thought of at first as only for the duration of the war, represented some sort of return to the Catholic fold (to which in any case Santayana had not belonged since childhood) would be a great mistake. In point of fact he did, towards the end, suffer a certain amount from the importunity of a priest who made efforts to win a late conversion, but though he continued to think of the church as a great human institution, and of the story of Christ as offering perhaps the finest symbol of the human predicament and the possibility of salvation therefrom, his allegiance to an entirely naturalistic account of things never faltered and, when he died in the convent in 1952, he resisted efforts to administer the rites of the church on his behalf.

Of course, Santayana's continuance in Italy during the war presented no problem, for he was a Spanish citizen, and though he had thought of moving to Switzerland, to keep more in touch with Cory and other American and English friends, this turned out to be impossible, as the Swiss would not let Spanish citizens have visas. Thus he spent the war years cut off from his closest friends, and in some financial difficulty, as his royalties were not accessible. It would seem that they were hard years.

As regards his sympathies in the war, it may be noted that he had had a life-long aversion to German nationalism and a love for England above all other countries, but that he had not been altogether unsympathetic to Italian Fascism. He deplored Mussolini's militant foreign policy, and certainly in later years considered Mussolini himself a bad man, but he thought that Fascist home policy was better than the likely actual alternatives.[41] In general, Santayana was against any ideology, Fascist, Communist, or Liberal-democratic, in any claims it might make to be of universal validity, and believed that a government was to be judged by the extent to which it met the most pressing natural, as opposed to the merely imagined, needs of the people affected by it. Above all, he believed in the right of every nation to develop its own particular form of life, in a world in which people could shift their national allegiances if need be.

After the war he saw a certain amount of various visiting American philosophers and other intellectuals, both old friends and new, and above all was able to see Daniel Cory and his wife again. His chief good, however, lay in the life of contemplation which he celebrated in his *The Realm of Spirit* and other works. Santayana's life and personality evoke very varied reactions; some have felt his detachment to have been inhuman, others have seen him as a kind of saint, offering a model for a certain kind of salvation. In any case his detachment lay in reliance on his own resources, and not in an indifference to the good of others, and it would seem that he was a good and kindly man as well as being excellent company. What matters in any case to the reader today is the vision of things expressed in his works, one I believe of a timely and abiding importance. Here we are concerned, I must emphasize, for the most part only with that part of this total vision which concerns the most general issues of philosophy. The corpus of his works remains as a source of insight and joy for those who approach it from many different points of view.

II

Scepticism

1 *Introduction*

The first work in which Santayana sets forth his mature philosophy is *Scepticism and Animal Faith*. The book was intended as an introduction to the ontological system presented at length in *Realms of Being*. In part it presents the epistemological background to that ontology, in part it adumbrates that ontology itself. In this chapter and the next we shall consider its main epistemological contentions.

It was not really Santayana's view that ontology requires epistemology as a basis, but he thought that the philosophical climate of his time was such that the ontologist must begin by disposing of all sorts of epistemological objections to his enterprise.[1] Only after he has considered the kind of right with which one can ever claim to know anything can the ontologist today set forth his view of how things are. This applies, especially, when the ontology claims to be, as Santayana's does, only a clarified version of the viewpoint of common sense, for alternative more metaphysical ontologies often justify themselves in part on the ground that they are less vulnerable than it to epistemological objections, to the challenge 'How if this is so, do you claim to know it?'

It would never occur to anyone, says Santayana, to initiate a criticism of knowledge, were it not for the existence of difference of opinion on various matters. The natural and original approach of the mind to the world is one of unperturbed dogmatism. People do not believe things because they have evidence. When something attracts the attention some fanciful account of its nature and origin leaps to meet it. It does not occur to the unsophisticated mind, to children or to simple peoples, to subject such fanciful dogmas to any canons of criticism. If everyone spontaneously came to the same conclusions as to how things are, the idea that one might *not have the right* to make certain assertions would never have arisen.

Still, people do disagree on a number of things, especially on some of the most crucial points regarding man's destiny. Hence a quest is instituted for some method of sifting what ought to be believed from what ought not to be believed, in short people turn to epistemology.

Once we begin to ask what gives one a right to believe anything, one is bound in consistency, to examine every one of one's beliefs to see what sort of right, if any, one has to hold it, including such basic beliefs as that one is a human being moving about in a material world. Indeed, the fact that many philosophers deny the truth, or at least the certainty, of this belief makes it especially desirable that a philosopher should not continue to hold it without considering what chances there are of its being false.

It is on the basis of considerations of this kind that Santayana undertakes to strain 'his dogmas through the utmost rigours of scepticism' (SAF, p. 9) to see whether he has any beliefs which are altogether beyond doubt. In fact he reaches the conclusion that he does not (SAF, Chapters III–XI). Thereafter he considers how one who is thus brought to the verge of total scepticism might recover confidence in most of those matters of ordinary fact which are commonly taken for granted. Let us now turn to the argument in detail.

2 *Solipsism of the present moment*

The serious epistemologist examines his every belief, including every item of so-called knowledge, to see whether, after all, it might not be mistaken.

There is no one right order in which to set about this doubting. He could doubt the physical facts first, leaving the historical facts standing for the present, or he could start by doubting the historical facts. 'Criticism, I have said, has no first principle, and its desultory character may be clearly exhibited at this point by asking whether the evidence of science or that of history should be questioned first' (SAF, p. 12).

As Santayana is using the term 'history' here, an historical fact is something purely mental, the fact that some mind had a certain thought, feeling or what not. This is not his own view of history, but the one he takes as implicit in some philosophical theories. Certain idealists and empiricists have accepted the fact that there are now many minds having certain different experiences, that a while ago there were many minds having certain different experiences, that a while before that there were many minds having different experiences again, and so on back moment by moment. Accepting 'history' in this sense, they have been prepared to doubt the existence of any other, e.g. physical facts.

31

But although the decision to:

> impugn the belief in physical facts reported by the senses and by
> natural science, such as the existence of a ring of Saturn, reducing
> them to appearances, which are facts reported by personal
> remembrance . . . [is that] . . . made by British and German critics
> of knowledge, who, relying on memory and history, have denied
> the existence of anything but experience . . . the opposite procedure
> would seem more judicious; knowledge of the facts reported
> by history is mediated by documents which are physical facts; and
> these documents must first be discovered and believed to have
> subsisted unknown and to have had a more or less remote origin in
> time and place, before they can be taken as evidence for any mental
> events; for if I did not believe that there had been any men in
> Athens I should not imagine they had had any thoughts.
> (SAF, p. 13)

Thus Santayana thinks that one would be more reasonable to
acknowledge the existence of the material world and doubt the consciousness of the other organisms in it, than to doubt the existence of
the material world while acknowledging the existence of a multiplicity
of minds in a common time. For one thing the evidence for other minds,
and perhaps even for my own past experience, is physical. For another
thing the concept of the temporal relations between mental activities
seems derivative from the concept of the temporal relations between
the physical events which are their objects or stimuli.

Since there is nothing within my experience to guarantee the existence of a real material world (some part of which it apprehends), or of
any other centre of experience, it seems that if I refuse to take anything
on mere trust, I shall end up in solipsism, that is in the belief that the
discoursing and feeling mind which I am exists, but that possibly
nothing else exists.

But solipsism of this kind is, according to Santayana, just as arbitrary
and perhaps incoherent as is the belief in history without 'physics'
(understood as an account of the world in its purely physical aspects).
The romantic solipsist thinks of himself as having had certain experiences in a certain order. But is there any clear ground for assigning a
certain order to remembered experiences other than one's knowledge
of the order in which physical situations unroll themselves? (If I have
a vision of my school days and of my Army days do I not know
their order because I know that one has the body and opportunities
of a child before one has the body and opportunities of a man?)
Does it, indeed, mean anything to say that one experience follows
on another, except that they are evoked by successive physical
events?

Though he sometimes seems ambivalent over this last question I think Santayana's answer to both questions is negative.

He is sure, in any case, that a being without belief in the material world will have no way of checking on the general reliability of his memory. Belief in any sort of record, natural or artificial, of past events will be impossible for him, and thus any trust in his own memory of the past will be the adoption of a groundless dogma. Since Santayana finally says as much himself about the basis of all knowledge claims, he should not be taken as putting this forward as a knockdown argument against romantic solipsism. He is simply insisting that the romantic solipsist, while he adopts a position psychologically less, not more, credible than that of the plain man, fails to retreat to a position having any greater rational security. The point which Santayana stresses is not so much that my own memories must be capable of support by the memories of others – a point urged subsequently by Wittgenstein – as that it must have support in physical evidences. Santayana accepts as meaningful the struggle of the solitary individual with his sceptical doubts, but claims that this individual can find no coherent resting place in a belief in nothing but his own unrolling mental history.

I am doubtful myself whether Santayana is right that there are no temporal relations between experiences except those derivative from the relations between their physical bases. Do not my experiences in a manner just slip into each other, and in that sense succeed each other? Perhaps the point is not of great importance at this stage, however, for this cannot be true of those experiences of mine which are divided by periods of unconsciousness, so that the temporal order of our 'experiential days' (by which I mean stretches of unbroken experience) must presumably, as Santayana claims, be an entirely physical order.

Presumably some influence of Kant is apparent in all this, but Santayana's position is really rather different from that developed in Kant's second analogy. Kant was concerned primarily with the distinction between a subjective and an objective succession, and, though certainly this is inconsistent with some of what he says, he seems to have held that the subjective succession was somehow something given. Santayana is concerned solely here with the subjective succession, that is with the temporal relations between subjective or mental events, and maintains that these are to be identified with those holding between their physical bases. Moreover Santayana is trying to decide what one may or must believe about the real world, not merely with presuppositions of experience which the philosopher regards as applicable only to a world of appearances.

Whether it could conceivably be true or not – and certainly Santayana thinks it has nothing to recommend it, as such – he is sure that it could not be believed with any steadfastness. If just one person existed, he could only have a sense of his own identity and of the temporal order of his experiences, if he falsely believed them to be experiences of a being not composed simply of experiences, who has a series of adventures in an 'external' world the moments of which are individuated by the fact that each moment owes its character to the previous one. Sometimes Santayana's position seems to be that though such a set of experiences might exist *in vacuo* they would not form a genuine temporal series.

Thus the romantic solipsist would have to give up his position at the first touch of criticism. Perhaps, we may add that if he thinks he is being criticized by someone else he has already given up his solipsism, but that there is no reason why he should not produce criticism of himself, or take seriously the opinions which the figures in his dreams put forward, without thinking there is any conscious or independently existing critic.

Solipsism of this standard kind, which Santayana calls 'romantic', is, then, an arbitrary stopping point for the sceptic, and one of doubtful coherence. The sceptic who continues to believe in the reality of his own past experiences, and even perhaps bases his expectations for the future thereon, has not given up every questionable belief but has a system of the world no more indubitable and considerably less coherent than that which he would have if he took himself as belonging to an independent physical world containing himself as one among many sentient organisms.

To say this is not, for Santayana, to rebut scepticism, but to show that the honest sceptic will press on to a more radical stance, which Santayana calls 'solipsism of the present moment'.

Such a sceptic who has given up all dogmas, rejects 'the postulates on which empirical knowledge and inductive science are based – namely that there has been a past, that it was such as it is now thought to be, that there will be a future and that it must, for some inconceivable reason, resemble the past and obey the same laws' as 'gratuitous dogmas'. He has no need of any such 'unwarrantable idea' as that of a past or future (SAF, p. 14).

The sceptic will, indeed, find within his present experience (that is, within what *we* call his present experience), a certain division into past, present, and future. Some of his images may have a certain quality 'of being somehow not in the foreground' which could be called their pastness, and others may have a quality which could be called their futurity. But merely to have these images and experience these qualities is not to believe. For belief there must indeed be some 'content' such as a complex of images, but there must also be a certain sort of active attitude towards this content. Thus the content may be temporal inasmuch as there is a before and after between its elements, and yet

34

there be no belief in any succession of events whatever. We shall explain this more clearly in what follows.

According to Santayana such solipsism of the present moment 'is an honest position, and certain attempts to refute it as self-contradictory, are based on a misunderstanding' (SAF, p. 15).

Some have tried to show that the position is incoherent by arguing that any language used by such a solipsist to formulate his position will contain implications incompatible with such solipsism. [2] If, for instance, the solipsist says that nothing but the *present moment* exists, he says something incoherent, for a moment can only be called present in contrast to other moments, which are past or future. But, says Santayana, such 'arguments confuse the convictions of the solipsist with those of a spectator describing him from the outside' (SAF, p. 15). The solipsist simply rejects the idea of there existing anything but *this* and *these*. If he steadies his attention by giving certain names to the different elements of the given, these names need have no further meaning or function. Presumably they are really only further elements in the given, each with a felt link to some other such element.

Santayana's position, then, is that one who doubted whatever is not in principle beyond doubt would become a solipsist of the present moment, contemplating the passing show of his own sensations, images, feelings, etc., without believing in anything beyond them, even in a succession of experiences of which they are the present members. Whether such a mental stance is possible or not, it is the only position in which one would avoid acceptance of all beliefs which could be doubted. Anyone who is not a solipsist of the present moment – and that includes all who speak to persuade – believes some things for which he can offer no properly rational ground.

Before we go any further we may note the following points.

1 Santayana hardly distinguishes between suspension of belief in anything but the passing show; a positive belief that nothing but the passing show exists; and a positive sense of the doubtfulness of any existence beyond. What he does say suggests that he thinks all three positions are possibilities, but that he has primarily the first in mind. [3] This is not, it would seem, a theoretical position at all, but Santayana might still claim that it is the mental stance at which one would arrive if one tried to be perfectly rational, at least as philosophers have usually understood that word, though clearly having reached the goal one would have forgotten the steps that led there.

2 Santayana's ultimate point is not to recommend solipsism of the present moment, but to insist that unless one is a solipsist of the present moment one cannot hold it against any theory of the world merely that it has foundations which cannot be demonstrated or verified.

In the end we simply find ourselves believing in certain facts, and there is no point in trying to discard these beliefs or in pretending we do not have them, unless we are prepared to do the same with all those beliefs which separate us from the solipsist of the present moment. Santayana stands in opposition to all ordinary philosophical scepticism.

3 For the purpose of the above argument it does not matter much whether in practice solipsism of the moment is a state one could ever actually reach, provided it is true that it would be the only state in which one's beliefs were not in part acts of faith. But Santayana sometimes seems to think it a state into which one can pass, with a certain intrinsic value of its own, and that on coming out of it one will have learnt something from the experience. Perhaps, if he had been pressed, he would have allowed that an approximation to the state will serve these purposes, and is all that is practically possible.

3 Doubting the existence of an experiential flux

The solipsist of the present moment has ceased to believe in the existence of change. That he does not believe that there is physical change goes without saying, for he has no belief in physical things at all, but that he does not believe even in a temporal succession of mental, nor yet of merely sensory, states seems more perplexing. Is it really true that temporal succession of any kind whatever belongs in the class of things dubitable, and would receive no credence from the really consistent sceptic? Santayana insists that this is true, and does so on grounds which are of central importance to an understanding of his philosophy as a whole. [4]

In one sense the sceptic will certainly be presented with change. Just as the content of his mental state may include shapes, colours, and smells, so may it include various sorts of movement and transition. But these movements or transitions will be specious rather than real. For real change to take place one state of things must pass away and be replaced by another state of those things. In specious change the earlier and later phases of the change are both simply aspects of a total single apprehended content. Any change which is immediately and indubitably present to my consciousness, as a colour or a shape may be, is a specious change, a certain temporal pattern taken in all at once. Real change can be believed in but cannot be immediately given, for in real change there is an earlier and a later phase of something and these phases are not simply aspects of a unitary totality.

We must distinguish between an immediate experience of change and a change of immediate experience. If I see a pendulum swing from left to right, and actually experience this change, I do not first experience the sight of the pendulum in one position and then experience the sight

36

of it in another, but I have a single experience of the pendulum in action. Were that single experience the only thing in the world, the world would contain no real change whatever, not even a mental change. For a real mental change to take place that single experience must give way to another experience. (The notion of its merely giving way to nothingness is identified by Santayana with its not giving way, and things not changing.) That change, however, is not something which can, in the same sense, be experienced, for the two distinct experiences cannot be different aspects of the content of one single experience. The second content will normally, so to speak, take up the story told by the first content, but if one experience really does give way to another the contents of the two experiences cannot simply be aspects of a larger content.

Thus the sceptic will have various forms of change present to his mind just as he will have colours, shapes, and sounds present to his mind (whether in the form of what an outsider would call sense experience or imagery). But these presented changes will no more be interpreted as the appearance to him of real changes than are the shapes interpreted as the appearance to him of real physical things, nor will anything thus present to his experience prove to him that his experience is itself in flux:

> If anything had an actual beginning, that first phase must have occurred out of relation to the subsequent phases which had not yet arisen, and only became manifest in the sequel. . . . In a word, specious change is not actual change. The unity of apperception which yields the sense of change renders change specious, by relating the terms and directions of change together in a single perspective, as respectively receding, passing, or arriving. In so uniting and viewing these terms, intuition of change excludes actual change in the given object. If change has been actual, it must have been prior to, and independent of, the intuition of that change.
>
> Doubtless, as a matter of fact, this intuition of change is itself lapsing, and yielding its place in physical time to vacancy or to the intuition of changelessness: [*or, surely, to the intuition of some other change*] and this lapse of the intuition in physical time is an actual change. Evidently, however, it is not a given change, since neither vacancy nor the intuition of changelessness can reveal it. It is revealed, if revealed at all, by a further intuition of specious change *taken as a report*. Actual change if it is to be known at all, must be known by belief and not by intuition. Doubt is accordingly always possible regarding the existence of actual change. (SAF, pp. 25–6)

Thus the perfect solipsist of the present moment will appreciate change and movement as a quality of that which is set before him, but he will not opine that the scene of change set before him is one of many such scenes set before him at different times.

Several comments are called for here:

1 When Santayana urges this point about change in the present connection he is evidently anxious to avoid using the technical terms he is soon to introduce for dealing with such matters, in particular the term 'essence', but in some ways the language he actually does use is a little misleading. I have followed him in trying to present the point in a fairly neutral way, not too implicated with his detailed doctrine of 'essence'. I should note, however, that in using the word 'content' to denote that which is present to consciousness in a peculiarly direct and indubitable way I have gone against Santayana's express rejection of this word as thoroughly misleading. For him, to talk of an immediately presented colour as a content of my mental act, or still worse as a mental content, went with a view of the mind as a *container* for which he felt a peculiar dislike. But I think that if one considers the use of 'content' or 'Inhalt' by such thinkers as Meinong the term is not inappropriate for Santayana's meaning.

2 The changes which Santayana calls specious correspond to some extent with what is usually called the specious present. However, I think Santayana includes under this heading not only what is immediately present to me when I perceive or even imagine a movement or other brief change, but also the way in which the temporal relations between any two events of which I am in any way conscious actually feel to me. Thus if I am thinking of the biography of Napoleon, then that which is immediately present to my mind, when I take in (however sketchily) the character of some long drawn out action of his, contains a kind of specious change which represents or symbolizes (as we shall see more fully later) the real changes he lived through. The sceptic, according to Santayana, could have these same thoughts, and thus have this sort of specious change present to him, without believing in it as real matter of fact.

Thus Santayana is able to conclude that if we confine ourselves to belief in what is presented in some quite indubitable way we will have no cause to believe in any real change. Certainly:

As I watch a sensible object the evidence of variation is often irresistible. This flag is flapping. This flame is dancing. How shall I deny that almost everything, in nature and in fancy, like the Ghost in *Hamlet*, is here, is there, is gone? Of course I witness these appearances and disappearances. The intuition of change is more direct and more imperious than any other. But *belief* in change, as

I found just now, asserts that before this intuition of change arose the first term of that change had occurred separately. This no intuition of change can prove. The belief is irresistible in animal perception, for reasons which biology can plausibly assign; and it cannot be long suspended in actual thinking; but it may be suspended for a moment theoretically, in the interests of a thorough criticism. (SAF, p. 27)

Having shown that the thorough sceptic will find nothing in the indubitably given to establish the existence of real change, Santayana finds it easy to argue that he will find nothing in it to establish the existence of any sort of substantial self, of an experiential flux or stream of consciousness, or even of an act of apprehension. An act of apprehension is an event with its own position in a temporal series. One could not believe in the existence of such an event without believing in the existence of other such events flanking it. A flux of experience consists of experiences in real not specious temporal relations to one another. The notion of a substantial self has no sense except as a persisting entity which stands in contrast with a persisting environment. The Cartesian argument 'Cogito ergo sum' he dismisses on the grounds that the sceptic will have no inclination to say, or at least mean, 'Cogito'. The outside commentator on the sceptic knows that the sceptic must exist in order to be in this sceptical state, but that does not establish his own existence for the sceptic, or show that he is irrational in rejecting it.[5]

4 *The possibility that nothing exists*

Surely there is one matter of fact regarding which each of us really has indubitable knowledge, and regarding which the sceptic can sow no seeds of doubt. 'This particular complex of qualities exists' I may say, mentally pointing to the complex directly given to my consciousness. But Santayana will not allow us even this crumb of indubitable knowledge about a matter of fact.[6]

Present to my consciousness, indeed, at any moment is a certain complex pattern in which qualities of various different sorts may figure – visual, tactile, auditory, emotional, for instance. This precise pattern could, in principle, be presented to the consciousness of more than one person; the pattern must be distinguished from any particular awareness of it. It has its own definite character, it consists in certain definite elements in certain definite relations to each other. That it so consists is a necessary proposition about it, in a sense a tautology. That is just what that pattern is. Consider the total appearance to me of the physical things in my vicinity. For this to be just the pattern or scene which it is, it was neither necessary for any part of the material world to exhibit it, nor necessary for anyone to envisage it. Just as four would be twice two, even if nothing at all existed, so would this pattern be those elements in those relations even if nothing existed at all, not even itself or the envisagement of it. If either some material things embody it, or some consciousness envisages it, it has a place in existence, but even if it has no such place, it still remains the pattern it is, the combination of certain elements in certain relations, for the intelligibility and point of saying that it exists depends upon the intelligibility of the supposition that it might not have existed. There is every reason to believe that there are some things which don't exist, some possible things which are not actualized. These things, which are absent from the world, must have their own definite character, if it is to be a truth that the world does not contain them. That the existing world contains the quality we call 'green' is a matter of fact which might have been otherwise. That the quality green (or a definite shade of green) is a definite quality which is either present in or missing from the existing world is not a matter of fact which might have been otherwise.

But what then is it for something to exist, if its character has being equally whether it exists or not? Santayana answers as follows: things which exist stand in external relations one to another such as mere consideration of their intrinsic natures will not reveal, and they are in real, not merely specious, flux. 'I am using the word existence . . . to designate such being as is in flux, determined by external relations, and jostled by irrelevant events' (SAF, p. 42).

He explains further that he is not so much defining the word 'existence' as characterizing the type of being or reality which he calls 'existence' in terms of its most striking contrast 'with other types of reality' (SAF, p. 42).

Actually present to the mind which has renounced all renounceable beliefs will probably be just some little scene, with its own emotional character. Normally it will have its own spatial and temporal quality, but this will prove nothing regarding any larger spatial or temporal context in which it figures. If it exists, it must have some fate, it must be either about to disappear or due to continue for a while subject to gradual modification in character, but to believe that this is so is to believe something not essentially implied in the scene itself.

Certainly the scene is related to its own elements, as, say, by containing the image of a yellow ball moving across a green field. But this relation of whole to part is an internal relation, quite distinct from the physical relation of whole to part. That just that scene, that particular pattern, contains that yellow ball, is a necessary proposition, not a contingent existential fact:

The sceptic has here withdrawn into the intuition of a surface form, without roots, without origin or environment, without a seat or a locus; a little universe, an immaterial absolute theme, rejoicing merely in its own quality. This theme, being out of all adventitious relations, and not in the least threatened with not being the theme it is, has not the contingency nor the fortunes proper to an existence; it is simply that which it inherently, logically, and unchangeably is. (SAF, p. 39)

Thus one who really succeeds in giving up every belief not established as true by something immediately experienced, will not believe in the existence even of that which, in fact, he does immediately experience, still less of his immediate experience of it. A real sceptic will deny the existence of every datum, everything he thinks of or imagines. The datum 'is the whole of what solicits my attention at any moment' (SAF, p. 35), whereas its existence is a matter of its being in external relations to things outside it, which nothing within the datum points to in an indubitable manner. That something exists cannot be known by intuition, or direct experience, nor is there any possible proof that anything exists. 'Belief in the existence of anything, including myself, is something radically incapable of proof, and resting, like all belief, on some irrational persuasion or prompting of life' (*idem*). This is not to say that things, including myself, don't exist. 'To bring me evidence of their existence is no duty imposed on facts, nor a habit of theirs: I must employ private detectives' (*idem*).

It is crucial to Santayana's contention that what is given immediately to consciousness cannot be given as in external relations to anything else. That this is true of the totality of what is given at any moment is perhaps obvious, that it is true of the various elements within that totality is less obvious. Why are their relations to each other all internal rather than external? Suppose that I see a yellow ball on some green grass, why is the relation between them internal?

Santayana's view on this matter is that it belongs to the essential character of each element in the totality of what is given at any moment that it is just that element in that totality. The yellow ball part of that total scene simply is that yellow ball part of that scene and could not be otherwise. Of course a yellow ball like that could figure in other scenes, but this is to say that other scenes can contain an element with a certain affinity to the yellow ball part of this scene, not that we have the very same form of being in each case. The point may come out more clearly by contrast with a relation which Santayana would call external. If you take the totality of what is presented at one moment you have a form of being which could occur twice and in one case be followed by presentation of one sort of development and in the other case be followed by another sort of development, without this making any difference to what the totality in each case essentially is. In contrast to this the yellow ball as a detail, say, to the left of one scene and as a detail to the right of another scene, is not in the same way the same thing in a different irrelevant context, for its place in its context is inseparable from what it itself is.

We shall pursue this subject more fully later. It may help, though, to point out that Santayana is saying much the same thing as an idealist such as F. H. Bradley expressed by saying that the whole is more real than the part, or that the part is a mere abstraction from the whole. However, Santayana has no wish to say that this is true in general, only that it is true with reference to the whole of what is presented at any moment to consciousness, and its parts.

We shall see, however, that this view gives rise to certain difficulties when we try to form a conception of a genuinely external relation, for, in Santayana's view, we cannot properly speaking imagine or intuit external relations. Our apprehension of the external relations between objects must be via intuited internal relations between those elements in the given which symbolize these external relationships. Real temporal priority, for instance, which is an external relation of one event to another can be apprehended only via intuition of specious internal temporal relations between elements in the given, and this apprehension depends upon our intent or belief somehow going beyond the character of what is actually given.

Thus a persistent sceptic will, according to Santayana, find nothing to satisfy him that anything such as is presented to his consciousness is in external relations, that is, exists, at all. The scene which comes before his mind at any time has its own character, and this he notices, but of the holding of external relations between it and something else nothing assures him. Nor does he find anything in the scene which shows that there is such a thing as his experience of it. Nor again is there any reason to ascribe existence to any of its elements. They are simply part of what is involved in the scene's character, not individual things in their own right in external relations one to another.

5 Essences as the sceptic's resting point

Is there nothing then which is indubitable, nothing of which one has a certainty quite immune to scepticism?[7]

Santayana's reply is that every matter of fact is dubitable, that nothing whatever can be known to exist, if we expect knowledge to be rooted in what is either logically self-evident or guaranteed by the indubitably given. There is, however, something which is indubitable, although it is not a matter of fact at all, and that is the actual character of the given. But we must be careful here. From the outside commentator's point of view that of which the sceptic is certain may be described as what is given or presented to his consciousness. From the sceptic's point of view, however, the fact that something is presented to a mind is by no means acknowledged. He merely savours the character of certain forms of being, this colour, this pattern, this idea, and finds it indubitable that they are what they are; he does not characterize them as experienced by anyone.

Santayana calls these forms of being *essences* and his account of them is central to his philosophy. His use of the term is somewhat akin to that of Husserl, but I do not think that this accounts for his use of the term (which is already adumbrated in *The Life of Reason*).

It is not to be thought that one can only grasp what an essence is, by considering with what one would be left after the most thorough sceptical reflections possible, but Santayana considers it one value of sceptical reflections that they may help us grasp the status of essence. (Santayana often thus uses 'essence' in the singular, without an article, to stand for essences in general.) As a later chapter is devoted to a thorough discussion of Santayana's doctrine of essence a rather cursory account must do for the present.

Essences are present to consciousness whenever we are conscious at all. Normally we do not dwell on them for their own sake, rather we react with feelings of fear, excitement, concern, and so forth which are relevant to them not as mere forms of being, but as characteristics or symbols of existence. If one suspends these normal reactions one becomes aware of them in a new kind of way. We see that they cannot change, or be other than they are (though our own relation to them continually changes). The view before me, that particular scene, cannot be otherwise than it is, though the opportunity for apprehending it may lapse. *That* scene simply is a pattern with that green hill to the left, that field of poppies to the right, and so on. *That* image of an unhappy childhood is what it is in an unalterable way, though it may only sometimes come before my mind, and may or may not come before the minds of others. To that scene, or that image, it is irrelevant that it was before the mind of a certain person at a certain time. The scene itself, the image itself, would be just as much a definite something which might present itself to some mind some day, whether I had ever contemplated it or not, whether or not it had aptness as a symbol for something before me or in my past.

In saying that the immediate objects of consciousness or intuition are essences, Santayana opposes the traditional view of British empiricism, according to which sense-data and images, conceived as private mental particulars, are immediately given. True, Santayana does on rare occasions call sensory essences 'sense-data', but these are universals, eternally available themes of attention, not particular existences, so that you and I and Julius Caesar may have intuited the very same one. Nor does Santayana support the idea that the contrast between sense-data and images marks some sharp contrast within the class of intuitables. Moreover, for Santayana the immediately given essences are not some sort of raw unorganized sensory material. The essence presented by a perceived object, say a cat, is the way it appears to me, and this is not a mere coloured shape, still less a two-dimensional shape, but something which can only be described as the appearance of a cat of that sort. But this does not preclude the possibility of my merely savouring the quality of this cat-essence, without further concern with the existence of any real animal which appears.

We do not perceive essences, we perceive material things (though the sceptic has no use for this idea). In ordinary life, the sensory essences which are intuited are not attended to for their own sake, are not that with which we are concerned. They simply serve as clues to the physical world in which we live. *Intent*, a key word in Santayana's thought, is directed on the material substance of which the essence is immediately, instinctively, and non-inferentially, taken to be a quality, appearance, or symbol. The assumed backing in nature of the phenomenon is the object of concern, not the unsubstantial phenomenon itself.

But though a positive belief in a material world existing independently of any consciousness of it is one of the main tenets of Santayana, it is not, of course, a belief of which the sceptic stands possessed at the stage we have now reached, when he merely intuits essences. He believes neither in the material world, nor in mind; in fact he believes in nothing. But his mind is not a blank. At every moment a definite selection from the infinite realms of essence is present to his consciousness and he can take in this for what it is.

Does Santayana think that one *knows* anything when in this state of mind? Santayana gives an explicit negative to this question in *Scepticism and Animal Faith*, though there are at least verbally contrary answers elsewhere in his writing. Yet he does regard intuitions as a kind of awareness *of something*, not as merely a matter of being passively affected somehow. So though there is no knowledge in what he regards – as we shall see – as the proper sense of the term, the mind does encounter an independent reality the being of which is strictly indubitable. This reality is independent in the sense that its being does not depend upon this or any other mental encounter with it. The intuited essence would be just what it is whether intuited or not, and it is its being, not the existence of an intuition of it, which is indubitable.

6 Does the given guarantee its own existence?

It is Santayana's claim, then, that though something is immediately given, this something does not, so to speak, carry its own existence, or the existence of anything else, with it. For something to exist it must not merely have a character, it must be in external relations to something, but the given is not given as in any external relations. To believe that it exists is to believe that it stands in external relations, and to believe this is to believe something not guaranteed by the given.

Some aspects of this doctrine will only become clear when we study Santayana's doctrine of essence more thoroughly than we can do now. For the present the following comments may be made.

1   Much of what Santayana has to say on epistemology will stand even if this extreme doctrine is rejected. If we agree that a certain sort of rationality pressed to its limits will lead to solipsism of the present moment, interpreted as nonbelief in the existence of anything but *this* (the present content) we may find cause to assent to Santayana's doctrine of 'animal faith', even if we are unconvinced as to the impossibility of indubitable knowledge that even *this* exists.

2   Santayana's view that, say, the colour *orange* has a kind of inevitable being, independent of whatever as a matter of contingent fact exists, seems correct. Had there been nothing orange, had even no one ever experienced the colour orange, *orange* (or each different shade of orange, at least) would have been a definite quality missing from the world, different from other missing or present qualities.

Santayana's point here is similar to that which underlies Meinong's theory of objects. It is still widely thought that the grounds for this theory were undermined by Russell's theory of descriptions. This, I believe, is a mistake though I cannot here discuss the matter in detail. But consider what the Russellian would say of my present example of orange. He could hardly deny that 'something is orange or nothing is orange' is a necessary truth, and this seems to admit that orange must have ontological status either as exemplified or as unexemplified. Consider a world in which nothing is orange. The Russellian can say: 'We need not allow that there are orange things which do not exist. Rather, we say, it is true of each thing that it is not orange.' But what is this quality which each thing lacks? Would it exist? 'You cannot say "Orange exists" or "Orange does not exist" for "Orange" is a logically proper name, not a description.' Does then a quality mid-way between yellow and red exist? 'Yes, there is a quality answering to this description, though nothing has it.'

There is much, I think, wrong with this whole Russellian treatment of existence, but even such as it is, it seems that in effect it must admit that there may *be* qualities and properties (including the highly complex property of being a twentieth-century king of France, for example) which are not exemplified. This is to admit all that in Meinong and Santayana seems odd to common sense; in all other respects they are closer to it, or to ordinary language, than is Russell. It is much more natural to say that there are possible objects and qualities which do not exist, than to invent a peculiar language in which you cannot say either that *blue* or *this* exist or do not exist, because 'blue' and 'this' are logically proper names.

3 It must be admitted, however, that Santayana's position is not altogether straightforward. One might think that on his view, although the given essence is not given as existing, still if it is in external relations, as on all but the sceptic's view it is, then it does in fact exist. However, his more considered view seems to be that given essences cannot exist, cannot be in external relations. It is their very nature to be self-complete and isolated forms of being. What may or may not exist is a substance of which they are an apt description, for it is only substances which can be in external relations. Of this more hereafter.

4 Leaving some of these subtleties aside, is it really true that in contemplating the given colour I receive no guarantee that anything exists whatever, that I am merely aware of a form of possible being? Even granted that there is the intangible kind of *being as a mere possibility* which every quality and property would necessarily have whatever might or might not exist, do I not, being aware of orange, have a complete assurance that something has that more substantial sort of being Santayana calls existence, whether it be the colour, the awareness of the colour, or whatever?

I confess I find it hard not to answer in the affirmative. I do not deny that one may so sink in 'pure intuition' that one makes no judgement of existence at all – but I cannot help a strong inclination to believe that if one raises the question, one can be sure beyond conceivable doubt that either this content, or the awareness of it (I need not here decide which), *exists*.

But there is a problem here, for Santayana does seem to be right that I do not have this sort of assurance of any context in which it belongs, and that is to say that I cannot have indubitable assurance that it belongs to any time, place, or enduring mind. But what sort of existence would it be that does not belong to any of these? Perhaps I should have to reply that a third ontological status is conceivable which is more than being as a mere possibility, and different from existence as an event or thing in time, space or mind – an isolated self-existence, and that Santayana confuses this with the first.

As to whether such isolated self-existence is a possibility I am in doubt. If it is not, I think Santayana's case is made. If it is, then Santayana's case can still stand in part, for he can still say that the given provides no indubitable assurance of existence of any ordinary sort.

III

Animal Faith

---

1 *The return from scepticism*

If knowledge or rational belief has to be based upon absolutely indubitable foundations, foundations which upon reflection one sees it makes no sense to call in question, then there can be no knowledge or rational belief regarding any matters of existential fact. Such is the conclusion at which we have seen Santayana arrive. But his philosophy is not intended to be primarily sceptical in its upshot, and we must now turn to the positive alternative he has to offer to such scepticism.

Santayana is most often referred to in books on epistemology as an example of extreme scepticism. These references seem to rest on a misunderstanding. On the whole Santayana's explorations of scepticism are designed to show the hopelessness of a certain ideal of knowledge, that for which knowledge must be based upon indubitable foundations, not to show the impossibility of knowledge on a more sensible interpretation of the term. In fact his position has a good deal in common with various recent attacks upon the view that for knowledge to exist it must have indubitable foundations. If it is in some respects sketchier than modern treatments of the subject, it is in other ways more radical.

Thus on the whole we should not call Santayana a sceptic. Yet it is true that he does thus describe himself from time to time, and speaks of scepticism as a worthy state.[1] There is, I think, a certain ambivalence in his attitude here. He has some tendency to think that scepticism would be the better path, but that since few of us are strong enough to live without reliance on the 'animal faith' we are shortly to explore, we may as well be honest about it and let our philosophy express this faith. But he also thinks it only a misunderstanding of the essential possibilities that we should be discontented with animal faith and look for more.[2] Moreover, the positive value he attaches to scepticism is not primarily that of a position in some manner rational, rather he sees it as an avenue to that pure intuition of essence which is a type of spiritual life.

Santayana's answer to scepticism lies in an appeal to what, in his colourful way, he describes as 'animal faith'. However much one may see the theoretical dubitability of all sorts of ordinary matters of fact, one is continually forced into believing certain things whether one likes it or not. When I intuit an essence of the type presented in perception, some physical thing is acting on me, and I am conditioned to respond in some way, say by an avoiding action. This physical response is reflected in my consciousness by my feeling towards that essence as to an existing thing (or at least to the appearance of such), such as is full of threats or potential benefit to my welfare. Santayana dubs this feeling 'animal faith' because it is the feature of our consciousness which is most conspicuously dependent on our status as animals in a treacherous environment. This, however, is to look at the matter from the outside. From the inside point of view, the fact is that however much one may aspire to the rationality which leads to scepticism, one will continually find oneself believing things for which one can give no reason other than one which begs the question. If one gives in to this pressure to believe, a world will present itself to one in terms of which one can explain why one has this impulse to believe, a world in which one is an animal having to cope with a difficult environment, and in which a differential responsiveness to the environment, of which belief is the conscious expression, is a characteristic on which one's survival depends.

In the latter part (Chapter XI onwards) of SAF Santayana describes one possible order in which the beliefs of common sense (described in philosophic language) might reassert themselves in the mind of one who had tried to be a sceptic. This is the path back from scepticism, but it is not a path determined by deductive or inductive argument, it is neither a rationalist nor an empiricist re-erection of human knowledge on logically sure foundations, it is rather a path in which resistance after resistance is broken down by the fact that habits of mind which one cannot long suspend have beliefs in matters of fact implicit in them.

One of the habits of mind which the sceptic will find most difficult to throw off is that of comparing what is before his consciousness now with something which was present previously. He may, for instance, have a sense that this same noise has been going on for some time, or that it has altered its character in some respect. These acts of comparison involve a belief, however vague, in a real flux of some sort in which essences figure for a time and then are replaced by others. There is no justification for this belief, other than one which begs the question, but it is in practice quite irresistible.[3]

Moreover, the sceptic will hardly avoid lapsing into some sort of consecutive thought, and this, according to Santayana, involves a belief of a more elaborate sort as to the relations between essences given now and ones given earlier. Even if reasoning is concerned only with internal relations between essences, rather than with any assertions regarding existence, it carries with it a sense of the passage of the attention from one essence to another, and as the fact of this passage, which is not merely specious, is never guaranteed by anything strictly given, belief in it rests upon no evidence which does not beg the question. [4]

These beliefs do not amount to a belief in a thinking self, according to Santayana, only to a belief in some sort of experiential flux, but some version of the former belief cannot now be long delayed. For as one notes these recurrences and connections in what is presented one will regain one's sense that an effort to learn something is going on. But a purpose carried over from one moment to another implies some sort of enduring self, so that here we have a further belief in the existence of something which is certainly not guaranteed by the given. [5]

These beliefs spring from inevitable habits of mind rather than from any particular presented essence. Santayana next considers a specific essence, that of shock, which, when intuited, as sooner or later it will be, carries with it a further increment of belief. *Shock*, which I take it there is no reason to distinguish here from any feeling of surprise, is the essence, the distinctive quality of feeling, which one experiences when something unexpected happens. [6]

That in which shock makes me primarily believe seems to be that I live in a world regarding which I have certain expectations such as can be fulfilled or disappointed. Santayana primarily stresses the further force it gives to the belief in my own substantial existence, as an individual for whom the flux of given essences is not merely something to be welcomed or feared as conforming or otherwise to its demands. But shock is also 'the great argument of common sense for the existence of material things' (SAF, p. 145) and though the belief in these seems to be taken here as more resistible than the belief in the self with its series of welcome or unwelcome experiences, it is not a belief which one can seriously resist for long.

Such in the sketchiest outline is the argument of Chapters XI–XVI of SAF. The following comments may be made.

1   The actual order in which Santayana shows the sceptic recovering his beliefs, especially when the chapters are analysed in more detail than has been done here, is in some respects curious. Santayana sometimes gives as a later stage in the recovery of belief what seems already contained in an earlier stage. But as there is no proper logical reasoning involved, and no one right order is insisted upon as the only possible route of such recovery, it is the general idea rather than the detail which matters.

2 When Santayana speaks of the recovery of belief in a substantial self, he means belief in an *I* which is more than a mere act of attention to essence, and more than a series of such acts. Santayana must hold, I think, that the expectations and hopes that one recognizes as belonging to this substantial self are revealed in these mental acts, but are not to be identified with them; he does not make this very clear but it seems implied in what he says, and fits in with aspects of his general philosophy of mind.

This substantial self is (on Santayana's view) in fact a certain physical organism, a living member of the realm of matter. However, Santayana supposes that the sceptic may have a sense of this substantial ego at a stage when he does not realize that the only proper candidate for this role is something fitly called physical. He may have had in mind the fact that a philosopher such as Fichte, whom he seems rather to have admired, believed in a substantial ego without any real environment, and have thought that such a philosophy represented a possible stage on the return from utter scepticism to common sense, more satisfactory than the position of a Humean empiricist who believes only in the flux of sensations.[7]

3 It may be thought that Santayana's position is little different from Hume, whose speculations drove him to scepticism but whom daily life brought back to the beliefs of every day.

Santayana distinguished his own position from that of Hume thus.[8] For Hume, the philosopher realizes that all there really is, is a flux of impressions and ideas, but he also realizes that as a result of certain principles of association, etc., a tendency to feign a more substantial world and self develops within this stream and in his lighter moments the philosopher feigns these things himself. Santayana, on the other hand, seriously believes that there is this substantial world. He admits that there is no proof of its existence, but nor is there any proof of the existence of the stream of impressions and ideas, or even of the existence of any one of them. He believes because he cannot help believing, but still he really believes, and does not believe that his belief is a mere tendency to feign. Nor does he believe that the philosopher should try to explain the growth of these beliefs in terms of processes in the allegedly more basic world of impressions and ideas, and the laws which govern them. Not only does this fragmentary world offer insufficient grounds for any such explanation, but since it is not merely in this fragment of a world in which Santayana believes he is not going to give it any such fundamental status in his philosophy.

This interpretation of Hume may not be entirely correct and Santayana's position may be nearer to some aspects of Hume than he realized. But that there is this aspect to Hume, and that Santayana's position is unambiguously distinct from it, cannot be denied. Moreover, as we shall see, Santayana's epistemology allows him to put a stress on the notion of substance of a quite unHumean kind.

4 Santayana exhibits the sceptic as returning to ordinary beliefs via stages which correspond more or less to those through which he passed on the way towards scepticism. Previously some of these stages seemed to be dismissed as incoherent. Is this judgement now rescinded?

By and large the answer seems to be as follows. They are all essentially unstable positions which point to either a reduction or an increase in belief. Even when internally incoherent they are still stages one can pass through. If one reaches them because one is doubting all one can doubt the same impulse will force one on to a still more sceptical position. If one reaches them, moving in the opposite direction, because one's mental habits, or the specific essences presented, simply force one to a certain minimal belief, the same pressures will carry one beyond them to a more substantial, and perhaps more coherent, body of beliefs.

5 Santayana seems rather to over-stress the place of shock in re-arousing a sense of one's own substantial self and the reality of one's environment. Surely it is not only when I am surprised by an unexpected interruption, but when I find myself responding to some quite usual stimulus, that I find my scepticism gone? This, I am sure, from the general tenor of this thought, would be allowed by Santayana.

A further point about 'shock' which calls for notice is this. Does Santayana hold that the feeling of shock, when say I suddenly feel the cat jump on my back, in part constitutes my belief that this was something unexpected or does it merely prompt the belief; and if the latter, is it a merely contingent fact that this essence of shock has such power to prompt belief? The following passage seems to imply each of these alternatives:

Nevertheless shock, like any other datum, intrinsically presents an essence only, and *might* be nothing more; but in that case the dogmatic suasion of it (which alone lends interest to so blank an experience) would be an illusion. The intuition [*surely he should have said 'the essence'*] would be what it is, but it would be nobody's intuition, and it would mean nothing. . . . Shock will not suffer me, while it lasts, to entertain any such hypothesis. It is in itself the most positive, if the blindest, of beliefs; it loudly proclaims an event; so that if by chance the change that I feel were merely a feeling within the unity of apperception, shock would be an illusion, in the only sense in which this can be said of any intuition: it would incite me to a false belief that something like the given essence existed. . . . Unless it is an illusion, which I cannot admit while I feel it, it implies variation in a voluminous vegetative life in which the sense of surprise is a true indication of novelty. (SAF, pp. 142–3)

Evidently there is a problem here, as to whether belief is merely the intuition of a special kind of essence, to which we must return hereafter. For the present it is sufficient if we can accept that though, when thus shocked, I form a belief, what I experience, even shock itself, gives no logical ground for this belief.

2   *Animal faith*

Having reached this stage in the recovery of belief Santayana claims that if we use the word 'knowledge' in a sensible way, we can describe these beliefs as knowledge. Certainly they do not amount to knowledge if by this be meant a kind of insight into fact which, in virtue of its own intrinsic nature, could not be mistaken, but such knowledge is something intrinsically impossible (though intuition of essence has some analogy to it) and should not be an object of repining. What is normally classified as knowledge is faith or belief in the existence of objects characterized or symbolized for us by the essences immediately present to our intuition, a faith the content of which is true, and not merely by accident but because it is the product of those objects on to which it is directed. Santayana is well aware that the claim that the beliefs we call knowledge are true itself rests on faith, but quite rightly considers this no objection. All assertions, including the assertion that a belief is a case of knowledge, rest on a faith without intrinsic infallibility, but since, if we are honest, we must admit that we have this faith, we need not avoid assertion expressive of it.

Santayana actually offers a kind of definition of knowledge, specifying three features as essential to it. (1) 'Knowledge accordingly is belief: belief in a world of events, and especially of those parts of it which are near the self, tempting or threatening it.' (2) 'Furthermore, knowledge is true belief.' (3) 'Finally, knowledge is true belief grounded in experience, I mean, controlled by outer facts.'

This account is similar to ones which have been advanced in recent times, for instance by J. Watling and D. M. Armstrong.[9] It differs from those accounts which insist in one way or another that the distinction between knowledge and mere belief lies in the reasons one has for the former, accounts which suffer, apart from further difficulties, from the fact that the possession of reasons for a belief presumably itself consists in knowing certain truths.

One can explain Santayana's position further, I think, by saying that I properly call a belief a case of knowledge if I believe it to be true and if I believe that it is not true by accident, but because it had causes connected with the truth of the proposition in which it is a belief. Hence though my knowledge is in a sense a mere belief, an act of compulsory faith, it is also properly described as knowledge by those who believe regarding it what has just been said, something which, if we are honest, we will admit we often do believe. Knowledge, one might say, is a kind of faith which we call knowledge because we have faith in it. It must be borne in mind, however, that the truth possessed by our knowledge is, for Santayana, rather a symbolic than a literal truth; the essences we ascribe to things are not their real characters but ones which appropriately do duty for these within our consciousness.

In any case what matters primarily to us at the moment is not Santayana's precise definition of knowledge but his reply to scepticism. This reply may be summarized roughly as follows: If you manage to do without all beliefs which are not self-guaranteeing or guaranteed by the given, I congratulate you, but we will have nothing to say to each other because you will be lost in a solitary swoon with no beliefs whatsoever. If on the other hand you do have any beliefs whatever, as you must have to speak to me, you must admit that ultimately you believe certain things merely because of a non-rational compulsion to do so. In that case you cannot reasonably reject belief in any particular type of thing because its existence is open to doubt. The proper path is simply to decide what you really, on reflection, do believe and then to organize your beliefs in a coherent way; such beliefs are rational in the only sense in which any beliefs can be. If this system of beliefs includes an explanation of why you have them, that is surely a great advantage. Thus the beliefs of a materialist or naturalist do far better than those of an idealist – who believes only in mental things or events. For the material-ist sees the compulsion to believe as having originated in the survival value it possesses for an animal in an independently existing environ-ment. This is why he describes this compulsion, or that to which it is a compulsion (for Santayana uses the term somewhat loosely), as *animal faith*.

On this view I would comment as follows:

1 It should go without saying that Santayana uses 'belief' in a wide sense to cover any case where someone holds that something is the case; not for a hesitant kind of opining which contrasts with the assurance proper to what we call knowledge. The propriety of this use of 'belief' has been disputed by some philosophers, but I think wrongly. Belief should be distinguished from mere belief; one who knows that it is Tuesday, *ipso facto* believes that it is Tuesday. Santayana is inclined also to use 'belief', not only for a fixed view of how things are, but for a momentary mental act of thinking that something is the case. Many philosophers have so used 'belief' but it has been widely challenged

in recent philosophy. However, unless it is denied that there are such mental acts, the dispute seems largely verbal.

2   Santayana calls himself a materialist and means thereby that the material world has an existence independent of consciousness, and that all causal efficacy is material. He does not mean that only material things exist, or that consciousness itself is material.

3   When we consider Santayana's materialism more carefully we shall see that it misrepresents him to say that *beliefs* have a survival value if by 'belief' is meant something purely 'mental', for strictly the survival value belongs to its physical analogue; but this is a subtlety hardly relevant at present.

3   *Substance*

We have now covered the essential principles of Santayana's epistemology, but there are some remaining themes it will repay us to look at. Chief among these is the vindication Santayana offers of the notion of substance.[10] 'All knowledge, being faith in an object posited and partially described, is belief in substance, in the etymological sense of this word; it is belief in a thing or event subsisting in its own plane, and waiting for the light of knowledge to explore it eventually, and perhaps name or define it' (SAF, p. 182).

I think we may say that something is a substance in this sense if, first, it can exist with its own definite character without being thought about by, or in any way revealed to the experience of, any sentient being, and if, secondly, when it is thought about it is external to the thought of it, in the sense that both object and thought could have had the same intrinsic character without the other existing. The rejection of substances in this sense is not only at the very heart of philosophical idealism but is also an important factor in a good deal of empiricism since the time of Hume. It is therefore quite a challenging assertion on Santayana's part that all belief is belief in substance. For it implies that the reasons given for rejecting material or spiritual substances are equally reasons for rejecting mental events and any other possible constituents of the world.

That all belief is belief in substance follows strictly from Santayana's analysis of belief. To have a belief is to take a given essence as somehow characterizing something beyond, and if there is a suitable object beyond, it is that which is believed in. Whether that something beyond exists or not makes no difference to the intrinsic character of the belief as a mental event, which turns rather upon the given essence which is, of course, not a substance. It is equally true that the something beyond could have existed without there having been this mental act directed on to it – that is really what is meant by saying it lies beyond.

It is particularly important, in this connection, to note Santayana's contention that mental events are not *ipso facto* objects of awareness. A mental event cannot be immediately given, since the immediately given is always an essence, so that it can only be cognized if another mental event constitutes a belief in its existence. (Santayana assumes that an act of belief cannot be a belief in itself.) From this it follows that mental events are all substances. They cannot be immediately given, and when they are cognized it remains true that they are external to the act which cognizes them, so that either might have been just as it was without the other. Thus Santayana can argue that even in allowing the existence of mental acts one is committing oneself to entities answering to the traditional idea of substances as entities independent of the experience of them.

Objectors to substance have objected above all to the existence of something which could never be experienced. If all that can be experienced are the appearances of material things, or of spiritual things, let us confine our serious belief (so such philosophers urge) to these appearances, regarding the substances as at best a convenient fiction useful in the organization of our knowledge of the appearances.

But Santayana insists that these very appearances, considered as mental or sensory facts, are themselves substances in the sense objected to. When it is objected that material substances cannot be experienced it must be meant that they cannot be immediately and infallibly given, since to say that they cannot be experienced in any sense, even by means of their appearances, obviously begs the question. But mental or sensory facts cannot be immediately given either, for these are supposed to be elements belonging to real temporal sequences while the only temporal relations that can be given are, as we have seen, specious ones, and there is nothing in the given which establishes the existence of any real temporal sequence, even one of mere sense data or qualities, at all.

Thus, according to Santayana, one will not avoid those features which have been held against the notion of substance merely by economizing on one's beliefs. Even a man who confined his belief to the stream of his own experiences would believe in something incapable of being directly given, and thus in something 'behind' any possible appearance. A real flux of experience demands transitions other than those merely specious ones which are a feature of the given essence. To recall or predict the unrolling of one's experiences is to take given images of transition as symbolizing real transitions which could never be immediate objects of awareness:

For my own part, having admitted discourse (which involves time and existences deployed in time, but synthesized in retrospect), and having admitted shocks that interrupt discourse and lead it to regard itself as an experience, and having even admitted that such experience involves a self beneath discourse, with an existence and movement of its own – I need not be deterred by any *a priori* objections from believing in substance of any sort. For me it will be simply a question of good sense and circumstantial evidence how many substances I admit, and of what sort. (SAF, p. 183)

If the essences before the philosopher combine urgently to persuade him of the existence of certain things, and if the memory of essences intuited in the past adds its persuasions (this memory being itself a particularly compulsive and basic belief) he has as much reason to believe in the existence of these things as he has to believe that his own past experiences once existed, or in the existence of himself, whether conceived as a pure consciousness or as some substantial agent. He feels an imperious summons to believe and, the belief once adopted, everything conspires to encourage its continuance. If sceptical doubts reoccur, he may remind himself of the risk essentially inherent in all knowledge claims, and by no means avoided by one who believes only in the flux of his own sensations or in mind thinking, and see that no strikingly new form of risk is being taken now that he begins to accept the belief arising in him of a vast world, properly called a material world, of interacting entities of which at one level he himself is one, entities which can be in closer or less close contact, which can break each other up or join together and so forth. He is simply giving in to the persuasive suggestions which these essences actually carry for him, and that is all that he, or any idealist or radical empiricist, was ever doing when he granted or assumed that such things as experiences, sensations, thoughts, consciousness, a self, or whatever, exist at all. One who accepts the validity of the pressing idea of a material world, in which his experiences arise as incidents in the life of an animal organism, has, though, one great advantage over the idealist or radical empiricist, namely that the world he posits (in full seriousness, not simply as some useful device for organizing facts about experiences) offers far more in the way of detailed explanation of how there arises this pressing urge to posit existences, whether mental, sensory, physical or whatever, than does the world of sensations following each other in a void which is alone posited with full seriousness by the radical empiricist, or the world of dreaming spirits, or spirit, which is alone posited with full seriousness by the idealist. The material world, once posited as a genuine and independent reality, can effectively explain the genesis of the act of positing in terms of its biological basis and connection with activities making for survival, though this does not, of course, from the point of view of the act of positing provide it with a justification of itself, especially as an act of positing cannot be aware of its own existence but only of the existence of previous acts of positing which it posits (normally, at least), as occurrences arising in physical situations, as its own existence may later be posited by other acts:

> The instinct and ability to posit objects, and the occasion for doing so, are incidents in the development of animal life. Positing is a symptom of sensibility in an organism to the presence of other substances in its environment. . . . The living substance within him being bent, in the first instance, on pursuing or avoiding some agency in its environment, it projects whatever (in consequence of its reactions) reaches its consciousness into the locus whence it feels the stimulus to come, and it thus frames its description or knowledge of objects. (SAF, pp. 184–5)

Having once given up the heroic effort to be sceptics, we should acknowledge our instinctive beliefs frankly and not be afraid to call them knowledge. On the basis of these primary instinctive beliefs we can erect a more and more satisfactory account of the world, the details of which will be checkable in a rational manner, that is, by their consistency with what we cannot, in the ordinary run of things, doubt.

The ordinary man's belief in material substances is not based on reasoning. The mental life for which belief in material substances is basic arises naturally in an animal adjusting itself to its material environment, and is indeed simply the focusing of this fact in consciousness. To take a sensory essence as an appearance of something capable of presenting a variety of other appearances is the normal original way of experiencing such an essence. There may be a problem as to how the physical life of the organism gives rise to consciousness but, granted that it does so, it is hardly surprising that the consciousness to which it gives rise is one in which the existence of physical things is taken for granted. Once the sceptic relaxes his forced abandonment of all belief whatever, the belief in substances will simply rearise in his spirit with as little foundation as ever. Nor need this be felt as a disgrace. If there is a material world, there is no other conceivable way in which knowledge of it could have arisen. Refusing to trust to one's instinctive beliefs is turning one's back on the only sort of knowledge a world could conceivably offer a mind.

Regarding Santayana's treatment of *substance* at this point we may note the following,

1   In general he does not use 'substance' in the present very wide sense and elsewhere he insists that there are no mental substances. Here, however, he is concerned to show that some of the objections typically raised to material substances apply equally to any sort of existent whatever.

2   His argument depends in part upon his own very special view of the

given, which he encapsulates in the slogan 'Nothing given exists'. Actually there is a certain ambiguity here, for Santayana seems at times to confuse the question: 'Are external relations given?' with the question 'Is the given in external relations?' What he means in answering the second negatively is that what is in external relations, and hence exists, is not the given essence but the intuition to which it is given, and this may be true, but insofar as he sometimes seems to derive this from his well founded negative answer to the first, his reasoning is imperfect.[11]

If one held, as against Santayana, that though the existence of the given is not given, it does in fact exist, one might claim that here one really has immediate experience of an existence, and that existences which can be known thus set a standard not attained by substances. But even if this were acknowledged, Santayana would still be right in claiming that a *succession* of such existences, in external relations to one another, has rather the status of a substance, and that therefore the most reductive sensationalistic ontology is still committed to substances. He could say the same to one who rejected even his view of existence, and thus claimed that the given was given *as* an existent.

The details of his argument rest, then, upon very specific views regarding the given, but its main upshot seems independent thereof.

3 In the arguments we have considered, Santayana is contending mainly against those who argue that we have a kind of evidence for the existence of so called appearances, which we do not have for the existence of the substances which, allegedly, they manifest. But one might object to material (or mental) substance on the ground not that evidence for it is insufficient but that we can form no proper conception of it. Santayana has a good deal to say on this but we shall postpone its consideration, only noting that for Santayana the fact that external relations are unintuitable means that existence of any kind necessarily has an aspect we cannot properly conceive.

4 It might be argued that Santayana, like Berkeley, confuses substance as that which contrasts with attributes with substance as that which contrasts with sensory appearance.[12] This is doubtless in part true, but the distinction could hardly be sharp for Santayana since on his view of belief or judgement this most commonly consists in taking the given appearance, which is a universal, as an attribute of something beyond.

4 *The uniformity and animation in nature*

For a complete return to the ordinary outlook of men there are two main remaining types of belief to be reinstated, belief in nature and belief in animation in nature. We shall not discuss Santayana's treatment of these topics in detail as the main character of his epistemology should be clear enough already.

By belief in nature Santayana means the belief, first, that the material world is *one*, so that all material substances stand in relation to each other,[13] and, second, that the substances in this world have constant ways of behaving so that adjustments found useful in the present will tend to be useful in the future. Consciousness reflects the adjustments which an organism makes to its environment, partly through inherited patterns of behaviour, partly through conditioning at the hands of that environment. Such adjustment can only exist between organism and environment if both have a certain constancy of nature. Consciousness simply finds itself with the beliefs which must be true if this basic condition of its existence is to hold. This gives it no reason for these beliefs other than one which begs the question, but for a mind which has abandoned scepticism it offers some explanation of the fact that it has them.[14]

Santayana's treatment of belief in the uniformity of nature is very general, and leaves a host of detailed questions untouched, but I see no reason why this topic cannot be dealt with adequately within the general spirit of his philosophy.

His discussion of belief in the animation present in nature is quite detailed and complex, with some interesting features we must pass over.[15] Here I may note his view that a particular body is regarded as the seat of my consciousness primarily because the sequence of my thoughts and feelings, and the character of the essences by which bodies in general are revealed to me, is evidently so closely linked with its destiny, and his view that the belief that other similar organisms are thus animated also (are linked with other such facts of thought, feeling, and perception), can be regarded logically as a special case of belief in the uniformity of nature. But though Santayana thinks that the stronger or weaker analogy between my own body and other bodies offers the best reflective grounds for ascriptions of consciousness, he offers a different explanation for the actual origin of this belief, seeing this in our tendency to project into an observed organism the thoughts and feelings which its behaviour arouses in ourselves. The arousal of such forms of consciousness in myself stems partly from the fact that my body tends incipiently to imitate what I see similar other bodies doing, and that this incipient behaviour brings with it feelings which I then project on to the body seen, and partly from the fact that I have myself often felt thus when I have seen another body thus behaving, in virtue of the fact that I am reacting to the same external stimulus as it.

It would take us too far afield to attempt an evaluation of these suggestions regarding the origin of the belief in animation in nature. We may note, however, that they are symptomatic of that side of Santayana's thought which makes him an important figure in the American philosophical movement known as *naturalism*, for they exhibit his wish to trace the origin of our beliefs neither to the intellectual insight stressed by rationalist philosophers nor to the kind of internal mental chemistry expounded by empiricist associationists, but to natural facts about the animal body and its environment.

It is tempting to say that these questions about the *origin* of beliefs belong to psychology rather than to philosophy and that now, at any rate, the philosopher can turn them safely over to the expertise of the latter; but if we have a view of consciousness or spirit at all similar to Santayana's (which we shall discuss later), the matter is not so straightforward, for we shall then hold that consciousness and its history is not properly amenable to scientific study, that a scientific psychology is a science of behaviour (together perhaps with its neuro-physiological basis), and that this psychology can only provide hints for the essentially literary activity whereby we try to seize the inwardness of mental life as it passes through its different stages.[16] On this view a characterization of the stages by which a child develops its conception of the world around it is neither a task for *a priori* reasoning nor for science as such. Santayana tried to do something of the sort in *Reason in Common Sense*. Today it is only those working in the phenomenological tradition who assay anything of the sort, though without the straightforward naturalistic ontology in the background which Santayana would have had underpin such studies.

Returning to the question of logical justification we may point out that for Santayana the character of my own consciousness is by no means my primary datum. What is immediately present is always an essence, and unless I am practising that unsustainable scepticism we have discussed previously, I take that essence as characterizing, as predicable of, some existence. This existence is normally some natural state of affairs, some fact in space and time; this is true even of most essences whereby I attribute mentality, for such essences as joy, fear, or suffering – when taken as predicates in belief or judgement – are predicated primarily of human beings or animals regarded as substantial physical entities. Although the application of such essences to myself, an animal whose existence is felt with special vividness, is more compelling than their application to others, Santayana does not see any utter contrast between the two cases. For one inclined to scepticism regarding the animation of other persons an appeal to analogy is relevant, but in fact the sense of others, and the sense of myself, as sentient beings are not easily separated parts of that natural view of the world which I hold, not because I have reasons for holding it, but because I simply find myself believing in it. Such seems the main upshot of Santayana's treatment of this theme.

Santanya distinguished what he calls 'discernment of spirit' from belief in the sentience of myself and others, at least he reserves it for a later chapter.[17] Presumably the latter involves a more precise sense of the ontological status of consciousness, a realization that there is, after all, a radical difference between the mere having of certain characteristics by a physical thing, animate or inanimate, and the presence of an essence to an intuition which takes it as the partial revelation of an existing world. When I recognize a being as sentient I presumably have some vague sense of the peculiar status of spirit, but I hardly distinguish the way in which shape and movement on the one hand, and sadness on the other, may characterize an animal. It will be better to reserve further discussion of these points till Chapter V.

Many philosophers in recent years, especially those influenced by Wittgenstein, have made a point of attacking the argument from analogy, the argument that I may and must justify my belief in the consciousness of others on the ground that physically they are analogous to myself, whom I know to be conscious directly.[18] It is difficult to say how relevant their criticisms are to Santayana's point of view, which is not that of their typical opponent; moreover, it would take us rather far afield to enter into their very complex arguments. We must confine ourselves to the following brief observations.

1   One rather simple point sometimes made is this. In the ordinary way if I infer that something has a certain character because it is observably analogous to something else whose possession of that character I have observed, this inferential knowledge is, at least in principle, replaceable by a knowledge based on direct observation: the inference from symptoms to a cancerous growth, for instance, can be confirmed by X-ray. When, however, I infer to another's consciousness I cannot, even in principle, confirm this inference by an observation of his consciousness such as that observation of my own from which I am supposed to have started.

This argument has always appeared to me pretty feeble. It is little more than a dogmatic use of the verification principle. Whatever may be said of the details of Santayana's epistemology, I am sure it has shown this much, namely that all belief rests upon assumptions of a substantial kind which can only be verified by procedures which also rest upon them. But their argument is in any case irrelevant to Santayana's position, since on his view my own consciousness as much as that of others is something believed in, not immediately given. Beliefs can to some extent be arranged in an order of compulsiveness, but there is no rock bottom of fact from which I start out. Hence there is not for Santayana the sort of contrast between the way in which I know about the consciousness of others and of myself.

2   Philosophers influenced by Wittgenstein have an intense suspicion of any talk about a realm of private mental events, though the issue is bedevilled, in my opinion, by confusion between different senses of

'privacy'. What they most object to is the notion that one is somehow primarily presented with a set of private facts on the basis of which, as a solitary ego, one constructs or infers a world in which other persons and public facts somehow figure. The critique of this view is presented essentially as an attack upon the possibility of a private language, for it is supposed that these private facts are recorded in a language which does not presuppose a social life with other persons.

Santayana's viewpoint is quite unlike that mainly under attack by such authors, indeed in some respects he is at one with them. He likewise utterly denies that one can regard the physical world and the sentient organisms within it as something inferred from, still less as something 'constructed' out of, more intimately known private mental facts, and even holds that I can hardly talk intelligibly of the occurrence of a mental event except as the experience of an organism specified by its 'external' character and place. His position is neither Cartesian nor phenomenalist, neither my own existence nor elementary sensory phenomena form the basis of knowledge.

All the same his thought does allow a place to the solitary philosophic ego which is alien to many contemporary philosophers. He allows the intelligibility of a scepticism which they would criticize as being incapable of linguistic expression.

It seems to me a just criticism of Santayana's philosophy that it is in some sense too individualistic. For all his emphasis on the biological foundations of knowledge and consciousness he leaves its social context very little explored.[19] Nonetheless most of his main tenets are compatible with a fuller realization of this side of things. For on the whole his message is simply this. If one looks for a certain sort of certainty, for which philosophers have striven since Descartes, one will slip first into solipsism, and then into a complete suspension of belief. That one could only have acquired the settled language in which to conduct one's philosophic meditations from life in a community does not affect this point, for facts about one's own consistent use of language, even the fact that one has a language at all, are as dubitable as other facts. One must distinguish here between what the sceptic reflects on, and the account of his reflections which may be given by the outsider. There are facts about his reflections which entail their incorrectness, but to believe in the existence of these facts is to have beliefs resting in part on animal faith, as Santayana calls it, not pure reason.

5 Santayana's epistemology in general

We have now explored the main features of Santayana's epistemology, his scrutiny of the foundations of knowledge. For all its dwelling on sceptical doubts the upshot of his enquiry is not sceptical, but lies rather in the recommendation to develop our view of the world on the basis, not of some supposed elementary data of consciousness, but of everyday beliefs which it is dishonest to pretend we do not hold. Ontology, for Santayana, is an attempt to clarify our ordinary or daily viewpoint, and to make it more precise, not to replace it by another.

As a defender of common sense Santayana's position is in some respects akin to that of G. E. Moore. [20] I think he differs, however, in a greater frankness regarding the non-rational foundation of beliefs. When Moore insists that we *know* certain propositions to be true, the word 'know' acquires a kind of mystic force whereby it is sought to repel scepticism. For Santayana the sceptic's position is in a manner invulnerable and even rational. We call our beliefs *knowledge* because we believe they are true, and the product of an appropriate contact with things, but the sceptic who says that they are, after all, only beliefs is in a manner right. In this I think Santayana goes more to the heart of the matter than Moore.

Bertrand Russell says in several places that the position of the absolute sceptic is irrefutable but uninteresting, because no one really adopts it. But Russell treats lesser scepticisms as interesting, because they might be believed, and thinks it a philosopher's task to refute them. Santayana's position, one might say, is that these lesser scepticisms are uninteresting (e.g. scepticism about other minds, about the natural world, about the uniformity of nature), because they leave a vision of the world which is no better grounded than the common one, yet lacks the rationality of absolute scepticism. Absolute scepticism is interesting because, however incredible, it is what one ought to adopt if one objects to ordinary beliefs as inadequately grounded.

Many philosophers seem to follow Russell in this matter. One may instance the discussion in Ayer's *Problem of Knowledge* where he worries away at the inadequate foundations of ordinary beliefs while taking the principle of induction more or less for granted, because to doubt this is to doubt so much as to make discussion impossible. It seems to me that Santayana is right that there is little point in playing at such half-hearted doubting.

Some philosophers look to the hypothetico-deductive method as a way of dealing with scepticism. [21] One does not claim to know anything for certain, one merely adopts testable hypotheses until such time as they are refuted. But whatever may be the merits of this as an account of scientific method, it hardly makes sense to apply it to the basic beliefs with which Santayana is concerned. One can only test a hypothesis if one takes one's own existence and that of the things around one in their main bold character for granted. To test the truth of these background assumptions is absurd, for all tests presuppose them.

Santayana's epistemology is incomplete in many respects, but I still think it a major contribution to the subject. Others have made many of the same points, but they have not brought out their fundamental importance as has Santayana. 'Investigate and reflect and then report honestly what you feel compelled to believe. If you are told that this compulsion is psychological rather than logical, then reflect that consistent resistance to such compulsion would lead to a suspension of all belief whatever – then report again.' That, in my own words, is, I believe, the essential message of Santayana's epistemology.

IV

The Doctrine of Essence

1 *Essences as the given*

One of the main tenets of Santayana's so-called *doctrine of essence* is that nothing is immediately given except essence, and that when I am conscious of any matter of fact some immediately given essence is acting as a symbol of it. If I am conscious at all, I am intuiting an essence, but this intuition may or may not be 'laden with intent'. If it is not I am merely dwelling on the essence for its own sake, and my intuition is 'pure'. If I have some sort of feeling of intent as I intuit the essence, then I am taking it as somehow bringing information of some matter of fact not implied in its mere being as an essence. Santayana's terminology is flexible and may be confusing to the pedantic reader. Sometimes by 'intuition' he means 'pure intuition', sometimes 'an intuition, whether pure or laden with intent'. In the latter and more common sense any mental act is, on Santayana's view, an intuition. Santayana does not himself use the term 'mental act', but I have frequently found it a useful term in the presentation of his doctrine.

I shall be discussing Santayana's view of intent later; here we must simply accept that there are two ways of taking the given – that in which we merely attend to it for what it is in itself and that in which we take it as somehow informing us of something beyond itself. In this first section I want to concentrate on Santayana's conception of essences as the sole given.[1] If we consider the application of this claim to perception we see that Santayana's position stands in obvious contrast both to the 'naïve realism' for which physical things can be given, and to the type of empiricism for which sense impressions or sense data, conceived as particular events or existents, are given.[2] His position also contrasts, of course, with those views which try to dispense altogether with the notion of the given.

I am not sure that Santayana ever offers a formal definition of the phrase 'the given', but I think it would be true to his intention, and will bring out the main point of his view, if we say that for something to be given one must be conscious of it immediately, that is one's consciousness of it must not be mediated by one's consciousness of something else, and one must be conscious of it indubitably, in the sense that one's consciousness cannot distort its character.

We have seen in the last two chapters that, according to Santayana, an attempt to doubt all that can possibly be doubted should lead to a state in which I am conscious of nothing but the immediate and indubitable, and that I am then conscious only of essence. It would be a mistake, however, to think that scepticism is the sole path to such pure intuition. I may reach it also in certain aesthetic or mystical experiences, when I merely, so to speak, 'drink in' the way things appear to me without any concern as to how things really are. This may happen, for instance, in the brief moment that I give myself up wholly to the beautiful smell of a rose, or to the beautiful pattern of a sunset. It may happen, again, if my attention is fascinated by the emotional quality of some situation. One is not then interested in something which belongs to a particular time and place, as does (say) that particular rose, but in a quality or pattern which could always be presented to another mind, if the right sort of conditions occurred. That specific scent which is all that is present to one's consciousness could not be destroyed, as can be that rose. Millions of years hence there might be a being whose consciousness was absorbed by this identical quality.

One might object that the immediate object of my attention is not the repeatable quality, but a particular case of it. Santayana would answer by insisting that what I dwell on so lovingly is the essentially repeatable quality, and that there is nothing in the given which can be distinguished as the particular instance. Certainly my experience of that quality is a particular event belonging to a certain place and time, but what I am delighting in is not the particular experience of the quality, but the quality itself.

It has sometimes been objected against this kind of view that I may experience two such identical qualities at once, and note that they differ solely numerically. To this Santayana would certainly reply that I am then aware of a complex essence having two like elements distinguished by their place within that complex, and that the whole complex, with those its elements, is an essentially repeatable essence.

In more everyday types of consciousness there still is a given and this given also consists of pure essences, but these essences are not dwelt on for their own sake but as characterizations of, or symbols of, existing facts. They serve as clues to the kind of behaviour requisite at the moment and taken as such clues they do not hold my attention but direct it towards further essences which will provide further clues.

It is not altogether obvious how one argues from the fact that only essences are given in pure intuition to the conclusion that only essences are given in perception or thought. I suppose Santayana would say that, at any moment, one can transform one's perception or thought into pure intuition and then recognize, on reflection, that one and the same indubitable element was immediately present to one before and after the transformation. This object can hardly be a physical thing, for it might have been present even though no physical thing of a relevant kind existed, and it is not a particular of any private kind, since there is nothing to prevent its being repeated in the experience of another person.

Santayana offers various traditional arguments against the possibility of 'intuitions of things', designed to show that my awareness of a physical thing presupposes an awareness of something else less dubitable, referring in this connection to illusions and hallucinations in a fairly standard way. (However some details of these arguments may stand open to criticism, the main points which, at their best, they seek to make, that there is a distinction between the character of the aspect or appearance which a thing wears at a certain time for an observer and the character of the thing itself at that moment, and that in hallucination there is an appearance but no thing, still stand. This is by no means opposed to common sense or ordinary ways of speech, both of which – as how could they not? – exhibit an unsystematic grasp of the contrast.)³ The real core of his thought, however, lies, I believe, in his sense of the essential externality of the relation between an act of consciousness and a physical thing. If Santayana is right, the complete nature of an act of consciousness can be specified while leaving it quite open whether there is any real physical existence of which it is a consciousness, though not whether there is any *essence* which provides its 'content' (though, as I have said, Santayana disliked this latter term) while, on the other hand, no events in the physical realm logically necessitate that there is any consciousness of them. If this is correct it does seem difficult to see how a physical thing could ever be immediately and indubitably present to consciousness.

Santayana's use of the term 'the given' is liable to mislead because this expression is apt to have meanings quite remote from those he intends. The term was perhaps ill chosen on his part, for these other meanings are perhaps the more natural ones.⁴

By a given element in perception may be meant some sort of indubitable information supposedly supplied in the perceptual process from which most of what we are ordinarily said to perceive is inferred. It should be clear by now that for Santayana nothing is given in this sense. The given essences are taken as characterizing and symbolizing facts beyond them but these facts cannot be inferred from the essences. One does not move from pure intuition of essences to intentful intuition either rationally or irrationally. The normal way of intuiting an essence is intentful. Pure intuition provides no basis for belief, it is merely intuition emptied of belief.[5]

Another meaning of 'the given' to be distinguished from that of Santayana is that in which it designates some supposed pure uninterpreted sensory core upon which the mind somehow works in order to provide the structured world we confront in perception.

Santayana acknowledges that there is a process of interpretation or synthesis something like what Kant describes, but this is not directed at something given to consciousness, nor is it a mental activity, if by this he meant something belonging to the realm of spirit or consciousness. Unknown physical processes in the brain operate on the physical messages brought by the sense organs in such a way as enables the organism to respond appropriately. The effect of this in consciousness is that a certain essence is intuited with intent. The given essence (I think we could say), is already an interpretation, not something to be interpreted.[6]

So far, Santayana is quite explicit, and it is sufficient to distinguish his view from many theories of the given which have rightly been subject to a good deal of attack in recent years. We are not to distinguish, at the level of conscious mind, between mere sense impressions, unorganized into objects, and the interpretation thereof.

It seems to be implied by this that the essence intuited when I perceive an object cannot be described, in most cases, simply in terms of colours, shapes, sounds and so on; that, for instance, when I see a horse, as a horse, an essence is given which can only be described as the essence of a horse (the specious essence, thereof, in Santayana's terminology, not the real essence). That this is so seems implied in Santayana's general treatment of the given, but I do not think he ever makes the point quite explicitly. It is in any case a point which needs to be made, and which fits in with Santayana's general outlook, and, more specifically, with much that he says in connection with the consciousness of space. One might point out, in the same connection, that when I look at a drawing the essence given is not in the normal case a mere flat arrangement of lines, but a version of the specious essence of the thing I see depicted, and will vary with my 'interpretation' of the drawing.

Though this does, on the whole, seem to be Santayana's view, he occasionally writes as though in pure sensory intuition I meet only with shapes and not with objects.[7] He may mean only that this tends to happen because the practical interests in terms of which I individuate and classify objects are then in abeyance. At any rate he surely should hold that it is also possible to have pure intuition of what we might perhaps call object-essences as opposed to merely quality-or-pattern-essences.

Maybe Santayana was not himself altogether clear how *intent* relates to *interpretation*. It is easy to run together the intent which must accompany my intuition of an essence, if that is taken as revelatory of a real existence, with an interpretation put upon some sensible form. If the two are identified then one will suppose that when intent lapses one is left with mere patterns or qualities. There are, as we shall see, various difficulties attached to the notion of intent, but I do not think the above identification is true to Santayana's main intentions even if he sometimes tends to it. Certainly he is as explicit as can be against the notion of the sensory core.

2 *Different sorts of exemplification*

So far we have considered essences almost exclusively as the immediate data of consciousness and vehicles of perception and belief. This, however, is only one of the two main ways in which Santayana thinks of essences as entering into the flux of existence, for essences may also occur as the characters of things.[8]

When an essence is the immediate object of intuition Santayana says that it is imaginatively exemplified by that intuition, the term covering exemplification in perception or thought, in fact as immediate object to any kind of consciousness, not merely in imagination as ordinarily understood. He tells us that he would like to speak here of 'objective exemplification', in the sense, echoing an old tradition, of exemplification merely as an object, but that since 'objective' has in modern times acquired a quite contrary meaning it might be misleading. When an essence occurs as the character of a fact or existence rather than as an object of consciousness he describes it as being formally or passively exemplified. An intuition formally exemplifies the essence of spirit while imaginatively exemplifying its immediate object. A physical thing formally exemplifies its own inner nature. We should note, further, that Santayana speaks of a thing as *speciously* exemplifying any essence which it regularly presents to the consciousness of humans or animals and in terms of which they identify it.

What more there is to be said regarding imaginative exemplification had better wait, mostly, till Chapter V, but a word is needed here regarding the role of the given essence when intuition is intent-ful, or, as Santayana puts it, 'is carried by intent'. I have said that this given essence is taken as *characterizing or symbolizing* an existence beyond. Are these alternatives or different expressions for the same thing? Santayana is often rather vague at this point in his thought, but what he seems to have held was that in belief a given essence is taken as a predicate of some reality beyond it, and that this consists in taking it as offering some insight into that reality's nature, either because the given essence is thought of as actually being a characteristic possessed by it, or alternatively as in some way suitably symbolizing such a characteristic. Presumably different minds would draw the line of distinction between these two at different places, the philosopher tending to interpret almost all cases in the latter way, the ordinary man thinking of the essences given in perception in the former way, and of the verbal essences (i.e. words) in the latter way, with the essences given in imagination lying somewhere between these two. It should be noted that Santayana hardly distinguishes sufficiently between the way in which essences given in perception bring tidings of the world and the way in which essences given in thought occur as vehicles of my judgement. When he speaks of essences being, or being taken as, appearances of things to us he presumably has the former case in mind. Here, as elsewhere, Santayana is so intent upon certain very bold and general distinctions that he exaggerates the homogeneity of what lies within each of his main categories. The assimilation in this case is not merely inadvertent, however, for on his sort of view the difference is only one of degree. In both cases the psyche is actively responding to stimuli originating outside it.

An essence is formally exemplified by being just what some thing is at a certain time. I offer the following as a somewhat personal elucidation of Santayana's viewpoint.

Consider some material thing just as it is at some particular moment, that is, discount its relation to other things and the way in which it appears to an observer, and consider just what it is that is lying within certain spatial boundaries at some moment. To tell the truth, the reader cannot really carry out this instruction, even if he is a physicist, any more than I can, for what an object is in itself must remain mysterious to us. Nonetheless, we can still play at the idea that we may really bring before our minds just what it is that lies within a certain region of space at a certain moment. If we do this, we will see that there is a sense in which what lies within that region of space might be lying in another region of space at just the same time, and might also lie within some region of space at another time, without its being true that identically the same material object is there as that with which we were concerned at first. This which might be in all these different places is that essence which our original material object happened to embody at the original instant, and it contrasts with the event of that body there and then embodying it. The essence, we may say, is the character or nature of that body at that moment, yet we can say this only if we exclude from the thing's character anything which is a matter of, though not, of course, anything causally dependent upon, its relation to things or events lying outside that region of existence at that moment. Note that the essence that a thing embodies at a particular moment is not some one specially privileged property among many properties predicable of that thing; it is just exactly what that thing at that moment is (insofar as this is something even in principle characterizable) considered apart from its relational properties. All its non-relational properties other than its total essence are elements in that essence. They are, indeed, themselves essences which the thing may be said to exemplify, but there is this difference between them and the total essence, that the object at that moment precisely is that essence figuring as an existent in virtue of lying in a particular set of external relations and as a distinct existent from its very self lying in a different set of external relations, if it happens to do so, whereas the included elements are only qualities of the object. The terms 'subject' and 'predicate' are appropriate for the contrast between the thing and these elements as it is not for the contrast between the thing and its total essence. If one considers an event or thing as it is in itself at a particular moment, apart from the external relations in which it stands to other things, one is considering its essence which, therefore, cannot exactly be contrasted with the thing as characterizing it. The thing at that moment just is the essence with existence or substance flowing through it (as we shall see more clearly later), thereby connecting it by external relations to other essences with existence flowing through them, external in that they do not turn on what these essences essentially are. Its duration is largely a matter of convention, since there is no sharp separation between substance being transmitted to phases of the same and to phases of different individuals.[9]

These are very abstract and general ideas about the nature of things to which sundry reflections point. We cannot fill the account out with specific and genuine examples of what is in question, for we never really know the true intrinsic essence of any object in nature, apart from that of consciousness itself, which in any case is only a natural object in a somewhat extended sense. We believe in the existence of enduring material things which we re-identify from time to time, and this belief, when reflectively thought out, amounts to belief that phases of existence pass into one another in this sort of way, but all we really know, according to Santayana, about the actual essences exemplified by these phases is very thin and abstract in character. Yet we do normally imagine them as though they contained the very qualities given to our senses, and can best grasp the above abstractions by filling them out in this way.

Although Santayana denies that we know the intrinsic essences of material things, he does not think such knowledge logically impossible. He insists that any essence whatever is intrinsically intuitable, were

71

there a spirit tuned to the right key, so to speak. [10] The converse is not true. Some essences, such as pleasure, beauty, and in general the emotional essences can only be exemplified imaginatively – that is their exemplification outside of intuition can only be specious. [11] Santayana offers no explanation of this fact, though it surely calls for one.

3 *The generic and the indeterminate*

It should be clear that Santayana's use of the term essence has little connection with that in which, according to some philosophers, each substance has an essence which it can never lose, and which contrasts with its accidents. For Santayana, on the contrary, there is no single basis on which to determine how long an individual substance survives – it depends on our purposes what we choose, in this sense, to regard as essential to an individual. Any distinguishable chunk of the world in space and time has its intrinsic essence, but there is no one correct division of it into such chunks. (We shall see, however, that at a level beyond practical use Santayana does suppose the world divided into distinct momentary phases of existence.)

The philosophical reader who has grasped this may still find himself looking for some philosophic term more familiar to him with which he can identify Santayana's use of 'essence'. If he is familiar with the writings of F. H. Bradley it may help him if I point out that when Bradley distinguishes the 'what' from the 'that' it is much the same as Santayana's distinction between essence and existence, and that Bradley's use of 'content' is also similar to Santayana's of 'essence'. Bradley and Santayana are poles apart in final outlook, but there are curious points of contact, as in their respective accounts of judgement and belief. What there may have been of direct influence it is hard to say.

Santayana's use of 'essence' is, of course, close to that of 'universal', particularly as used by the early Moore and Russell with whom Santayana had discussed these things while at Cambridge (England) in 1896. [12] But though essences certainly are universals, the notion that what Santayana primarily had in mind were such entities as *horse* or *being a horse* would be mistaken. He tries from time to time, in a rather half-hearted way, to do justice to such class-universals, and to fit them under the heading of essence, but essences are certainly not introduced primarily to explain the use of general terms. [13] The essences he mainly has in mind are quite specific natures or forms of being, universal in the sense of being intrinsically repeatable, and not tied down to a given locus, rather than as being generic. There is, among some philosophers, a tendency to confuse the distinction between the specific (this precise shade, the precise overall state of an animal at a certain moment) and the generic (red in general, *horse*) with the distinction between the universal and the particular. But the specific, even the precise present state of an animal, is something intrinsically repeatable not tied down to one locus and is as much opposed to its particular instances as is the generic. Santayana's essences are certainly universals, but he tends to take a Berkeleyan view of the generic and to say that to have a general idea is to take some specific essence before the mind as symbolizing some range of objects rather than a single one. As to the question what determines membership of this range, Santayana remarks briefly that general terms are associated with impulses which will find satisfaction in certain objects and not others, and that it is as all satisfying some human impulse that they are united.[14]

Are we to take it that for Santayana there are, in the language of W. E. Johnson, only determinate universals not determinable, shades of red but no such thing as redness, absolutely specific sorts of horse but no such thing as horsehood? Though Santayana does not use this terminology, much of what he says suggests an affirmative answer.[15] Nonetheless it is clear that this is not really his view, for he insists, as against Berkeley, that one can intuit indeterminate essences. If I see or imagine a triangle, for instance, the intuited figure may definitely have three sides without these sides being of any definite lengths relatively to one another; if I see or imagine a coloured object the intuited colour may simply be yellow and nothing more precise than that, and so on.[16]

Santayana's view here is akin to that of those philosophers who claim that sense-data or images may be indeterminate in certain respects, though for him it is indeterminate shapes or colours which are intuited, not objects possessing them. The subject is a difficult one, but there is much to be said for this claim. Is it not plausible to say that the taste I experience when drinking tea actually is, in some sense, lacking in the determinateness of the taste present to a tea-taster? If once the possibility of such indeterminateness is admitted there seems no *a priori* limit to it, so that even if Berkeley could not imagine a triangle which was 'neither equilateral, equicrural, nor scalenon, but *all and none* of these at once' (i.e. which was indeterminate in these respects) perhaps Locke could.

Santayana still wants to insist that these indeterminate or vague essences (which, with verbal inconsistency, he often calls generic essences) are in some more fundamental sense absolutely specific. They may be indeterminate in respects in which we expect determinateness but they are still individuals with an exact nature of their own.

It is not quite clear what sort of importance Santayana attaches to this possible indeterminateness of essences. Does he think that one must be able to intuit a mere triangle in order to understand the word 'triangle'? On the whole I take his view to be that there is no necessary connection between degree of indeterminacy and generality of use. If my intuition of it is connected with a generic impulse its reference is general whatever its degree of determinateness, so that the vehicle of my reference to triangles in general, or to horses in general, can equally be a generic or a specific image, or simply the verbal essences 'triangle' or 'horse' without further intermediary.

Are we to conclude, then, that (on Santayana's view) there are not such essences merely as horse, red, triangle, and so forth? If we do so we will go against some of his explicit utterances. These may be explained, at least in part, by reference to the observation he sometimes makes that we must continually talk of different essences as being one essence when the affinity they bear to one another is such as to make their difference irrelevant in the present context. (Thus we treat various essences given to sight or in the experience of movement, or in some more purely intellectual fashion, as all being the same essence 'circle' because of their complete formal affinity for certain purposes.) At all events, whether he sticks to it quite consistently or not, I believe the main tenor of his thought is such as I have indicated.

There is no doubt that Santayana's treatment of these matters is sketchy. He is concerned only to show the sort of way in which they may be treated, not to work out the details. His real interest in essences is as objects of pure intuition and as eternal possibilities which have a being independent of the fluctuations of existence.

4 Complex essences

Much more interesting than his treatment of the matters just discussed is what Santayana has to say regarding complex essences.[17] Such essences consist in elements in certain relations to each other and these elements are themselves essences. The pattern of the French flag, for instance, consists in red, blue and white stripes of a certain shape side by side; a triangle consists of three straight lines enclosing a space. The appearance to perception of almost any object is complex in the same kind of way, as is especially obvious in the case of sight.

We have already seen that the relations between the elements of such a complex essence are internal, inasmuch as the being that element in that whole is precisely what such an included essence is. Of course, Santayana recognizes that, on the face of it, one can make a detail in a complex pattern an object of attention on its own, but he insists that, strictly speaking, we are then intuiting a different essence with an especially close affinity to the detail, such as makes it proper to call it the 'same'. This applies equally when we seem to discern a common element or part in two different essences, as for instance a straight line present in two different figures. It will be useful, for future reference, if I introduce my own term for Santayana's idea here and call such essences *virtually identical*.

The following passage on logical implication puts the point rather clearly:

> I have said that logical implication is explicit inclusion of a part in a whole; but what is inclusion? When one essence is said to include another, an identification has taken place *in discourse* between an element in the inclusive essence and the whole of the included one; but no essence can *be* another, so that in this identification (which is the first principle and condition of reasoning) there is something non-logical, not to say absurd. . . . Not that identification need be erroneous . . . since in discourse assimilations are inevitable; but the point is that the most proper identification is still the act of calling one essences which are individually two: a trick of discourse and language. (RB, p. 88)

In quoting this passage, I have omitted Santayana's actual examples of such apt but in part fictitious assimilation as they represent a feature of Santayana's thought which will seem most perverse to many modern readers and which is not at all essential to the main point. The illustrations are in fact the aspects of unity and of Pure Being which are supposed to be an element in every essence, and in each other, which aspects are strictly different but kindred essences when the essences in which they figure as elements are different. Various less abstruse examples are given later in the same chapter as, for instance, when he says:

> Essences have no origin, and in that sense no constituents; their elements are only their *essential* features which define them and are defined by them. A straight line may be intuited alone, say by an organic motor impulse felt in a dream: you traverse it, you have immediate acquaintance with its absolute nature. You may think that you find it again by inspecting the edges of a triangle; but here the object, 'straight line' has become the object of a different sense, sight, and appears in a context, the visible triangle, absent before, and strictly excluded by the original intuition expressing only a motor impulse within the organism. The identification of the straight line there with the straight line here is therefore intentional only, not actual. It expresses an affinity between the two intuitions, their partial equivalence in discourse; and perhaps the separate occurrence of the first may have contributed, through the preparation and enrichment of the psyche, to the present complexity of the second. (RB, p. 89)

Santayana also indicates that essences can have elements which cannot be considered as parts in relation to other parts. Any colour includes what he calls *light* (which here means *brightness* of some degree) and any thought or feeling contains *life* (which here seems to mean consciousness or spirit) but there is no such thing as the rest of the essence, something which would be left if the brightness or life were removed. His view seems to be that the brightness present in one colour is *virtually identical* with the brightness present in another in the same way as certain 'parts' of two essences can be virtually identical. Santayana seems also to imply that an element virtually identical with the brightness in some given colour is intuitable alone, and that in the same way a solitary version of any element distinguished in a given essence is, in principle, intuitable. His discussion of this centres on qualities, and mainly on the very special and controversial case of *being* and it is difficult to be sure how far the points made there can be generalized. Are we to take it, for instance, that the indeterminate three-sidedness or triangularity of an imagined figure, or of a figure as perceived, can be called virtually identical with some element one can notice in every triangle? The answer seems to be an affirmative one, and if this seems odd, I suppose Santayana would remind us that there is no absolute truth in the settlement of such issues of identity, only a pragmatic convenience.

This, it will be noticed, bears on the issues about the generic discussed in the last section. Santayana would seem to hold that, at least in many of the cases where many essences are covered by some generic term, there is a separately intuitable essence, such that each of these other essences includes a distinguishable element, virtually identical with it, and that the term covers each such element as well as the solitary essence, under the fiction that they are one and the same. This appears to extend, without rescinding, the view of the generic so far considered, for the fact that one word or image represents all these kindred or virtually identical essences may still spring from the fact that they are all indications of something which satisfies a generic impulse, i.e. a state of need which can reach quietus in a variety of different though kindred ways.

Santayana is much concerned to insist that all essences are equally *primary*, as he puts it, and in so describing them, he means, in particular, to oppose complex essences to complex ideas as conceived by empiricists in the tradition of Locke, for whom they were somehow put together by the mind out of simple constituents passively received. As against this, Santayana maintains that in the realm of essence, taken as the realm of all possible forms of being, the complex essence with its elements has no different status from that of the solo versions of this element. The status of a complex pattern is not that of something which could be made out of more basic elements together with a separately conceivable universal of relationship, but of a definite form of being in its own right. Furthermore, intuition, and identification, of the complex may precede or succeed intuition of simple essences virtually identical with its elements as the accidents of circumstance, physiology, or psychology, determine. Whether, for instance, a child learns to recognize a circle or a wheel (in which the former is an element) first is not to be derived from the nature of the essences involved.

In saying this, Santayana is also attacking the other great, but somewhat opposite, empiricist doctrine of abstraction.[18] Obviously one cannot, on his view, abstract essences from things since the things are only presented via the essences, but one cannot, in general, explain our recognition of the less determinate features of things in the world by talking of abstraction from the more determinate. It is just as possible that an indeterminate essence of movement strikes one first as that some determinate type of movement does, and, in any case, each essence is a quite specific form of being in its own right, with its own precise degree of determinateness or indeterminateness, whether we take it as characterizing one or many things.

Santayana's discussions undoubtedly suffer from the almost complete lack in his works of any philosophy of language. He is not in much worse case here than many earlier philosophers, especially the British empiricists with whom in spite of important divergencies he had much in common, but at the date at which he was writing there was less excuse for this. His wish to root his philosophy in biological fact seems at times to have centred his attention on those features of consciousness which have no appearance of being peculiarly human. After decades of an almost exclusively linguo-centric philosophy Santayana's approach certainly offers a relief, but on some topics, and especially on such matters as generality of reference, it means an inevitable vagueness of treatment. But what makes matters worse is his tendency, already noted, to assimilate perception and thought. Thus in discussing whether simpler or more complex essences are first distinguished he hardly separates the question as to which are first discriminated in perception and the question as to which are first used as symbols in thought. One might also complain that he confuses mere passive presentation of an essence in perception with its discrimination, but this would be less just, for it seems that for Santayana the circular shape (say) of an object could not be spoken of as intuited unless it was to some extent fixed as an object of attention.

In spite of these deficiencies Santayana is making some important points, especially in his insistence that all essences are primary. He is surely right in claiming that any given quality or pattern, including the total impression on us of any object we perceive, is an individual unity, identifiable by its unique overall character, which, though it can be analysed into elements cannot be regarded as composed of them, as also in his insistence that as unrealized possibilities the complex and the simple (or simpler) are on a level. If there is no literal truth or falsehood in these matters, this seems at least a more appropriate way of looking at them than the alternative. It compares favourably, for instance, with the logical atomism for which basic names should designate only the simple, while the complex should be identified only through definite descriptions.[19]

Santayana's discussion of complex essences could be regarded as a poetic rendering of the facts pointed out by gestalt psychologists, but I think he is right to set them out in an ontological and epistemological context. Philosophy has always been concerned to identify the most basic realities in the universe, and Santayana is insisting that the unities he calls complex essences are at any rate the realities most familiar to us, far more so than the simples into which philosophers have often tried to resolve them, or than any universal plenum without natural boundaries between thing and thing. More instructive than a comparison with gestalt psychologists is one with the philosophy of F. H. Bradley, for a complex essence is very much the sort of non-relational many-in-one of which he spoke. Yet Santayana, as we shall see, was far from thinking that the universe as a whole could properly be thus regarded.

5 Pure Being

In *The Realm of Essence* a whole long chapter is devoted to pure Being. His treatment of this essence seems often to have disturbed sympathizers with Santayana's general outlook.[20]

Santayana sharply separates Being (or pure Being) from Existence. Being is the maximally indeterminate essence, related to essences in general as colour (or 'light' in one sense of the word) is to shades of colour in general. Being is present in unexemplified essences as much as in exemplified essences, and, if nothing existed, it would itself be unexemplified. Existence is utterly different, being a status which essence may or may not possess, not an essence itself nor an element contained in essences as such (Santayana sometimes talks of *existence* as having its own essence or nature, identifiable, I think, with the common quality of all external relations, but he insists that existence, unlike Being, is distinct from its essence).[21]

Whatever may be thought of some of Santayana's more detailed discussions of pure Being the general point seems to me a helpful one, though use of the words 'Being' and 'existence' for the contrast is optional. The point could be expressed by saying that though Kant and others are essentially right in maintaining that existence is not a predicate, this leaves open the possibility that there is an absolutely general predicate, Being, which is implied by all other predicates, a predicate which can otherwise be put as *being a distinguishable something*. We may think of it as at the top of any classificatory tree either of existents, or of possible types of existent. It is certainly open to argument whether there is some quality, Being, which all things have in common, but the vacuity of this conception cannot be established by analyses of the conception of existence.

For Santayana *Being* is both an element present in every essence and also an independent essence intuitable alone. This is meant to be understood in terms of the theory we have been considering, and means, in the terminology we have proposed, that in each essence there is an element virtually identical with *an element* in every other essence, apart from that very special essence, pure Being on its own, with *the whole* of which it is virtually identical. To intuit this solo version of pure Being is said to be an uncommon accomplishment, but detection of the pure Being within determinate essences is not so difficult. Presumably the art of recognizing it is somewhat like the art of recognizing the same hue in different degrees of saturation and tonality. The discrimination of this element of pure Being in every essence one intuits, and perhaps its eventual intuition in isolation, is said to be the goal of many spiritual exercises, and its achievement to be the supreme good for a certain class of mind, but Santayana is careful to preserve his ethical relativism in this connection, and to say that its value depends upon the particular needs of the individual psyche.

That Santayana is discussing a type of experience which actually occurs seems hardly doubtful. The sense of something one and the same at the heart of everything experienceable can sometimes haunt a mind far from mystical, and the surmise that some forms of mystic experience consist in an intensified version of this feeling, leading finally to absorbed attention to some maximally indeterminate 'essence' which seems to be this common element in isolation, seems reasonable. In allowing so much, have we allowed Santayana's thesis?

May not the feeling, however strong, of something one and the same in everything experienceable represent an illusion? May it not rather be that in certain states of mind one *responds* in the same way to everything and wrongly takes this as the discovery of a common something always present? Moreover, even if there is something in common to all the essences one intuits, does it follow that it must be present in all essences whatever?

Consideration of the first of these two questions is complicated by the notion of virtual identity, as I have christened it. For Santayana there is no cut and dried truth as to whether two essences contain a common element. We merely say that they do if we feel a strong affinity between elements found in each of them. (Perhaps even the very idea of each essence as containing *elements* means no more than that the affinity between the different whole essences is only partial.) The question then would seem to be: Does talk of pure Being suitably express a feeling one may come to have regarding the affinity of all essences? not: Is there really and truly such an essence? We have already inclined to an affirmative answer to this first question.

A doubt may still be felt as to whether anything suitably called pure Being on its own can be intuited. I can see no reason why there should not be, though I would add this, that there might be various *different* strangely indeterminate essences all with an equal claim to be so called, and virtually rather than strictly identical with one another.

Our second question above remains unanswered. To discriminate an essence and call it pure Being is to claim that in all essences whatever, not merely those one has come across, one would find something virtually identical therewith. But how can one know this? How can one know that some strange new experience might not present one with something so utterly different that one could find in it no affinity at all to what one has thus described?

Santayana might say that this only shows that one might mistake something more specific for pure Being itself. But if this is always so, how be so sure that there is any essence suitably called 'pure Being'?

In fact Santayana appears to have two different sorts of reason for maintaining that there is such an essence as pure Being. On the one hand are reasons which, in a very broad sense of the word may be called empirical, namely that we seem actually to find such a common element in all essences we scrutinize, that something deeper and more elementary than colour, smell, extension, pain and so on seems to be present in them all, so that each can be seen as a special determination thereof. This is empirical inasmuch as it is a kind of induction from an 'ideal experiment', but its result purports to be more than contingent, to generalize from an intrinsic, not an extrinsic, feature of each examined essence to a feature of the eternal realm of essence in general. On the other hand stands a reason more abstract or logical, namely the idea that essences are essences because they have a property of essence-hood, that they are distinguishable possible somethings because each has the property of being a specific something, a property which can be labelled more briefly 'being'.

One is certainly inclined to see confusion in Santayana's thought here. Is there not a category mistake in identifying the higher-order property of being an essence with some sort of quality or essence present in every other essence?

This may well be so, but though Santayana's account of pure Being is often presented in a confused way, its basic point is perhaps not vulnerable to such an objection. For may it not be that to find a partial affinity between all essences and to describe this as awareness of their all containing *Being* precisely is simply to note that they all have in common the property of Being specific somethings? Is it even absolutely evident that one might not pass therefrom to a state of mind in which one contemplates an object so indeterminate as appropriately to be called pure somethinghood or Being?

It would take us too far afield to pursue this difficult subject further. That there is a certain confusion, an element of that playing on words which seem always an aspect of philosophical discussions of *Being*, in Santayana's discussion (which has many details I have passed over), I do not doubt. Yet this peculiar playing on words, in Santayana's case as in that of other philosophers, does seem to communicate a state of mind of some peculiar value.

To sum up. For Santayana every essence has Being, is a definite and distinguishable something, and in that sense *is* whether it exists in any instance or not. Being or somethinghood can be an object of special attention, either as an element in some other essence or on its own. By 'Being' may sometimes be understood the realm of essences in general as being the totality of all that has Being. At other times it means this common property or element of somethinghood. 'Pure Being' sometimes means the latter in contrast to the former, but at other times the term 'pure' serves mainly to indicate that it is not *existence* which is in question.

6   *Do essences have natures?*

Santayana often says that each essence has its own individual character which determines its (internal) relations to all other essences.[22] Is there some confusion here? What is this character? His language sometimes almost seems to suggest that each essence is an instance of itself, a way of looking at universals the difficulties of which Plato himself long ago exhibited.

Santayana was once charged with making this sort of mistake, of thinking, for instance, of loveliness as itself lovely. He replied that though not lovely, it was loveliness itself, and that this was better.

His language may sometimes be misleading, but I think his position on this score is really quite clear. He speaks of each essence as having its own idiosyncratic nature or individuality as a way of emphasizing that each is what it is, and this is different from what any other is. An essence is not an instance of itself, rather it is itself, but it is very different to be one essence from being another. The quality red (meaning here some specific shade of red) is not a red surface, and is red only in the sense that it is identical with red. Still, it is not to be thought of as some characterless abstraction, it is that unique idiosyncratic quality which

81

contrasts in a definite way with blue. In saying that each essence has its own nature I think Santayana means no more than that each is its quite distinctive self and thereby different from every other essence.

Complex essences could be said to have natures in a more straightforward way than simple ones. Each complex essence is those elements in that relation. When Santayana speaks of *the definition* of an essence he seems to mean the way in which it is thus composed of other essences, not any verbal formula. If there are simple essences (and Santayana assumes there are), they would not have definitions. Insofar as they contain elements (as every other essence contains being) they could perhaps be spoken of as having the property of containing such and such an element, but if by *a nature* be meant *a definition* they would not have one. Nonetheless I think it is quite natural and proper for Santayana to speak of every essence as having its own distinctive nature, as a way of emphasizing that it is an idiosyncratic individual with definite contrasts and affinities to every other such individual.

In view of various recent philosophical discussions it may be as well to point out that given essences, as conceived by Santayana, can hardly be described as ineffable. He describes various ways in which one can intend or refer to an absent essence, i.e. one not at present intuited, either by reference to the circumstances in which it has been or might be intuited or by its internal relations to other essences.[23] It would, in short, be quite wrong to suggest that any essence is indescribable, for there is always much that can be said about it either in terms of its external, or more intimately in terms of its internal, relations. There is a sense, indeed, in which, according to Santayana, one must, in following any description whether of existences or essences start from essences immediately given in intuition, and not otherwise specified, for thought essentially consists in taking present essences as somehow applicable to something beyond. Nonetheless these essences can themselves always become objects of description, even when one does not intuit them, and presumably even for those who have never intuited them, provided there is some shared common starting point, as, granted the basic assumptions of animal faith, there is bound to be in animals of the same species responding to the same external stimuli. Certainly the specification of an absent essence is no adequate substitute for immediate acquaintance with it in intuition, but one can hardly therefore call it ineffable. On the contrary, its internal relations with other essences can be made a matter of explicit study.

7 *Internal and external relations*

Though Santayana seems never to make the point very explicitly, it is quite evident that two rather different sorts of relation are included for him under the heading of internal relations. [24] The first type of internal relation comprises all the relations which hold between the elements of one total essence (such as is not merely an element in another essence) and between each of these and the whole. Secondly, there are relations of contrast or affinity such as may, indeed, hold within a complex essence, but may hold also between essences which either *are* or *belong to* different total essences, *separate* essences as I shall find it convenient to call them. Such are more or less the same as what Hume called relations between ideas. Examples are relations of contrast between different colours and the geometrical relations between different figures (most obviously those envisaged as having Euclidean spatiality). These two types of internal relations are surely very different (though they over-lap), but they share the two inter-connected features, first, that each essence being what it is they cannot but hold, and, second, that they hold independently of any existential facts. Even if nothing existed each possible pattern, for instance, would consist in certain definite elements in a certain definite arrangement, and would contrast with other such possible patterns in certain definite ways. I shall call relations of the first kind holistic, and of the second kind contrastive.

We have already seen that, according to Santayana, existence and the being in external relations are equivalent, and in the light of the preceding the reasons for this thesis may have become clearer. Consider a certain (total) essence, it does not matter whether it is simple or complex. That internal relations hold between its elements or between itself and other essences does not imply the existence of anything. Suppose, however, that it stands in relations which do not thus follow from its mere nature, then indeed it belongs to a world in which things hang together in an arbitrary contingent way, and this is as much as to say that it is an element of existence. Moreover, if it does not stand in any relations other than those implied in its own nature, then there is nothing to distinguish it from a nonexistent mere possibility, for all the truths about it will be necessary.

We have spoken just now of an essence standing in external relations and thereby belonging to existence, but is it supposed, strictly speaking, to be the essence itself or some fact (a word which, in Santayana's terminology, means some concrete phase of existence rather than some-thing which 'is the case') which exemplifies it, that stands in these external relations? Santayana's language on this point is not consis-tent, [25] but I think one may sum up his position sufficiently for the moment by saying that the fact is the essence *qua* element in a system of external relationships. One may say either that an essence, when in external relations, becomes a fact, or that not the essence, but only the fact exemplifying it, stands in these relations. Of course, even on the first way of putting it two different facts may have the same essence, since one and the same essence becomes two different facts by being in two different sets of relationships.

It is well to note that on Santayana's view the existence of something consists in its being the case that the intrinsic and probably unknown essence of that thing at various moments stands in external relations, rather than in its being the case that the essence in terms of which I think of it so stands. I can truly say that the present Queen of England exists but her existence consists, not in some essence specified by this definite description standing in external relations, but in the unknown inner essence of a certain sentient organism doing so. It is as well to point this out as Santayana's theory is likely, otherwise, to be connected in the wrong sort of way with discussions centring on Russell's theory of descriptions. For Santayana, I should think, the use of singular terms expresses my sense that I am responding to some existence aptly thus symbolized, and this sense may be correct or incorrect, but it is not the essence which is that symbol, or other essence it brings to mind, which may or may not be in external relations.

Santayana does not distinguish between existence and occurrence, so that for him a 'fact' or event exists as much as a man. This may scandalize philosophers much concerned with ordinary language, but really it seems quite reasonable to contrast occurrence and existence under one term, as ways of being which are contingent, with the eternal being possessed by essences, whether exemplified or not. For Santayana an ordinary thing exists at every moment when some fact which is a phase of it exists. The most fundamental external relations are the ones between such facts, both those which consist in one fact taking over from another, and those relations which make facts collateral with one another. Santayana speaks of this as implying that there is to the facts something beside their essence, namely the substance which they transmit to further facts, but it is doubtful how far this is meant to be more than another expression for the holding of these relations. In any case, I don't think it incompatible with speaking of the fact as its essence standing in external relations, for we say that the fact is the essence with substance passing through it.

Thus the world of existing things consists in the holding of external relations between essences at the character of which we can only guess. Moreover, it is not only those essences, but even more the external relations between them, which are mysterious. It is intrinsically impossible that an external relation should be intuited, since all that I intuit at a moment belongs to one over-arching complex essence. The most one can hope is that some holistic internal relations may give an inkling of the character of some external ones. In particular, the sense we have of one event passing into another probably gives some hint of what it is for one fact really to give way to another fact, so that, without being mere aspects of a single totality, they are externally related to each other temporally. But we shall return to these themes later.

The question naturally arises whether Santayana regards relations themselves as a species of essence. In fact he does on occasion explicitly classify them as such, yet one cannot but feel that they do not answer to much that he says of essence. For one thing, he has a strong tendency to think that for any distinguishable essence there is a solo version intuitable alone, yet it is difficult to take this as a possibility in the case of relations. He seems, however, to suggest at one point that relations are always essentially elements in complex essences.[26] I suppose *virtually* identical versions of the relation *on top of* (for example) could be found in various different such complexes. More importantly, it would be difficult to maintain that relations enter the field of existence only by standing themselves in external relationships. A Bradleyan regress seems to hover here. It might seem better to say that external relations belong of themselves to existence, and internal relations to the realm of non-existential being.

Though the textual support for it is sketchy, I would suggest that the view which makes best sense of Santayana's position is as follows. Internal relations (at least of the holistic kind) are essences, but essences which only have status as elements in complex essences. Thus an infinite number of virtually identical versions of *on top of* could be found in an infinite number of complex essences. External relations, on the other hand, are not essences and not universals, so that the external relation between two particulars cannot hold also between another two particulars; they are, nonetheless, either individual instances of, or perhaps rather they each in some way correspond to, some one internal holistic relation. There are passages in Santayana which suggest such a view and, obscure as it is, I think it may point in the right direction.

Santayana says on various occasions that even if we knew all the essences exemplified in existence, existence itself would remain something not fully graspable by the mind, that it is an unintelligible surd. He is echoing the Platonic view that the world of becoming is only open to an inferior kind of awareness, that of opinion, and that knowledge is only of the Ideas, though for Santayana the place of opinion is taken by knowledge and that of knowledge by intuition. One may see him also as anticipating a major theme in existentialism but it must be emphasized that Santayana is saying something more than that there is no ultimate reason why existence should have this character rather than that, though certainly he does say this. He is saying not merely that the existence of anything is contingent, but that the difference which existence makes to an essence is not conceivable, not expressible in terms of essence. There is a good deal to suggest that this is really the same point as that which we have suggested emerges from his treatment of relations, namely that the external relations between essences which give them existence are ultimately unintelligible.

Santayana is not ashamed of the mysteriousness which external relations possess on his account, for he thinks he is right to find a certain opaqueness to consciousness at the heart of existence. What he does not make so much of is a certain obscurity which attaches to the status of contrastive internal relations on his account. Contrasts and affinities may, of course, hold between the elements of a complex essence, and in that case they are holistic as well as contrastive, and may be regarded as elements within that essence, but contrasts between *separate* essences seem to require different treatment. Sometimes Santayana seems to imply that, in fact, contrasts and affinities only really hold within a complex essence, and that when they are said to hold between separate essences this is because these correspond to the elements in some such complex. Such a view is, on the face of it, incoherent, for this correspondence, or virtual identity, as we have called it above, is itself an affinity holding between these distinct essences. Sometimes Santayana, showing an uneasy awareness of this problem, seems to suggest that the contrastive relations between distinct essences are ultimately fictitious, inasmuch as the virtual identities on which they depend stem from a virtually arbitrary act of identification, a view similar to some strange views some find in Wittgenstein. However, his usual, and surely wiser, view seems to be that, though my awareness of the contrasts or affinities between distinct essences must be mediated by awareness of such contrasts and affinities between elements, within a single essence, each of which corresponds to one of them, nevertheless the cognized relations of contrast and affinity, as also this relation of correspondence or virtual identity, have an independent and eternal being such as the essences themselves do. These points are only dimly hinted at by Santayana, but I suspect that he was explicitly conscious of the issue as one he had not resolved to his satisfaction. A comparison of his published with his unpublished (or posthumously published) writings reveals a tendency to keep the polished prose of the former free of the tortuosities of matters not quite resolved.

8   *Beauty as a liberator of essences*

The beautiful is itself an essence, an indefinable quality felt in many things which, however disparate they may be otherwise, receive this name by virtue of a special emotion, half wonder, half love, which is felt in their presence. The essence of the beautiful, when made an object of contemplation by itself, is rather misleading: like the good and like pure Being, it requires much dialectical and spiritual training to discern it in its purity and in its fullness . . . I will not stop to discuss these complications: however apt to become entangled itself, the beautiful is a great liberator of other essences. The most material thing, insofar as it is felt to be beautiful, is instantly immaterialised, raised above external personal relations, concentrated and deepened in its proper being, in a word, sublimated into an essence: while on the other hand, many unnoticed Platonic ideas, relations or unsubstantial aspects of things, when the thrill of beauty runs through them, are suddenly revealed, as in poetry the secret harmonies of feelings and of words. In this way innumerable natural themes of happiness, which no one could possibly mistake for things, become members of the human family, and in turn restore the prodigal mind, perhaps long wasted on facts, to its home circle of essence. (RB, pp. 8-9)

Unfortunately *The Sense of Beauty* is probably Santayana's most widely read book today. A discussion of Santayana's later and somewhat divergent treatment of beauty is desirable, not only as extending our account of his doctrine but as suggesting how his ideas on this topic developed. [27]

Santayana tells us that one of the main ways in which attention can come to linger on essences rather than be intent on things is the presentation to spirit of some essence under the aspect of the beautiful. If one is entranced by the beauty of something which one sees or hears, one's whole attention centres with loving care on the precise given character of that with which one is confronted, and one is not concerned with the irrelevant factual context in which this thing is embedded. If I find a landscape beautiful, curiosity as to what lies on the other side of those hills, or of the causal potentialities or hidden parts of the things around me, is suspended and I merely drink in the given essence. Santayana is rightly insistent that while one is concerned with a work of art, say a painting, as a physical object with a certain history one is not concerned with beauty. When a painting is found beautiful one finds delight simply in the immediately given eternal essence, the being of which is quite independent of any facts about the century in which that physical surface was painted or of its subsequent path through space.

What is found to be beautiful, then, is a given essence, not the physical thing which presents it. Santayana emphasizes that any object I perceive or think about equally presents a given essence which is my symbol of it, whether that essence is found beautiful or not, and such essence always could be made an object of attention on its own account. In general, however, we do this only when that essence is beautiful or fascinating in some kindred way.

It is, then, the sense of beauty which most typically leads one to contemplate the given essences as the eternal objects which essentially they are, and to cease thinking of them merely as items in a network of external relations, that is, as contingently existing facts. Thus attention is concentrated on the absolute appearance of things and not on their history, location, potentialities and so forth. Santayana sometimes writes as though the essence thus liberated for contemplation were the very essence of the existing thing itself, but his considered view is, of course, that it is only the essence which characterizes the thing for human consciousness. One must not forget, however, that the appearance upon which attention is fixated in appreciation of the beautiful is not an ephemeral private mental particular, but a certain complex form which is an eternally possible object of contemplation by mind in general.

That what one finds beautiful is something rightly felt to be eternal is something very important to Santayana. One delights in the idiosyncrasy of some form which could not be otherwise than it is, and which therefore calls forth no active response such as is appropriate to a changeable thing which may be moulded in an effort to satisfy the will. There is an echo of Schopenhauer's theory of aesthetic experience here, as being the suspension of the will at the sight of itself objectified as a Platonic idea.

Santayana is far from saying that beauty is only to be found in the sensory appearance of things, and that representative aspects of art, historical associations, scientific knowledge of the substances present in a scene, and so on, may contribute nothing to the experience of beauty. What he insists on, simply, is that if such things really belong to the beauty apprehended, then their essences are elements in a complex essence in the contemplation of which the spirit rests with joy, and are neither taken merely as facts the further ramifications of which in the existential flux one is panting to pursue, nor belong merely to a fringe of associations which determine the reaction, without themselves being the object of concentrated attention. As regards representation, what is found beautiful in, say, Greek sculpture is the essence of a certain sort of ideal human being, not simply certain geometrical shapes. In a religious painting it may be the essence of a certain nonexistent (in Santayana's view) transaction between God and man which is brought before the mind as beautiful, not merely a patchwork of colours. This essence will not be presented to a mind which lacks a certain sort of cultural background, so that one's whole cultural and religious experience, and one's historical knowledge, may certainly be relevant to one's intuiting an appropriate essence in presence of the physical picture. The point is, however, that one delights in what is, as a result of whatever processes, here and now completely presented to consciousness, and does not take an interest in this presentation as a clue to matters which will become fully present only to later thoughts, or which will be distributed among them, so as never to be fully present to any.

This might seem to imply that one who walks round a sculpture to see its other side thereby shows himself discontented with the essence first presented and cannot be responding to the sculpture's beauty, an idea which seems rather absurd. Yet the matter is a difficult one, for it does seem true that when really transfixed by beauty one strives to keep one's point of view and sense of the thing unchanged. However, Santayana often insists that the true lover of beauty is content with a brief vision of the eternal and is far from any greedy hanging on to it. His point would seem to be roughly this. While absorbed in the beautiful one's activity both physical and mental becomes trance-like, rather than laboriously purposeful, and yields essences continuous with one another in such a way as to constitute ever deeper versions of the vision first vouchsafed. This deepening and enriching of the original version through essences which belong with it essentially is far from the practical frame of mind in which one, as it were, cross-examines an essence and its successors as witnesses on points of fact.

For Santayana, 'beauty' is predicated of essences rather than of things. Why is this? He does, after all, insist that such essences as *hard*, *large* and *black* are properly predicated of things, in spite of the fact that the essences thus named strictly belong to things only for human or animal consciousness. Why should not beauty also be an essence which characterizes things – rather than essences – for human consciousness?

One should avoid pedantry here. Santayana insisted that language was and should be highly flexible and objected to any idea that philosophic insight is best advanced by some rigid verbal formula. In saying that essences rather than things are beautiful, he is not making the absurd claim that 'This material object is beautiful' is essentially 'ill-formed', but saying that the sense of beauty fixes attention on an essence for its own sake rather than as the supposed character of some variable material complex.

Another apparent inconsistency is more serious. Sometimes Santayana insists that no essence is beautiful in itself, and that its beauty is cast upon it by the adoration of some contemplating spirit. On another occasion, however, he talks of the inalienable beauty of the essence present to one who finds the Venus de Milo beautiful.

It is quite clear that for Santayana no landscape, painting, musical performance, or whatever, considered as a physical fact to which different minds may respond in different ways, has or lacks beauty in itself. Some such facts may be particularly fitted to arouse the sense of beauty, but if two persons diverge in what they find beautiful there is no fundamental sense in which one can be right and the other wrong.

Consider, however, the case of a physical surface which presents exactly the same essence to two observers, something at least in principle possible. Is that essence, then, beautiful or unbeautiful in itself? Certainly Santayana would never say that a consciousness could be mistaken in failing to find beauty in an essence with which it was presented, so the question is not whether there could be a beauty to such an essence which only one of the parties felt. The question, rather, is this. Could the parties be described as intuiting the same essence, though only one of them felt beauty in it?

Though he does not spell it out in the same laborious way I believe Santayana's position is, in effect, as follows.

When I find an essence beautiful, its beauty is a quality suffusing the whole and quite essential to its being the essence it is. *That* beauty is an essential element of that essence, and any essence without that beauty is another essence. On the other hand there may be, and indeed must be, an essence which though essentially different as a whole, because thus unsuffused with beauty, is still the same in every other respect, and is thus virtually identical with the content of what, in the first essence, is suffused with beauty. Someone intuiting this second essence may be said, with equal justice, either to be intuiting the same essence as I intuited, while not finding it beautiful, or to be intuiting a different essence. In saying that the essence I intuit is beautiful one may be ascribing beauty to that in the first essence which is virtually identical with the second essence, or one may be ascribing it to the whole of the first essence. If one speaks in the former way one must say that essences are never intrinsically beautiful, because the same essence may always be beautiful for one intuition and not for another. If one speaks in the latter way one must say that an essence, if beautiful at all, is intrinsically beautiful. Both ways of talking have their point. The first emphasizes the identity in everything except beauty which there may be between two essences, the second emphasizes the radical transformation there would be in what is immediately present if it gained or lost beauty, and that this beauty is no feeling on my part which stands over and against the object of awareness but is essential to its individual nature. This account not only removes an appearance of inconsistency between some of Santayana's comments on beauty but is, I believe, only a more explicit statement of what Santayana himself seeks to convey in his more elliptical way.

Santayana's position in *The Sense of Beauty* is naturally classified as a 'subjective' one. On that early view, beauty was a quality of our reaction to an object wrongly taken as a characteristic of the object itself. The later view is more subtle, and it would be misleading to call it either objective or subjective.

In the first place, Santayana's later view is that 'beauty' names a certain definite quality suffusing some of the essences we intuit. To ask whether this quality is 'objective' has no clear meaning. It is certainly not an element in the actual character of any physical existent, but equally it is not an element in the actual character of spirit. It is not literally true of anything at all, and can be exemplified only as an object of contemplation. Whether thus exemplified or not, it is a distinct individual in the realm of essence with its own special idiosyncrasy. If it is asked whether anything is beautiful intrinsically or whether beauty attaches to things only arbitrarily in the 'eye' of some beholder, one must answer thus. An existing thing can be beautiful only in the sense that as a matter of contingent fact the specious essence it wears for some observers is a beautiful one. This it does when it brings a certain sort of equilibrium or alert quietus to the organism. (That such equilibrium produces such intuition is not a necessary truth, but the intuition of beauty is an intrinsically suitable expression of such a physical state.) The essence itself, however, is intrinsically beautiful, inasmuch as its beauty is a main feature in what essentially it is. Nonetheless other observers, or those same observers at other times, might well intuit an essence which diverges from this one only (though what an 'only') in being devoid of its inalienable beauty.

This doctrine, it seems to me, does justice to what relativists and subjectivists have wished to say about beauty, but also recognizes that one who is absorbed in beauty is absorbed in a perfectly definite reality, which is no more itself composed of human reactions than are numbers composed of the thoughts of mathematicians.

It may be objected that there is no one quality which suffuses all the essences we would call beautiful. But here one may recall Santayana's general view about the identity of essences, according to which all such identities other than that between a single total essence (or a definite element in some one such totality) and itself are really only close affinities which we so describe when we wish to assimilate them but which we can deny when our purpose is otherwise. (Santayana's doctrine of essence could perhaps cope with the concept of 'open texture' along these lines.) On this view the question whether the beauty present in one essence is the same quality as that present in another has no definite answer. Santayana himself sometimes speaks of each beautiful thing (or rather essence) as having its own beauty, sometimes as having the same quality as all other beautiful things. Perhaps Santayana exaggerates the identity or affinity, but I confess it does seem to me that if one tries to recall the moments when one has really been entranced by what it seems right to call a thing of beauty, there is a real affinity between what one was aware of in each case, which justifies a properly qualified talk of a common quality of beauty.

Some modern philosophers would say that 'beauty' cannot name an intuited quality, or even a range of kindred qualities, because if so we could never be sure we all attached the same meaning to the word. This argument, however, applies almost equally to all words which Santayana would think of as specifying essences, and is really only a special case of the problem of other minds.

We have seen something of Santayana's treatment of this topic. In observing other people I incipiently mimic their responses to the things around them and this produces a sense of what I would be feeling in their place, and a belief that this is what they feel. This belief fits in with the overall assumption of the uniformity of nature, and can be confirmed or otherwise in specific cases on the basis of assumptions I cannot honestly dispense with. In the case of a quality such as beauty, moreover, Santayana would not altogether disagree with those who think that application of the word essentially belongs with a certain mode of behaving, for, as we shall see hereafter, Santayana held, if somewhat tentatively, that the intuition of certain essences is in some rather essential way the appropriate expression in consciousness of certain behavioural propensities, though certainly the intuition is one thing and the behaviour another.

Of course the attention Santayana gives to questions of communication, and of philosophy of language in general, is quite inadequate by today's standards. On the other hand, it is worse to trim our notion of what can be said to some *a priori* theory of communicability than to ignore such issues. This, I suspect, is the case with those who say that 'beauty' could not be used as Santayana professes to use it. Santayana has certainly not said the last word about *beauty* but his account seems helpful and correct so far as it goes.

9 *The doctrine of essence*

Santayana's so-called doctrine of essence is not so much a single theory as a variety of interconnected theses all making use of a certain concept, that of an essence. But this is not the only reason why one cannot ask whether it, the doctrine in general, is *true*, for it is not the kind of doctrine which is either straightforwardly correct or not. It is, rather, a certain way of looking at things which may or may not be helpful in bringing out certain aspects of reality. Even if it is thus helpful, it is hardly likely to be the only way in which essentially the same features of reality could be brought out. These points are not simply those of an external commentator, for they are made by Santayana himself.[28]

We have commented on many points of detail as we have gone along. The most basic points of all may be summarized in the following four propositions.

1 The immediate object of consciousness is always an eternal form of

being. It is eternal inasmuch as it cannot cease to be something available for intuition, should a suitable mind arise, and inasmuch as even if never intuited, it is still a definite something with essential relations to all other such somethings. These somethings may be called 'essences'.

2 Every existing thing is, at each moment of its existence, the actualization of a quite definite form of being which is eternal inasmuch as it cannot cease to be available as a form which might be actualized again, and inasmuch as even if it had never been actualized it would still have been a definite something with essential relations to all other such somethings. These somethings may be called 'essences'.

3 Affinities may hold between what are strictly different essences such as justify calling them the 'same' essence, at least for certain purposes. A chief example of such 'virtual identity' (as we have called it) is that which may hold between the elements of distinct 'total' essences.

4 The same essence may be exemplified as the immediate object of intuition and as the character of some existence at a certain time. The logical possibilities here are very wide, the actual cases where this may happen are very limited indeed, though this depends somewhat on whether strict or only virtual identity is in question.

Our own attitude to these propositions may be summed up as follows:

The main serious alternative to proposition 1 is the view that the immediate objects of each person's consciousness are particulars of some kind (say sense impressions or images) which instantiate essences, not essences themselves. It is rather plausible to say that the divergence between Santayana and such a view is merely verbal, that both sides admit an element of particularity and an element of universality, and that the argument as to whether the particularity belongs only to the act of awareness or also to its object (or for those who prefer not to talk of an act at all only to the object) concerns only forms of expression. If this is so, then Santayana's seems to have the advantage, for it avoids the problem as to whether the presented particulars are in some disturbing sense 'private' or not, but decision as to whether it is so would require a more extended discussion of rival theories than we can undertake in the present context. In any case, that there is a given in a sense pretty close to Santayana's, and that *in principle* what is given on one occasion may be identical in character with what is given on another, seems hardly susceptible of intelligent denial, and will perhaps only be denied by those who confuse Santayana's sense of the given with an alleged 'sensory core' or with a something supposed to provide the first premisses of empirical knowledge.

Proposition 2 also seems hard to deny. It would seem a rather vacuous observation were it not that its implications are denied by so many philosophers, who seem to lack the sense that a real existence must be a definite something in its own right if it is to stand in relation to other things or be an object of knowledge.

Proposition 3 serves quite well as a stop-gap account of matters of only secondary interest to Santayana; as anything more it is inadequate. Santayana hardly attempts to specify the circumstances under which it is appropriate to treat different essences as the same.

Proposition 4 will be considered in later chapters, and is mentioned here only for completeness. All four propositions, indeed, will acquire a fuller significance in the light of matters still to be discussed.

V

Spirit and Psyche

1 *The psyche*

Santayana distinguishes four main ontological kinds or realms of being; essence, matter, truth, spirit. The three realms other than essence represent, in effect, three different ways in which essences can become something more than merely possibilities. The realm of spirit is composed of intuitions which actualize essences as objects of awareness, besides formally exemplifying their own distinguishing essence of spirit or consciousness. The realm of matter is composed of a comprehensive system of facts in dynamic external relations one to another, each of which formally exemplifies some essence. The connections between these facts, and between the various sub-systems of such facts, are the basic unifying factors in the cosmos, for moments of spirit, considered apart from their grounding in this system of physical facts, would be quite isolated one from another. The realm of truth is composed of essences which apply to systems of interconnected facts without exactly ever being exemplified all at once by anything, but of this more hereafter. For present purposes we need concern ourselves only with the other three realms.

A casual glance at this list might lead one to expect that, for Santayana, the human mind would belong to the realm of spirit, and the human body to the realm of matter, and that his position would be that of a Cartesian dualist. Such, however, is not really his position.

The two key factors in what we may call his *philosophy of mind* (though he uses no such expression) are the notions of the psyche and of spirit. Although he tends to use the terms 'mind' and 'mental' as though they referred only to spirit he takes many of the attributes other philosophers have wished to ascribe to mind as attributes rather of the psyche. Indeed Santayana does not really think in terms of *spirits* at all. The realm of spirit comprises all intuitions (i.e. conscious mental acts), the grouping of intuitions together as those of one person is not intrinsic to the realm of spirit as such, but derives from their connection with an individual psyche, and this, as we shall see, belongs rather to the realm of matter than that of spirit.

The realm of matter is a scene of constant change, its various parts continually exchange one essence for another. Santayana uses the term 'event' for a succession of changes in anything distinguishable as a continuous thing or group of things. Each event has its own essence consisting in the precise character and order of the phases passed through by the things which figure in it, and Santayana calls such an essence 'a trope'.[1] Tropes, unlike other essences, cannot be exemplified 'all at once', but only piecemeal.

An event is a particular, its trope an essentially repeatable universal. Santayana emphasizes (RB, p. 296) that the tropes exemplified within a certain time and place are indefinitely many and heterogeneous in character, holding on all sorts of different scales and levels. Laws of nature are tropes of a particularly pervasive kind, such that their partial exemplification is a reliable sign that the rest will follow. Santayana might with advantage have made a clearer contrast than he does between the generic and the specific in explaining these points, for a law of nature could hardly be the complete essence of a particular event but at most some aspect it has in common with all other events of the same broad type. One might in any case object that the law is not the trope, but the assertion that the trope once started will work itself out. Perhaps Santayana could reply that such an assertion is the assertion that that trope has the status of a law. Even so, this is, for various reasons, a doubtfully adequate account of laws of nature in general; but the point is not of much importance for present purposes, since the recurrent tropes in which Santayana is mainly interested are patterns more apparent to common observation than are the more basic laws of nature – the regular succession of the seasons, the alternation of day and night, and all the regularities on which ordinary prudence is based. Among these are the main regularities apparent in the lives of plants and animals, the usually repeated cycle of birth, maturation, and death.

The distinctive tropes exhibited by living beings, by plants or animals (or by their *lives*, as one should more strictly say), have the peculiarity that, though it is by no means uncommon for them to receive an only partial exemplification, the plant or animal will, in a wide variety of circumstances, do whatever is required (that is, will exemplify such lesser tropes) if the chances of the trope's continuation are to be at a maximum. Such tropes, at least when conceived in a way which Santayana regards as appropriate but in the last resort mythical, are what Santayana calls *psyches*.[2] In this semi-mythical conception the trope is thought of as imposing itself on the matter which exemplifies it, or somehow watching over the substance of the plant or organism and making it do what is required if the trope is to be carried out.

Santayana indicates rather vaguely that the psyche has various different levels and echoes the old tradition of a vegetative, an animal, and a rational soul; yet he is primarily concerned to emphasize the continuity between physiological and psychological activity, seeing both as operations of the psyche, as activities necessary if certain master tropes are to be carried through, and as in that sense teleological. Nonetheless he can hardly have meant to deny that there are important differences between them, and indeed their distinction is presupposed when he speaks of the psyche as that which, however erroneously, is thought of as a self independent of this particular body, for he must be thinking here of the psychological psyche. In fact, though he does not put it in this form, he gives us what amounts to a theory of the distinction between physiological activity and behaviour.

Both sorts of activity are at one level teleological and at a deeper level mechanical, but the adjustments to the environment we call behaviour are mediated by complex internal representations of the environment (presumably in the brain) such as give rise to consciousness[3] and, in particular, to an envisagement *sub specie boni* of the organism's goal, that is the upshot such adjustment will have if it successfully maintains the tropes which 'control' it. Santayana holds that this envisagement, this conscious deciding or willing, is never strictly a cause of behaviour but only a symptom or, as he puts it, 'expression', of that to which the behaviour, or its inner physical causes, is tending, but insofar as these, and indeed all other acts of consciousness too, stem from and express the psyche's workings they count as the psyche's acts. Thus it is the psyche which is most properly called the subject of consciousness. (In spite of this, Santayana sometimes understands by the psyche's operations only its physical, especially its behavioural, manifestations, as when he claims that the psyche, but not the spirit, is the proper object of a scientific psychology.)

Santayana often speaks as though the psyche were fixed for each of us at birth and that all our doings represent the nearest approximation possible to some genetically determined blueprint or master-trope. However, he does also speak of the psyche as indefinitely pliable. This seems to mean that the original blueprint is highly generic, and that it becomes gradually more and more specific, and sub-tropes (or as we might say 'sub-programmes') are gradually incorporated in it, determining their own special branches of behaviour, when their exemplification has become the most effective way of conforming to the abstract master-plan.

The assumption seems to be made in all this, that the organism's activity is determined by the requirement that certain directions of change be persevered in, but he should, surely, have allowed that the requirement may sometimes be rather that some single state be persevered in so far as possible. This state would not strictly be a trope in Santayana's sense, but he can hardly have meant to exclude it from the psyche. Preservation of such states may, I suppose, be more fundamental than persistence in a certain predetermined direction of change.

Actually, Santayana holds, in any case, that at the most fundamental level of explanation, if that is ever reached, nothing comparable to the psyche will figure, and regards the notion of tropes which have a tendency to work themselves out so far as circumstances allow, as an impressionistic man's-eye view of the world. Probably everything ultimately rests on the way matter operates (not necessarily in a wholly deterministic fashion) at a level far below that of such units as *plant* and *man*. The following passage sums up many of Santayana's reflections on this theme, though usually he inclines more strongly to the mechanistic side of the controversy which he here describes, rather arrogantly, as stupid, meaning really only that it is a question of scientific fact without the 'moral' importance sometimes attached to it:

Science as yet has no answer to this most important of all questions, if we wish to understand human nature: namely, How is the body, and how are its senses and passions, determined to develop as they do? We may reply: Because God wills it so; or Because such is the character of the human species; or Because mechanical causes necessitate it. These answers do not increase our scientific understanding in the least; nevertheless they are not wholly vain: for the first tells us that we must be satisfied with ignorance; the second that we must be satisfied with the facts; and the third, which is the most significant, that these facts are analogous in every province of nature. But how close are these analogies? Mechanism is one habit of matter, and life is another habit of matter; the first we can measure mathematically and forecast accurately, the second we can only express in moral terms, and anticipate vaguely; but that the mechanical habit runs through the vital habit, and conditions it, is made obvious by the dependence of life on food, on time, on temperature, by its routine in health and by its diseases, by its end, and above all by its origin; for it is a habit of matter continuous with other inorganic habits, and (if evolution is true) arising out of them. In any case, life comes from a seed in which it lies apparently dormant and arrested, and from which it is elicited by purely mechanical agencies. On the other hand, the seed reacts on those agencies in a manner as yet inexplicable by what we know of its structure; and its development closely repeats (though perhaps with some spontaneous variation) the phases proper to the species.

To this mysterious but evident predetermination of normal life by the seed the ancients gave the name of soul; but to use the word soul suggests a thinking spirit, or even a disembodied one. It is totally incredible that a thinking spirit should exist in the seed, and should plan and carry out (by what instruments?) the organization of the body; and if so wise and powerful and independent a spirit lay in us from the beginning, or rather long before our birth, how superfluous a labour to beget us at all, and how unkind of it to dangle after it, in addition to its own intelligence, these poor blundering and troubled thoughts of which alone we are aware! Evidently the governing principle in seeds is no soul in this modern sense, no thinking moral being; it is a mysterious habit in matter. Whether this total habit is reducible to minor habits of matter, prevalent in the world at large, is the question debated between mechanical and vitalist psychologists; but it is a stupid controversy. The smallest unit of mechanism is an event as vital, as groundless, and as creative as it is possible for an event to be; it summons fresh essences into existence, which the character of the essences previously embodied in existence by no means implied dialectically. On the other hand, the romantic adventure of life, if it is not a series of miracles and catastrophes observed *ex post facto*, must be a resultant of simpler habits struggling or conspiring together. However minute, therefore, or however comprehensive, the units by which natural processes are described, they are equally vital and equally mechanical, equally free and (for an observer with a sufficient range of vision) equally predictable. On the human scale of observation it is the larger habits of living beings that are most easily observed; and the principle of these habits, transmitted by a seed, I call the Psyche: it is either a complex of more minute habits of matter, or a mastering rhythm imposed upon them by the habit of the species. Many Greek philosophers taught that the Psyche was material; and even Plato, although of course his Psyche might eventually take to thinking, regarded it as primarily a principle of motion, growth, and unconscious government; so that the associations of the word Psyche are not repugnant, as are those of the word soul, to the meaning I wish to give it: that habit in matter which forms the human body and the human mind. (SE, pp. 219–22)

When Santayana says that the psyche is a myth he is in some way downgrading explanations of activity which refer to it. When he says that it is a useful and inevitable myth he is saying that this type of explanation is all the same the one most properly made use of in daily life.

His critique of explanation by reference to the psyche seems to turn on two really very different points, which it would have been well if he had distinguished more clearly. When one explains an organism's activitities by reference to its psyche (that is, by reference to its goals or purposes) one (partially) identifies a master-pattern, or system of patterns of activity and development, as one to which it seems to conform so far as circumstances allow, and one treats this master-pattern as a sort of power which keeps the matter of the organism in conformity to it so far as possible.

The first inadequacy Santayana finds in such an explanation seems to be this. The habit which organisms have of conforming to patterns of this sort derives from much more basic habits of matter, and it is to these more fundamental habits that a true explanation would appeal.

Such habits are more fundamental for one or more of the following to some extent independent reasons: they are more pervasive and these habits of the organism are simply their consequences in peculiar conditions; they hold more rigidly and are not mere tendencies; they are patterns exemplified by physical things as they actually are rather than by things on the scale and with the qualities with which they appear to human consciousness, whether perceptual or intellectual, though of course they determine all patterns cognizable at the human level. Santayana sometimes runs these points together, but elsewhere, though it is not his way to list them in this bald way, he notes that they are independent of one another. The last condition is the most fundamental for him and it is to be noted that he thought it likely (but certainly not necessarily true) that no human explanation would reach the patterns at this level.

The second defect Santayana finds in explanation by reference to the psyche is that the latter is treated as though it were an existence exerting force of some kind upon the organism, when in truth it is merely a pattern it tends to exhibit. Such defect, it should be noted, could, on the face of it, arise equally with explanations of the more fundamental kind just discussed (though perhaps it arises more naturally with patterns to which matter tends to conform than with those to which it always or merely sometimes conforms) for here also it would be possible to treat the law or pattern in conformity with which one 'fact' influences another, as a further 'fact' exerting its own influence. Santayana, indeed, sometimes says that laws of nature are mythical in the same way as the psyche, because they are thus conceived. In spite of this, he is far too prone to assimilate these two really quite different senses in which he regards the psyche as 'mythical'.

One may agree readily enough with Santayana that it is a confusion to treat a pattern to which a thing's activity conforms or tends to conform as another thing acting upon it, but why should this confusion be built into the word 'psyche', and, as he sometimes maintains, into the phrase 'law of nature' also? The latter term, at any rate, can surely be used without any such confusion, and one may well ask why Santayana does not simply recommend a similarly confusion-free use of the word 'psyche', or, if the word is too much imbued with this confusion, why he does not recommend another term altogether?

The answer is, apparently, that the psyches of human beings are their very *selves*, that I am my psyche, and that, though I may be in the last resort a partly mythical entity, I can hardly therefore give up speaking of myself. Santayana does not stress the paradox in this way, but it seems to be present in his thought. The consciousness which arises from the state of my organism at any moment understands by the terms 'I' and 'You' (or perhaps we should say, is, in part, an understanding of the terms 'I' and 'You' as meaning) something deeper than any act or series of acts of consciousness, and something more recondite than the organism, in whose activities it manifests itself.

Santayana has many reasons for denying that you and I are the series of our mental acts, of the instances of spirit pertaining to us. [4] Chief of these is that the self is a thing of indefinite hidden potentialities, while a series of acts of spirit is just what it is and cannot, with any clear sense, be said to have had the potentiality of being otherwise; the self, moreover, can often be said to have had purposes by no means fully expressed in its conscious acts. It is not so obvious why Santayana does not simply identify the self with the organism, but among his reasons seems to have been the distinction which most people feel to be at least possible between the fate of the former and the latter; transmigration of souls, survival of bodily death, two selves in one body – all these seem consistent with the self as it thinks of itself. Santayana evidently concludes that by oneself one means (or spirit in one means) a system of controlling purposes, or, what is the same thing, a system of tropes which one's actual mental and physical activity realizes, at each moment, so far as circumstances allow, conceived of as a kind of invisible thing. (Presumably it is the psychological rather than the biological psyche which is primarily in question here.)

As I have remarked, Santayana, not being the sort of metaphysician who takes a delight in shocking common sense, does not emphasize the paradox inherent in asking us to recognize that we ourselves are in some sense mythical. Certainly there is an air of paradox in this, but no real incoherence. If one asks who it is who really sees the world in this way, the answer is that this vision of the world is present in many acts of spirit, and these are not myths. One can say that *spirit*, or that many an act of spirit, sees things in this way. The ordinary language philosopher may object that it is people who have visions, not spirit or acts of spirit, but this only shows that ordinary language must sometimes be modified for the expression of philosophical insights.

Where I think Santayana's account is seriously deficient is in explaining the ways in which what is really only a form, or system of forms, is treated as a thing. He tells us that this consists in regarding it as a power, but what is surely equally essential is that it is treated as having a history, as being subject to change, and as having an identity which is not simply qualitative or formal. These points are interconnected. On the face of it, identical twins could have their behaviour under the control of identical master-plans or tropes, yet their psyches would count as different, and this is in part because psyches are thought of as evolving, so that the sub-tropes which the fortunes of each child associate with the original master-trope are thought of as accretions to the original psyche, something which would not make sense in reference to an essence.

Santayana's conception of the psyche derives in great part from his reading of Aristotle.[5] The curious thing is that in developing the theory he does not seek to remove what he regards as its ontological confusion in treating the form of an animal as a power presiding over it, but rather seems to argue that such a confusion is implicit in the ordinary and inevitable notion of a soul or self. It would be more plausible, surely, to say that the psyche or self is conceived of as an existence which acts, so far as possible, in conformity to a certain system of tropes which can be called its purposes, than that it is the system of tropes itself conceived of as an existence. Such an account would make sense of the conceptual distinctions between the self and the organism, since it could be an open question for consciousness how far the, so to speak, core exemplifier of these tropes was the organism itself or something else physically, or in some metaphorical sense, inside it; moreover on Santayana's own view of identity across time,[6] the present phase of the organism and the self could be identical, without the organism and self exactly being so, since an existence of a given kind lasts as long as a succession of facts somehow follow on one another conforming to the right essences, which could be different for the organism and the self. But though Santayana virtually employs this conception in some of what he says about the psyche, his explicit account is as given above.

2 *Santayana and behaviourism*

Behaviouristic theories were beginning to gain ground at the time when Santayana's ideas on mind developed. As a complete account of the human person any sort of behaviourism appeared as quite absurd to

Santayana. His 1922 review of J. B. Watson's *Psychology from the stand-point of a Behaviorist* still has relevance as an amusing exhibition of the theory's absurdities.[7] However, Santayana was largely sympathetic to a kind of methodological behaviourism in psychology, and in some respects his own account of the psyche even approximates to certain types of philosophical behaviourism. It is interesting to note, in this connection, the curious analogy there is between his account of the psyche and Gilbert Ryle's account of the mind. Just as Ryle (in his famous *The Concept of Mind*) says that the mind is not a substance or thing but a system of behavioural dispositions, so Santayana says that the psyche or person is not a substance or a thing but a system of tropes or behavioural patterns. Just as Ryle seems sometimes to be in doubt as to whether the mind is some kind of logical fiction or whether it is a perfectly good reality merely misrepresented by certain philosophers, so Santayana seems to be in doubt as to whether the psyche is essentially a myth or whether it is a perfectly good reality merely liable to be misconceived as a substance. There are other similarities too. They are both anxious to attack the idea that the mind or psyche acts on the body in some quasi-mechanical way, and wish rather to assimilate its explanatory role to that of a set of laws governing the behaviour of the organism. In such a passage as the following Santayana's dismissal of 'mental machinery' is strikingly similar in tone to much of Ryle, though the last sentence reminds us that in recognizing the existence of immaterial acts of spirit (which, in a different sense of 'of', are also the psyche's acts) Santayana keeps his eyes open to a kind of fact on which Ryle takes a somewhat shuffling attitude:

> The psyche is a natural fact, the fact that many organisms are alive, can nourish and reproduce themselves, and on occasion can feel and think. This is not merely a question of the use of words: it is a *deliberate refusal to admit the possibility of any mental machinery*. The machinery of growth, instinct, and action, like the machinery of speech, is all physical: but this sort of physical operation is called psychical, because it falls within the trope of a life, and belongs to the self-defence and self-expression of a living organism. How should any unsophisticated person doubt that the movements of matter have the nature of matter for their principle, and not the nature of spirit? (RB, p. 332)

If Santayana had identified mind and psyche his position would have been still closer to that of Ryle. He did, in any case, regard the psyche, and the psyche only in its publicly observable manifestations, as the proper object of scientific psychology, holding that spirit, the actual quality of our consciousness, was only open to an intuitive literary kind of study, which he called 'literary psychology', whose aim was to communicate how it felt to live through various experiences, and which could not become an exact science.[8] The words 'mind' and 'mental', however, he reserved (mainly) for this latter realm, the realm of spirit, partly perhaps because without 'mental' there is no useful adjective meaning 'pertaining to spirit', since 'spiritual' connotes only the purer forms of spirit.

For myself, I think there is little point in arguing as to the proper use of 'mind'. In ordinary language the word occurs mainly as a mere component in various idiomatic expressions; outside such cases its use is always bound up with some controversial theory. The statements Ryle chooses to analyse, presumably as being 'about the mind', seldom contain the term, and if Santayana treats these as concerning not the mind but the psyche or person he does so with as good a right, though in fact he usually avoids the term, doubtless because it tends to blur the distinctions on which he means to insist.

The important thing, in any case, is the distinctions recognized, not the terminology used. Santayana's account of the psyche is impressionistic, and leaves numerous relevant questions unanswered, and is probably wrong-headed in various details. On the other hand, the broad distinction he makes between the psyche and the spirit seems a valuable one, such that if something along its lines were accepted one could clarify many a discussion about *mind*, by asking which of these two is meant. If Santayana is right, it should always be the psyche that is meant when *mind* is treated as an object of properly scientific study. The descriptions of the stream of consciousness at which William James was so adept really belong to literature since their subject matter cannot be directly experimented upon by the investigator.

Santayana sometimes suggests that most psychological expressions have a double meaning, referring on the one hand to observable activities or propensities of the psyche or organism, on the other hand to certain unobservable acts of consciousness – a view he professes to derive from Aristotle.[9] In view of this one must suppose that he would have looked favourably on the many recent attempts to analyse psychological expressions in behaviouristic terms, a line of enquiry of which *The Concept of Mind* remains the classic case. He would, I should suppose, have taken these as providing material for elaborating his own concept of the psyche, for although he describes the psyche as a system of tropes which exhibit teleology, in a publicly observable sense of the term, he certainly thinks of such less obviously teleological terms as perception and knowledge as being, in one sense, publicly observable features of the psyche, because essentially instruments whereby it pursues its goals.

In insisting that the fact of having goals is a publicly observable feature of an organism, Santayana sometimes comes close to the account of teleology which has quite recently been elaborated by Charles Taylor in his *The Explanation of Behaviour*. Taylor argues that teleological systems are not those whose activities require to be explained by some occult entity called a purpose, but those which, as a matter of observable fact, will do, in a wide range of circumstances, whatever is required to bring about a certain result (though when he says that, in 'intentional' systems, it is the requirements of the intentional not the real environment which matters, the observability of the facts is less obvious).[10] Santayana holds that an organism has a purpose insofar as its activities are observably modified so as to conform to some master-trope. He (unlike Taylor) regards it as all but certain that the teleology of organisms is ultimately explicable in mechanistic terms.

Another feature of Santayana's account of teleology which is of some interest, is his suggestion that the distinction between teleology and mechanism lies to a great extent in the way one looks at things. To say that objects, of whatever kind, are governed by a certain law of nature and to say that they are striving to conform to a certain pattern of activity, differ only in that one chooses in the latter case to regard such conformity as the object's *good*.[11]

It is only if reference to the essentially unobservable is introduced, and the question is as to whether the object itself (and not simply the observer of it) feels that such conformity is a good, that we have a properly factual, though even then not a scientific, question.

One might think that there must be observable differences between those objects to which one ascribes such consciousness of good and the others, and that these supply an observable contrast between the teleological and the mechanical; nor is it hard to derive from Santayana himself some suggestion as to what these observable differences may be. Two stand out. The individuals one most typically thinks of as conscious seem, as a matter of ascertainable physical fact, to modify their behaviour according to the kind of messages they receive, and have in the past received, from the environment, and it is an essentially physical and verifiable hypothesis that this is via internal physical representations thereof which are then built up. Moreover, the tropes which seem to govern their behaviour are not absolute laws, such as govern mechanisms, but rather patterns to which they approximate so far as possible.

Santayana does not deal with these points at all systematically, but I think he may have still thought of the contrast as less than absolute because, after all, every physical item is liable to internal modification according to its environment, and thus in a manner represents it, and because even the most mechanical laws can perhaps be described as ideal patterns to which things conform insofar as other factors do not interfere.

Santayana's main contention is, in any case, independent of any decision as to the sharpness of the essentially observable difference between those things in nature which we typically think of as having purposes and those which we do not, for it is this. At one level organisms are simply parts of the physical world and their behaviour can be studied and explained without reference to their presumed 'inner' consciousness. Whether the patterns or laws by reference to which the details of their activity may ultimately be explained are of a special type, distinct from the laws governing other physical things, or not, they are still essentially publicly observable patterns exhibited by publicly observable things, and we are not broaching the realm of spirit or consciousness in referring to them. It would be well if this essentially valid point were grasped better at the present day. There are many philosophers who repudiate what they call behaviourism but who are apparently as dead as the behaviourist to the specific nature of spirit or consciousness, merely giving a less simplistic account of man *qua* object among objects in the world.

Santayana holds that this is what man must be so far as any scientific study goes, but he also insists that it is in his own peculiarly qualified awareness of things, that is in his consciousness or spirit, that the whole value of a man's existence lies. While largely sympathetic to this point of view, I do not think that Santayana explains at all adequately why consciousness or spirit cannot be referred to as such in a scientific psychology. The claim that its presence and quality is not detectable by observation, but only by sympathetic intuition, seems hardly to justify its omission from the scientific account of things, when, on Santayana's own view, this rests at every point upon unverifiable assumptions. If Santayana is essentially right in this, I should suppose it is because the fluidity of consciousness is such that its different forms cannot be denoted by a language whose terms possess the fixity of meaning appropriate to a science. Its character is conveyed rather by the literary artist who suggests and insinuates his insights in words which will never mean quite the same in other contexts.

There is some difficulty in evaluating Santayana's account of the psyche since it is not quite clear just what it is designed to establish. In the case of the doctrine of essence one can ask whether there are, in the relevant sense, such beings as he characterizes under this term, but one cannot ask quite the same question with regard to the psyche, because the entity is admitted to be in some sense mythical. Sometimes it looks like a highly impressionistic suggestion as to a way of looking at things which should be helpful in biology and psychology, and it does contain what seem to be essentially guesses concerning what science may one day reveal, as, for instance, in its stress upon the innateness of the individual's main goals. Still, Santayana would claim that it is essentially only a restatement of what the most ordinary observation will reveal to anyone. Is it then the identification or analysis of some ordinary concept, and, if so, what word usually connotes it in daily life? On the whole, I think we may take it thus as an account of what each of us really thinks of as his real self and as the self of others. Taken as such, it is hardly adequate. Santayana says very little about memory in his description of the psyche, yet it is hard not to think that a large part of what I mean by myself is a being with certain memories. It seems odd, also, to think that the self is, somehow, an *essence* mistaken for a power though, as I have indicated, I would not reject this merely because of a certain verbal difficulty in saying *whose* mistake it was.

As a matter of fact, I suspect, that none of us always means the same thing by the word 'I' or by 'you', even when talking to the same person. If I am asked who it is who means these different things, I reply, much as before, that there are thoughts which belong to *me* in each of these senses, and that it is for these thoughts that the meaning of 'I' varies. As a very impressionistic adumbration of one such meaning, thus of one account of the 'self' (and of the 'mind' too, I should add, because in certain senses of these words they refer to the same thing) I think we may grant Santayana's account a rather limited measure of success, especially in the way in which he contrasts it with spirit.

3 *The glory and the impotence of spirit*

The agent in action and the subject in experience is (for Santayana) the psyche, and the psyche, though not exactly a material thing, is a pattern or complex of patterns exemplified in the material world. We have suggested that Santayana might have done better to have said that the psyche was the organism itself, *qua* exemplifier of such a complex pattern, and in effect Santayana often himself adopts this position.

The internal and external activities of the psyche give rise at every moment of waking life to what Santayana calls moments of spirit, meaning what would more commonly be called states of consciousness. These moments of spirit are not facts or events in the physical world and cannot be identified with anything which could be found within a human head or in any other place. The totality of such moments is what Santayana calls the realm of spirit.[12]

These moments are each the intuition of some complex essence, with or without intent. The division of the stream of a man's consciousness into such moments is not merely conventional for Santayana; each takes in a certain totality, normally a stretch of specious space and time, in a single synthetic glance.[13] But though at this level the realm of spirit divides up, of its own nature, into distinct 'moments' or 'facts', there are no individuals at a higher level than this with boundaries determined by characteristics intrinsically spiritual. Santayana occasion-ally talks of *spirits*, but he certainly thinks that what makes all the intuitions of a single person the intuitions of a single spirit is the fact that they emanate from the activities of a single psyche. If, therefore, we think of the realm of spirit in abstraction from its physical basis, there is no more cause to speak of many spirits than of the one spirit.

An intuition is to be distinguished from the essence of which it is the intuition. All the same, Santayana usually maintains, as we have seen, that there is nothing which can be said to have the intuition other than the psyche or organism from whose activity it arises. He does, indeed, sometimes speak of *spirit* (rather than of *a spirit*) as having intuitions – as fearing, enjoying, suffering[14] (all of which, taken in reference to spirit, refer to types of intuition). Occasionally he also speaks of *a spirit* as suffering or whatever, but he prefers to speak of 'spirit within me' or 'within you' as doing so.

It is not too easy to say to just what the word 'spirit' refers in such locutions. Is it, perhaps, the generic essence of spirit which is one and the same in all those intuitions which exemplify it?[15] But can one speak of an essence, even the essence of spirit, as rejoicing or suffering? Certainly one could not do so with literal correctness, but perhaps just as the psyche is for Santayana an essence mythically depicted as a sub-stance so is spirit, in this sense, the essence of spirit mythically depicted as an individual.

In using such locutions Santanaya is certainly deliberately echoing the language of such mystics and idealists as speak of a single world spirit. I think Santayana would justify the usage as drawing attention to a valid point of some ethical importance, namely that the distinction between different subjects of experience has no basis when experiences, or intuitions, are considered for what they are in themselves, and apart from their grounding in a fundamentally different kind of existence, the physical, and that, therefore, if, considering them as they are in them-selves, we express our reflections in the subject-act terminology which it is so hard to avoid, we had better speak merely of spirit as the subject.

One is tempted to say that Santayana's language here is not that of the disinterested ontologist but one who wishes to convey a certain way of looking at things. The suggestion of such a remark, however, is that there is a way of describing such things which represents the bald truth, and that departures therefrom distort the facts in the interest of special attitudes. But perhaps if Santayana is right that the class of all intuitions does not sort itself out into those of distinct subjects by its very nature, then any theory as to the subject of such acts represents a way of classifying them corresponding to a particular interest. One such inter-est, that of the practical organization of life, bids us distinguish them as the acts of separate psyches; another such interest, that of reflecting on the nature of intuitions in themselves, bids us put them all together as the acts of one subject. (Conceivably a legitimate interest could be served by seeing (say) the intuitions of all Frenchmen as the acts of France, but with this Santayana would have little sympathy.) Certainly the former has an epistemological priority, since, broadly speaking, we can only know of an intuition's occurrence via knowledge of some individual psyche's activities, but the latter might have 'spiritual' priority. Indeed it is because Santayana thinks that the 'spiritual' point of view, as expressed in religion at its best, is the point of view for which the realm of spirit is regarded in its own intrinsic nature, and apart from its physical grounding, that he uses the term 'spirit' rather than consciousness.

Spirit is essentially impotent, according to Santayana.[16] The causal explanation of events in the realm of matter, and hence of human behaviour, lies wholly in antecedent physical facts. Events in the brain, but not the moments of spirit which arise therefrom, belong to causal chains. Santayana is careful to point out that this does not mean that reasoning and deliberation are inefficacious, for these terms do not only denote certain forms of spirit, but refer also, in a summary fashion, to essentially observable facts as to the way in which the psyche learns from and takes account of its experience (where 'experience' refers to actual physical transactions between organism and environment) and perhaps also to the presumed physical mechanisms which underlie these facts:

> When, for instance, I say or assume that reflection and reason
> have important consequences, I am not contradicting my doctrine
> of the material inefficacy of consciousness or spirit. Reflection and
> reason are forms taken by life, they are psychic processes in
> organisms, involving all sorts of physical relations and potentialities.
> They are not clear hypostatic *results* of these processes such as
> consciousness and spirit are. That a man is reflective or rational
> appears in his whole behaviour during long stretches of time; an
> idiot does not speak or act like intelligent people. . . . In a word,
> the psyche must not be confused with the spirit. (PGS, p. 541)

Santayana's language sometimes brings him closer to the behaviourism of a philosopher such as Ryle, sometimes to a central state materialism such as that of Armstrong; that is, sometimes he seems to think of 'reason' as referring to facts of a behavioural kind, sometimes to a presumed inner mechanism accounting for these facts; probably he would have thought an attempt to decide between the two would show a pedantry such as the flexibility of language renders nugatory. One might complain also that he leaves it vague when he is describing ordinary use of these terms and when he is recommending a new one.

Yet to press such objections is to treat Santayana's philosophy as an attempt at conceptual analysis of the modern kind, when it is intended rather as a first order description of the actual facts as they present themselves to a clarified common sense.

Santayana's materialism is not worked out with the kind of detailed reference to different psychological terms with which philosophers such as Ryle and Armstrong develop their views. He is defending a general thesis against general objections. I do not think this makes his work vacuous. The claim that the truth lies in a certain general direction can be rationally supported by one who makes no pretence to having charted it in detail.

In any case, at the time when Santayana was writing (long before the days of the computer) a mechanistic theory of the mind – or of the psyche, as Santayana would say – could never be more than impressionistic. The chief merit of Santayana's treatment of this topic is his clear recognition that the ground for insisting that there is a non-physical dimension to man's being, such as he calls *spirit*, is not that it is required for the explanation of his physical doings but that, only by reference to it, can we explain what matters, what is morally significant, in the fate of human beings. The actual reasons Santayana gives for holding that my conscious states arise from brain activity without reacting on it are less than conclusive, often indeed they seem to beg the very point at issue, but, for us today, when a mechanistic interpretation of the human being looks ever more and more promising as an essentially empirical hypothesis, his development of epiphenomenalism may commend itself as the one thesis which does justice to the best of what is meant by those who deny that man is a machine without forcing us to be obscurantist about the significance of neurophysiological and artificial intelligence research.

Having said so much I shall not attempt to summarize all the reasons Santayana offers from time to time in favour of spirit's inefficacy. It may be as well, however, to consider a line of argument which stems from certain general considerations regarding causality.

Evidently Santayana had some difficulty in satisfying himself as to the correct account of the causal relation, but he certainly strongly tended to a view for which it consists in the gradual transformation of one state of affairs into another through a sequence of essentially observable intermediate phases, according to a law of universal validity. [17] On this view nothing can properly figure as a cause if it is so radically different from the effect as not to be observable in the same sense as that is, or if it is such that there could not be facts intermediate in character between the cause and effect. Combining this with the ascription to consciousness of a character utterly distinct from that of material processes, and with the belief that consciousness is essentially unobservable, he argued that it could not be a cause of such physical goings on as constitute human behaviour.

The obvious objection to this argument is that consciousness, by the same token, cannot be an effect of physical goings on, in the brain or elsewhere. Santayana does not ignore this, and sometimes says that strictly speaking consciousness is not an effect.[18] On the other hand, while the scientific attempt to explain physical events, including human actions, cannot properly look beyond the processes of transformation just explained, the fact that moments of consciousness occur must be left entirely unexplained unless one sees them as somehow grounded, though not in a strictly causal way such as science could ever chart, in physical facts. It is this non-causal grounding to which Santayana refers with the phrase 'hypostatic result' in the passage quoted above; I shall consider its meaning shortly.

Even without the special stress which Santayana puts upon the notion of gradual transformation, the contention that consciousness is unobservable in some much more fundamental way than are even the unobservables of science (whose actions can be registered in various quasi-perceptual ways) and that science, as a study of the functional relations between events which are all observable in at least a broad sense of the word, will never need to take account of it may well commend itself. I suspect, however, that the reason one thinks of consciousness as so peculiarly unobservable is that it seems nonsensical to suppose that it might reflect light, or in any other way act on a sense organ or scientific instrument, and this, even if true, is clearly a *petitio principii*.

The claim that consciousness is so different in character from any physical facts that it can hardly belong together with them in any single process of transformation seems less question-begging. The mere fact that one can hardly think of a moment of consciousness as *in a place* seems to show this sufficiently. Unfortunately Santayana's own account of location in space undercuts this, or makes it another *petitio principii*, since, in the last resort, proximity in real space is (for him) a matter of immediacy of causal interaction. Santayana would still, perhaps, insist that the essence of a moment of spirit is so different from that of a physical fact that the one could never count as a modified version of the other, and as capable of taking over from it in the ways that members of a causal sequence must do.

But even granting this, Santayana's case seems rather weak. If it is true that facts in the realm of matter may conjointly ground the occurrence of a fact in the realm of spirit, as Santayana holds they may, why should not a fact in the realm of spirit be among those which ground a fact in the realm of matter? The difference it would thus make in the realm of matter would not be causal in Santayana's sense, but this seems a mere quibble.

Santayana's words sometimes suggest the weaker but better supported claim that the determination of the states of an organism's consciousness is so little amenable to scientific test that they cannot enter into scientific theory. He needs to show, however, why the faith involved in all scientific enquiry will not suffice to satisfy us sufficiently in this too. In any case, Santayana wishes to show that spirit actually is impotent, not that its potency is untestable.

But though both these and other arguments he uses are far from conclusive demonstrations of the impotence of spirit, he does seem essentially right in his contention that spirit is hardly the sort of thing to figure in any scientific explanation of behaviour. In practice we cannot get agreement about its character or presence as we can about the character or presence of physical facts, nor, in spite of various limited successes in 'psycho-physics', can it be adequately characterized in terms of measurable properties such as may enter into functional relations with physical forces. If this is true, the prospect of a genuinely scientific account of human behaviour is one with the prospect of its elimination from the causal story. That nonetheless it would remain the most important of realities is well brought home to us by a philosophy which denies it all causal efficacy from the start.

It is this essentially moral insight into the independence of spirit's value from any alleged efficacy it possesses which mainly inspires Santayana's epiphenomenalism. He did not, of course, invent this doctrine, which had already been advocated by such thinkers as T. H. Huxley and Shadworth Hodgson.[19] It had, however, usually been regarded, even by its proponents, as essentially a gloomy theory, representing the consciousness which is what essentially we are for ourselves as a passive victim of brain processes of an essentially mechanical kind, suffering from the vain delusion that it controlled its own destiny. Santayana, on the contrary, cherished epiphenomenalism for bringing home to us the *true* dignity and worth of consciousness which does not consist in the work it accomplishes but in the moral significance it gives to what would otherwise be mere meaningless happening. For without spirit's living sense of the goodness of that at which the psyche aims, and of the evil of its frustration, it would simply not matter how far the psyche in a certain sense 'prospered' or not. Here surely Santayana is right, and right as against any conceivable form of behaviourism or physicalism, however sophisticated. Even though one can take words like 'purpose' and 'motive' in the kind of way they utilize, and even though it is only in such senses that they need occur in a behavioural science, the facts that the words cover in these restricted senses only have any value, and are worth bothering about, because they are, as Santayana puts it, 'expressed' by facts in the realm of spirit. That it is in this that the importance of spirit lies stands forth much more clearly once we cease to think that it has the importance of an agent that gets things done.

The moral aspect of Santayana's epiphenomenalism comes out clearly in his attack upon William James's defence of the efficacy of consciousness.[20] James claimed that consciousness would have atrophied if it served no useful purpose in the economy of the organism, and Santayana quite rightly points out that this would not be so if it necessarily goes together with certain mechanisms of adaptation to the environment. Santayana sees James's use of this argument as really expressing a New England puritan's and pragmatist's distaste for anything not useful, whereas, for Santayana, consciousness need serve no other purpose than that of giving a moral significance to life to justify its existence. One wonders whether Santayana's suggestion that for the pragmatist, consciousness, if not useful, must 'be a bad habit, deranging or weakening the organism, like masturbation'[21] is not applicable to the suspicion of so many modern philosophers of private experience as a nasty solitary thing they will not admit to in public.

Santayana is ready to admit that the manner in which the physical world has given rise to spirit remains to a great extent mysterious. He certainly wants the relation between the physical processes in the organism and its consciousness to be an intimate one. On the other hand it is not a properly causal one. There can be no transformation of physical energy or substance in to moments of spirit. Nor can one even call in aid spatial or temporal relations between organism and these moments of spirit in explaining how the one belongs to other, since the moments of spirit are only in physical space and time in a derivative sense, inasmuch as they can be spoken of as occurring at the place and time of their physical basis. What, then, makes a certain mental act the act of a certain organism at a certain time?

Santayana's answer to this question is anything but easy to grasp. On the face of it, two different features seem to contribute to this relation as he sees it.[22] First, the occurrence of the intuition must be due to physical facts in the organism, so that without them it would not have occurred. Second, the intuition must be an appropriate 'expression' of the state or situation of the organism, that is it must be the intuition of an essence which has some special affinity to the essence of this latter. Though Santayana doesn't point out this contrast, the former relation seems to be some sort of external relation, the latter some sort of internal relation.

If one asks in what sense the intuition is due to the state of the organism it seems that almost every plausible answer is ruled out by some feature of Santayana's system. We have already seen that it has nothing to do with the transformational process with which Santayana identifies causation. One might hope to explain it in terms of a counter-factual, and say that the intuition would not have occurred if the physical event had not done so, but Santayana rejects the idea that counterfactuals can constitute an ultimate form of truth. Sometimes Santayana even tends towards a 'double aspect' view and says that the moment of spirit is in some sense the same event as its physical basis in another aspect, [23] but common as such views are they explain little unless the relation between the aspects is explained and we cannot attribute to Santayana any view for which these aspects are not in some sense also distinct facts. The only possibility remaining seems to be that certain universal truths hold, to the effect that for every physical fact of a certain kind there is a moment of spirit whose character is related to it in a certain way, and that the occurrence of every moment of spirit is a special case of some such truth. It must be borne in mind, however, that the truth is not that such a moment of spirit exists at that time, since it only belongs to that time in the sense that its physical basis does.

The difficulty in elucidating this first feature of the relationship between the moment of spirit and its physical basis may tempt us to interpret it in terms of the second alone. If we do this, however, we shall have difficulty in explicating the situation when two different creatures, even at different times, intuit the same total essence (a situation Santayana explicitly allows as possible) [24] since granted that there are two distinct intuitions there will be nothing to settle which belongs to which creature, seeing that the same ideal relation will hold equally in each case. Although it would fit in with certain of Santayana's views to say that the intuitions are two only in the sense that there are distinct organisms whose states are equally expressed by what would otherwise be merely one intuition, this solution seems pretty weird. Thus I doubt whether Santayana would or should have dispensed with the first more external feature of the relation between an intuition and its physical basis, however difficult it may be to explain it.

Santayana's account of what I have called the internal feature of the relation between the intuition and its physical basis, such as makes the former an expression of the latter, is far from explicit, but I think one can distinguish two aspects thereof. First, the given essence may function as a kind of map of the organism's environment. The distribution of the elements in a single specious space and time may correspond to the distribution of corresponding elements in the real spatial and temporal environment. (It would be no easy task, however, to say in what sense these elements correspond, if one cannot first presuppose – on the basis of more external physico-mental links – the location of intuitions and say that the former are normally only intuited when the latter are present. We should note also that such an explanation of the correspondence makes it a relation which has external as well as internal features.) Second, an intuition may have an emotional quality or may set the scene, of which it is an intuition, in an emotional light, which is the intrinsically fitting expression of the disposition of the psyche towards some state of affairs representable thereby, as is, for instance, the felt fearfulness of a scene to the organism's behavioural tendency to remove itself from its present surroundings. It is in this sense that the envisagement of a state of affairs as *good* expresses the psyche's impulses towards it and it is only a psyche whose impulses are sometimes thus expressed which, for Santayana, has aims or purposes. That states of consciousness may be thus intrinsically suited to express behavioural tendencies seems, to me, to be true. It goes against some current beliefs, and it may be dismissed as an unacceptable synthetic *a priori*. It should be noted, however, that the claim is not that the existence of a fact of one character synthetically entails the existence of one of another character, only that certain essences, whether exemplified or not, have this peculiar sort of affinity one to another. Certainly this view gets no clear statement in Santayana, but I think it is what he means when he talks of intuitions expressing the psyche's impulses.

Thus Santayana leaves the relation of moments of spirit to their physical basis in considerable obscurity and can hardly be said to have solved this aspect of the body-mind problem. He may, nonetheless, have been working along the right lines. Any adequate theory must surely do justice, as his does, both to consciousness as something distinct from any processes discoverable inside an animal's head (as that also in which the whole value of existence lies) and to the strangeness of asking science to include anything not found there or elsewhere in its explanation of animal behaviour, considered as a physical fact.

Santayana seems once (cf. 'System') to have tended towards a different solution of this problem and to have held that the consciousness of animals consists really in certain facts in the physical world identified in their inner essence. Since he always held that the physical world is a system of facts, each possessing an unknown essence, in external relations to one another and characterized for us by the essences they present to intuition, such a solution might seem to have been a natural one. If he had surmised further that the inner essence of all ultimate facts is really in some sense spiritual or experiential his position would have been close to that of Whitehead. It would also have had some similarity to that of Herbert Feigl, though it would have been far from that of those modern 'brain-mind identity' theorists who simply try to explain consciousness, in any proper sense, away. It is not altogether clear why he abandoned this view. He seems to have held that reflection on one's conscious states somehow exhibits them as not capable of being in the relevant external relations. He might also have argued, and with a good deal of force, that the physical basis of an act of consciousness is likely to be a complex of basic facts (or 'natural moments') in external relations to one another and that an intuition (an organism's total state of consciousness at a certain time), is self-evidently not a compound of this sort, but an essentially single fact whose elements – or rather, whose immediate objects – are related only internally. [25]

4 *Intuition and intent*

Santayana's language often suggests that an intuition would be completely characterized if one could specify the essence of which it was the 'objective' or 'imaginative' exemplification. On the other hand he does not think that all intuitions are 'pure', consist in mere absorption in the given essence; on the contrary, most are 'laden with intent', take the given essence as characterizing or symbolizing something beyond. Moreover he talks of spirit as believing, desiring, suffering and so forth as well as merely intuiting. Does not this imply that the quality of intuition varies as well as its objects?

Sometimes Santayana writes as though there were just two types of intuition, those exceptional ones which are pure, and those more usual ones which are carried by intent, or as though the one difference between intuitions, apart from their objects, lay in the degree of their 'intentfulness'. Since he tends to identify 'intent' with 'belief' this would seem to suggest that there are no distinct sorts of mental act known, say, as desires, hopes, or what not. I think we can best make sense of his position if we take it that all intuitions which are not 'pure' contain an element of belief even if they are further characterizable as desires or whatever. This seems reasonable. A state of mind in which one desires something must, it would seem, also be one of belief in the existence of a situation which may or may not be susceptible of a certain modification. It seems to be this aspect of belief, present in all states of mind in any way directed to the real world, with which 'intent' is identified for Santayana. Intuitions carried by intent are concerned with something not given and are thus self-transcendent in a much stronger sense than a pure intuition can be said to be, even though the object of the latter is also something other than itself. Santayana would be criticized by some modern philosophers for using 'belief' to cover certain momentary acts of consciousness rather than some sort of long-term disposition or state, but whether one approves this verbal usage or not the fact of such self-transcendence on the part of momentary states is one which it is absurd to deny and baffling to elucidate.

In some few passages Santayana seems almost to suggest that the difference between a pure and an intent-laden intuition lies not in the quality of consciousness but in the latter's being a symptom of a certain readiness for appropriate action towards something connected with the intuition's cause.[26] His true meaning, however, seems to be that in intent-laden intuition the given essence is felt about in a way which is appropriate towards an existing fact or thing but not to a pure essence,[27] and that the occurrence of feelings of this sort is symptomatic of, or 'expresses', some readiness for action on the part of the psyche. 'Intent' tends to cover, for Santayana, both the presence of these feelings and the psychical (in the sense of: pertaining to the psyche) basis thereof, but he seems to have had no real doubt that these feelings had their own distinctive character which suffices to distinguish pure and intent-laden intuitions as intrinsically different sorts of moment of spirit.

The single word 'intent' suggests that there is some one and the same feeling present in all intuitions which are intent-laden, and maybe Santayana sometimes thought of this as a not further definable ultimate. On the other hand, other passages suggest that there is a range of quite varied feelings all of which are different cases of intent, alike in that they are quite inappropriate to a pure essence. (Or at least are inappropriate to an essence considered apart from some natural or dialectical context in which it has figured, for Santayana specifically asserts that an 'absent essence' – i.e. one not presently intuited – can be intended as the essence occurring in a certain, presumably intended, context.)[28] In terms of Santayana's account of the generic it would be senseless to press too hard the question whether they contain any common element, but Santayana tends to represent them all as different sorts of anxiety or care. Feelings of anxiety, in any case, are prime examples of what Santayana has in mind. For he maintains that it does not make sense to feel anxious about a shape, a sound, or an image as such (or even about an emotional feeling or pain as this reveals itself to pure contemplation when this is sustained) so that to feel anxious about these presentations is to take them as somehow more than pure forms of being, as somehow belonging to a world of facts full of threatening potentialities. Santayana tends to emphasize negative and unpleasant emotions in this connection but I do not see why various forms of pleasurable excitement should not be included among those feelings towards the given which are not appropriate to it in its role as pure essence. The various different forms of 'mental act' which include intent represent, it seems, broad classifications of a continuum of such subtly varying feelings. In desire, for instance, some essence is intuited under the form or aspect of the good. When all such feelings are absent we have pure intuition, though Santayana seems somewhat ambivalent as to whether this means the absence of all feelings whatever towards the given or allows for the presence of calm contemplative feelings. The latter seems the more promising alternative, and makes better sense of the notion that any essence can be an object of pure intuition, for we can think even of a feeling of anxiety or hate as being itself the object of feelings of pure intrigued attention.

It should be obvious from preceding chapters that Santayana does not think of intuition as somehow initially pure and becoming intent-laden as these feelings grow up. On the contrary, pure intuition is a late and rare flower of a consciousness which arises as the care-laden product of psychical adjustments to the environment. Essences are symbols before they are objects of attention in their own right.

Presented in this way it looks as though for Santayana an intuition is characterizable under two headings, first in terms of its immediate objects, second in terms of the emotional quality of its awareness of them. Unfortunately for this neat scheme Santayana certainly regards these emotional qualities as objects of intuition themselves,[29] and even seems to hold that they can become objects of 'pure' intuition.

On the whole I think Santayana's position can be presented as follows. Here, as elsewhere, it is hard for the commentator to be sure how far he is himself developing a theory along lines vaguely adumbrated by Santayana, and how far he is reporting on Santayana's clearly worked-out view. Santayana is not given to the dry analytic statement, his mode of communication works by suggestion and metaphor, yet if one claims therefore that a view has not been carefully worked out one wonders why so many passages work to introduce the same views into the reader's head.[30]

There seem to be two components to the total essence complex which is present to an intuition: there is what we may call the object essence, and there is the aspect under which it is presented, but while certain essences can only be exemplified as objects, others can be exemplified either as aspects under which other essences are intuited, or as objects appearing under further aspects. No such word as 'aspect', however, does entire justice to the facts, and to redress it we may sometimes think of these aspect essences as a kind of colouring which may pertain to object essences virtually identical with object essences otherwise 'coloured'. A good deal of apparent inconsistency in Santayana's discussion of intuition seems to arise because sometimes he means by 'the given', 'the object of intuition', and so on, the totality of *the object essence under some definite aspect* and sometimes merely the object essence. The whole difficulty as to whether intuitions differ only in their immediate objects, for instance, seems to turn on this. In terms of this scheme we can say that the different sorts of mental act represent broad classifications of the aspects under which object essences may be intuited, and that, in particular, intuitions carried by, or containing, a feeling of intent are those in which the aspects are emotional qualities such that they are hardly appropriate to the essences intuited under them as such.

These aspects certainly include, and are perhaps identical with, the class of all those essences which Santayana calls 'moral'. One intuits an essence under a moral aspect whenever one is in any way valuing or disvaluing it. Moral essences are, for Santayana, all different species of good and evil in a broad sense, varying from one another not merely in degree but in kind, for it would seem that for Santayana such a feeling as anxiety consists in the intuition of essences under a certain species of the aspect of evil. (For Santayana, we should note, a 'feeling' is sometimes a certain essence, sometimes an intuition of it.)[31]

I said earlier that for Santayana such essences as beauty and pleasure are capable only of imaginative exemplification, and not of formal exemplification, and complained that Santayana offered no explanation of this. Santayana's language seems often in motion towards a type of explanation which would have much to recommend it, but which conflicts with certain of his doctrines. The suggestion I have in mind is that the difference between imaginative exemplification and formal exemplification should actually be equated with the difference between exemplification either *under* a moral aspect or *as* an aspect (under which some other essence is exemplified), and exemplification apart from any such moral aspects. Something rather along these lines would seem helpful, for one thing, in explaining what we mean when we think of an event as one in consciousness or not. When we think of an ultimate physical fact as having a character but as being unconscious I suspect we mean that while its existence consists in the actualization of some quality or form, that quality or form is neither a case of valuing of any kind, nor is itself immediately valued. (If I am asked how I know that this is true of such facts I would reply that indeed I do not *know* that they are not in their inner nature cases of consciousness.) It would also explain how all essences other than the moral ones could be exemplified either formally or imaginatively, since this would turn merely on whether they were or were not so to speak coloured by a moral essence. But though Santayana may sometimes tend to such a view it contradicts his belief that essences imaginatively exemplified are not the *character* of that which exemplifies them as are formally exemplified essences, since it would imply that really the total essence, *object essence under moral aspect*, is the character of the moment of consciousness, is what, apart from its external relations, it is.

Santayana's theory, that intent consists in greeting the given with

feeling such as those of care or anxiety which are simply inappropriate to its character as pure essence, can be evaluated apart from a
decision on such subtle points. Those will be more sympathetic to
it who have grasped and struggled with the extreme difficulty of
the issue and who have thereby come to realize that it is probably
only soluble after certain widespread philosophical prejudices are dis-
carded.

Chief among these is the idea that there cannot be intrinsically
suitable ways of feeling in certain situations, that anything can go
with anything, without this producing any essential 'jar', a Humean
prejudice from which Santayana is by no means free himself. It goes
against this prejudice to say that a feeling of anxiety cannot be appropriately directed to what is actually experienced, and must have as its
proper object something somehow at a remove which may be experi-
ienced by a later state of oneself but is not experienced now; yet if one
considers the quality of anxiety without such preconceptions this will
seem a natural claim. We are in fact returning to the point made previously that certain emotional qualities of consciousness are intrinsically suitable to certain dispositional states of an organism, for the
present account of intent really amounts to saying that it consists in
feelings which are suited to an organism adjusting itself to a represented environment.

The tendency among contemporary conceptual analysts would be to
allow that there are essential, but not exceptionless, connections
between the having of such feelings as anxiety and certain behavioural
tendencies, but to see this as a matter of logical implications built into
the meaning of the words, which are by no means mere names for
intrinsic qualities of feeling. This is quite different from the view that
certain pure qualities, quite apart from the implication of any words
which may refer to them, are *suitably* felt in certain situations and not
in others. It is this latter view which I find in Santayana though without being developed at all explicitly, since he himself has a strong
tendency to the view with which it clashes. Yet as noted before it
does not imply a necessary connection, or even a necessary tendency
for certain things to go together, only that certain sorts of thing, if
they are taken together, have a certain congruity.

I am myself by no means devoid of a suspicion of such congruities,
yet I am equally averse to the explaining the appearance of them away
by appeal to the implications of terms in a particular language, or
indeed in any 'linguistic' way. Unable to satisfy myself that any account
of the way in which consciousness somehow takes the given not as
a form of being in its own right, but as the revelation of a beyond of
which fresh givens will present fresh aspects, but sure that this must
be a feature of consciousness as it actually is at a moment – since if I

really judge, I must judge within a moment – I can merely note that it is a more plausible account than most, to say that I judge or intend, when the given is qualified by feelings unsuited to it as such. Santayana's treatment of this topic is hardly the last word, but I do not know who has said the next one. Too many dealings with the problem elaborate neat conceptual schemes and tidy terminologies while avoiding encounter with the ultimate problem. To distinguish carefully, between mental act, content, and intention, for instance, is a good beginning, but the charting of the relations between the three becomes too often a recondite formal game.

5 *Determination of the intended object*

So far we have considered what it is that makes the difference between a state of mind which refers beyond itself or rather beyond its own internal and immediate object, and one which does not; we have not considered in virtue of what some particular item in the great world beyond is that which the state of mind intends.[32]

Santayana directs his account mainly to cases where one believes something about a particular thing or fact, past, present, or future. In such a case one intuits an essence with intent, and this intuition arises from processes in the psyche (which are ultimately physical) such as constitute a more or less successful adjustment to some particular fact; the intuited essence is then functioning, as he puts it, as one's description, at the level of spirit, of that fact, and one is predicating the former of the latter. In the simpler cases one's body is actually acting in some manner which, if not frustrated, would terminate in some physical manipulation of the intended object, but, without analysing it in more than a highly impressionistic way, it is evident that Santayana thinks behaviour, or its incipient internal physical stages, can – quite apart from anything contributed by spirit – be taking account of some definite fact past, present, or future, in a sense which can be roughly understood in the light of the account of the psyche we gave previously. However, Santayana does sometimes remark that a condition of an intuition intending some removed fact is that the essence present to it has some aptness as a description thereof,[33] and I think one perhaps gets nearest to Santayana's intentions by saying that for a thing or fact to be intended by an intuition both the conditions indicated must to some extent be met, that is, the given essence must have some aptness as a 'description' of it, and the intuition must express the psyche's adjustment thereto. Certainly the ideal case of literal knowledge would be, for Santayana, one in which the very essence formally exemplified in a removed fact was also imaginatively exemplified in an intent-laden essence which expressed the way in which a psyche's behavioural tendencies took account of it.[34] In actual fact the given essences are seldom more than appropriate symbols for the essences of the removed facts, such appropriateness turning on various features, such as a similarity or identity in formal structure, their being such as are regularly intuited when the psyche adjusts to such an object, or some more recondite sorts of affinity.

It is evidently a consequence of Santayana's theory, and one which he explicitly draws, that no belief, in the sense of intentful intuition, can be erroneous through and through, once granted that it occurs as the mental act of a real psyche.[35] Such an intuition is bound to express the adjustment of the psyche to something, and is to that extent correct in its positing of some reality. The psyche's own blind adjusting to a surrounding environment is raised to the light of consciousness in the feelings of care and anxiety which constitute our sense of being plunged in a really existing world; moreover, the individual object which is intended must to some extent be correctly characterized, error consisting in the presence of further incorrect attributions. It seems that for Santayana all false existential beliefs could be described, alternatively, as cases where some part of the world has been misconceived in a particularly radical fashion.

The most obvious deficiency in this account lies in its concentration on singular judgements. There are indications, however, that Santayana thought that universal judgements are characterizations of the cosmos as a whole, that is of the total reality to which the intuition belongs (what Santayana calls a 'relative cosmos'). Although such a doctrine requires more justification than Santayana gives it I personally believe it has much to recommend it, and that if 'subject' be taken in a wide enough sense the much denigrated view that all judgements are ultimately subject-predicate in form is correct, and that always in thought one is characterizing to oneself either reality as a whole or some limited portion thereof.[36] In tending to this sort of view Santayana probably shows the influence of thinkers of the Hegelian school. We shall have more to say of this in our chapter on Truth.

The nature of reference to an individual thing has been much debated among logico-analytic philosophers, especially in connection with the functioning of singular terms. For some philosophers all ordinary proper names and other singular terms refer to a single object, if at all, because it alone satisfies a certain description, sometimes thought of as formulable in completely general terms, which would identify that same object whensoever and wheresoever used. For various other philosophers the object referred to by a singular term is such, in large part, because of some 'natural' relation in which it stands to the user of the term on the relevant occasion, so that the language user is thought of as in dynamic connection with that of which he speaks.

On the whole Santayana's viewpoint seems nearer to that of this second group of philosophers.

But though there is certainly a relationship between the kinds of disputes to which I am referring (of which the controversies between Quine and Strawson are a prime example) it would misrepresent Santayana to treat his theory as directly concerned with the significance of singular terms or any other parts of speech. For, in the first place, Santayana is as much concerned with the reference beyond of intuitions which are quite non-verbal. His theory, indeed, would seem, in intention, as applicable to the consciousness of animals as men, and indeed it is an aspect of his wish to put man in his biological place that in his whole treatment of mind he has a certain tendency to ignore anything which could not be attributed to animals on a generous conception of their mentality. In the second place, even in verbal thought (whether in dialogue or monologue) I suppose he would hardly have us think of one part of the sentence as carrying intent and the other as summoning up the predicated essence. It would be true rather that the whole sentence, together with whatever images it summons up, is an essence attributed to a beyond, as somehow characterizing it in virtue of being shot through by intentful feelings. Doubtless Santayana's whole theory remains incomplete and in certain respects untested until it is brought into connection with a more careful philosophy of language than he ever attempted, but, apart from some few casual and uncrucial remarks, Santayana is far from encouraging us to equate his distinctions between the different aspects of thought and reality with distinctions between the jobs performed by individual words.

Once granted Santayana's account of the psyche and the spirit, an account of *intending* along the lines he suggests seems virtually inevitable. It leaves innumerable matters of detail vague, but it must surely point helpfully in the right direction given that starting point. The same may be said of the theory of the psyche and of spirit in general, if one once grants that consciousness as such has no explanatory value, that it is the apex of existence from the point of view of value, but that so far as the attempt to chart scientifically the causes of things, including human behaviour, it can be ignored. As I have said, Santayana's own arguments for the inefficacy of spirit seem inconclusive or worse. On the other hand the whole direction of modern experimental psychology, together with the new science of artificial intelligence, seems to presage a future in which man can be understood as a mechanism without reference to his consciousness (though the word may confusedly be used for certain features of such a mechanism as it comes to be understood). If that is so, and if we are not to lose our sense that after all consciousness is a unique kind of existence utterly distinct from any physical system, I believe that we will have to move towards a philosophy of mind close to that of Santayana, and will appreciate more and more his insistence that the value of consciousness lies in what it essentially is and not in the physical work it does or does not accomplish.

VI

The Material World

1 *Treatment of matter in* The Life of Reason

Santayana tells us that the truth of materialism became obvious to him at an early age.[1] In calling himself a materialist he did not mean that he believed that material existences were the sole reality. His was not a materialism of the myopic sort which finds its present chief exponents in certain Australian philosophers.[2] In calling himself a materialist he affirmed his belief, first in the real existence of the material world as something independent of mind, the essence of which lies neither in its being thought about nor in its postulation subserving the ordering and anticipation of sensory experience, and second in its being the only efficacious reality, so that all causes are physical.

The first major statement by Santayana of this materialist creed is in the five volumes of *The Life of Reason*. Key chapters for this theme are 'How Thought is Practical' in volume I and 'Mechanism' in volume V. In the former he states the epiphenomenalist position which we have already discussed, and in the latter he speaks of the moral character of materialism.

But although many affirmations of such a materialism are made in these volumes, there are also statements regarding the status of matter of a rather different and seemingly opposed kind, such as seem idealistic, or perhaps pragmatist, rather than materialist. Thus he often talks as though material existences were the products of certain sorts of mental activity, being imagined composites of various disparate qualities which happen to go together in our experience.

According to the Santayana of *The Life of Reason* there are two stages in the development of thought out of an original chaos of experience (James's 'blooming, buzzing, confusion'). The mind first learns to treat similar sensations as re-occurrences of one and the same quality. Such qualities are called concretions in discourse, where 'discourse' means, as it always does for Santayana, a stream of thought which may or may not be verbal. Subsequently to this, it is able to compose objects out of these recurrent qualities by regarding those which tend to occur together as constituting some one and the same object. Such objects are called concretions in existence. After that, it is possible for the first process to take over again, and treat similar objects (concretions in existence) as re-occurrences of some one and the same universal, such presumably as the different species of animals, thereby creating a higher order concretion in discourse. Theoretically, the process can go on and on, and ever higher orders of concretions in existence and in discourse be created.[3]

Concretions in discourse are evidently the progenitors of the later *essences* but differ radically from them in that they seem to be regarded as somehow constructed by the mind out of similar particulars, whereas the later Santayana insisted that particulars are similar only because they are instances of a certain definite nature, which would have been just what essentially it is, had these particular particulars never existed. A similar contrast seems to hold between the subjective slant of what is said about material things under the title of concretions in existence, and the completely mind-independent status always allotted them in the later writings. In both cases, however, there are also affirmations of a more realist character, and in the case of material things at least, these would seem to represent the more fundamental view.

It is often unclear in *The Life of Reason* whether Santayana is tracing the ontogenesis or the phylogenesis of some aspect of rationality, perhaps because some doctrine of recapitulation is assumed according to which the child constructs the ordered world of adult experience along the same lines as the race did in the past.[4] Such an assumption must strike one as very hazardous. It hardly seems likely that the consciousness of an adult primitive man, or of any non-human mammal, is very close to that of the helpless infant human being of a civilized community before he learns to speak; at most there may be a few interesting analogies between the two.

On the whole, when we find Santayana discussing questions concerning the order in which different conceptions develop, he would seem to have the individual's development mainly in mind (but he may be assuming also that the minds of primitives only reach the earlier stages of the process, and that with the advance of civilization the individual is led more readily through each phase by his culture). This is presumably what he means when he says that the more elementary concretions in discourse must come before any concretions in existence, for since the latter are combinations of concretions in discourse, their construction must come later.

Developing this thought, he says that sensible qualities such as red, round, and hard, should not be called abstractions from physical things, for we must have identified them before we could put them together to compose the notion of individual material things:

> Roundness may therefore carelessly be called an abstraction from the real object 'sun', whereas the peculiar optical and muscular feelings by which the sense of roundness is constituted – probably feelings of gyration and perpetual unbroken movement – are much earlier than any solar observations; they are a self-sufficing element in experience which, by repetition in various accidental contexts, has come to be recognized and named, and to be a characteristic by virtue of which more complex objects can be distinguished and defined. The idea of the sun is a much later product, and the real sun is so far from being an original datum from which roundness is abstracted, that it is an ulterior and quite ideal construction, a spatial concretion into which the logical concretion roundness enters as a prior and independent factor. Roundness may be felt in the dark, by a mere suggestion of motion, and is a complete experience in itself. When this recognizable experience happens to be associated by contiguity with other recognizable experiences of heat, light, height, and yellowness, and these various independent objects are projected into the same portion of a real space; then a concretion occurs, and these ideas being recognized in that region and finding a momentary embodiment there, become the qualities of a thing. (LRI, p. 168)

There are really two points here, of which one seems to be a correct piece of philosophy, and the other a very doubtful piece of psychology.

The philosophical point is this. Individual objects can only be re-identified from time to time in virtue of their characteristics, so that the notion that one arrives at all universals by abstraction from common sense particulars, such as chairs, trees, and heavenly bodies must be mistaken. The doubtful piece of psychology is the claim that I first learn to recognize rather elementary universals, like specific shapes, colours, textures, and so on, then construct particular things out of them, such as this thing, that thing, and the other, and then finally arrive at universals such as *chair* and *tree* by learning to regard various resembling thises and thats as fresh instances of them. This is certainly not the only possible order of development and it seems unlikely to be an actual one. For instance, one might come to recognize such universals as chair, person, face, dog, and so on before such universals as red, round, hard, and before any particulars at all. Subsequently,

one might distinguish individual chairs partly by their spatial surroundings (by the sort of thing surrounding them) partly by noticing
differences of detail (thereby identifying new universals) and the sense
qualities by abstraction from the complex universals. Since the consciousness in question may well be preverbal, the order in which words
are learnt is not decisive on this issue.

Enough has been said to give some idea of the rather different
spirit of Santayana's approach to these things in *The Life of Reason*
from that of the later writings which have been our main object of
study. Above all, there is the tendency in *The Life of Reason* to write
as though material things were somehow constructed or composed by
the mind. In the passage quoted above Santayana does say, indeed,
that it is the idea of the sun, and not simply the sun, which is a later
product than are certain qualities, but he immediately goes on to
say that 'the real sun . . . is an ulterior and quite ideal construction,
a spatial concretion'.

Is this mere looseness of expression, or did Santayana really sometimes think of material things as being constructed by the mind,
rather than as being objective realities saluted by it?

Santayana wrote a new introduction to the 1922 edition of *The Life
of Reason* at a time when his ontology was reaching its final form.
He suggests there that in *The Life of Reason* he was taking the transcendental view, inasmuch as he was charting the development of, and
the character of, the mind's ideas of things from the developing
mind's own point of view, and that this led to an idealist tone of
voice much of the time, but that he never doubted that the real physical
world had a real history long antedating any consciousness of it.
He was, one might put it, practising an ἐποχή (epoche) akin to that
of Husserl, except that he thought that this constituted an ignoring
of most of the truth of things, and did not regard it as a more valid
mode of thought than the ordinary as Husserl seems to have done. The
result was that he often spoke of nature, the sun, or what not, when
it would have been more correct to have said *the idea of* nature, of
the sun, or of what not. He allows that this becomes particularly
confusing where he talked about mind as being a residue left over
when other things have been allocated positions in space, as though
the mind itself had not arrived till its conception of itself was formed.
All the same, he is inclined to think that the way of speaking adopted
was essentially innocent:

Shall I be blamed for giving the same name to the idea of nature
and to existing nature, to the category of mind and to existing
mind? I admit that, if the words are pressed, they become
confusing; and yet at the play I might innocently say to a friend:

'There is Hamlet coming on the stage. What a get-up! He looks more like Bunthorne.' Clearly the phenomenon I should then be calling Hamlet would not be the real Hamlet, neither the Danish prince nor the presumable ideal in the mind of Shakespeare. This Hamlet is only the absurd actor playing Hamlet for the time being. Why should the verbal ambiguity be more annoying if in reviewing the life of reason I confidentially turn to the friendly reader, whom I suppose to be watching the same drama, and say: 'See mind and nature coming on the scene. What a travesty the green-room of fancy has made of them! Here is nature tricked out in will and purpose like a moral being, and mind tumbling about in motley and gibbering!'

One should also perhaps quote the beginning of the next paragraph, to redress the balance:

This drama, as I conceived it, was far from being a mere comedy of errors, to be treated satirically; it was a chequered experience from which wisdom might be gleaned.

But was the Santayana of 1904 so completely free from the idealist and pragmatist conceptions which he explicitly rejected in his later writings, as in 1922 he said that he had been? Perhaps we must take his word for it, and certainly there is much to support it in *The Life of Reason* itself and in writings preceding it. Nonetheless, the apparently idealist or perhaps rather pragmatist line of some of what is urged in these volumes, is something which could not be removed by minor verbal alterations.

A curious point in this connection is that Santayana sometimes describes the material world which we postulate as lying behind and explaining our sensations as Platonic in its status, and associates this with calling material things, or the material world, 'conceived realities, on an ideal plane', 'intelligible objects', 'universe of mental discourse' 'imaginary construction', 'figment of reason', something 'constituted in its ideal independence by the assertive energy of thought', 'an ideal term', and so on. These terms are all taken as applicable to the material world and its components in the chapter of *Reason in Common Sense* called 'The Discovery of Natural Objects'.

In these passages Santayana is contrasting the series of ephemeral events which constitute the matter or substance of my inner life and the inferred stable entities belief in which it prompts and which is supposed to provide its explanation, and claims that, according to which of them they prefer, philosophers designate one or the other by the eulogistic term 'reality' while dismissing the other as somehow illusory. Santayana urges, as against this, that we should recognize both for what they are rather than argue as to which is to be commended as the more *real*, though he also says that if the word 'reality' is to be reserved for one of them it is more appropriate to apply 'so Platonic a term as reality' to the intelligible objects which are inferred.

Santayana describes these objects as intelligible (rather than sensible) because he holds that such objects cannot be directly encountered in experiential immediacy, and are met with only in the sense that their existence is affirmed by rational thought. What is thus encountered supplies the only evidence we have for our belief in the latter, but our belief in the latter is a belief in something which goes beyond any of its sensible manifestations.

Although Santayana talks of these intelligible objects as being inferred, it is clear that even at this stage he held that nothing in our experience can be regarded as strictly proving even the probability of their existence. He would have expressed himself more clearly had he used his later terminology, and said that these objects are posited. However, precisely this positing of objects, which once posited serve to explain the experiential flux, is one of the activities coming under the heading of reason. To take immediately given entities as representative of objects beyond themselves is the very essence of speculative reason.

In this sense, then, material things are known by *thought* or *reason* and not by sense, and that is why Santayana says that we are being Platonists in taking them as more real than their sensible appearances:

> It is this rationalistic or Platonic system (little as most men may suspect the fact) that finds a first expression in ordinary perception. When you distinguish your sensations from their cause and laugh at the idealist (as this kind of sceptic is called) who says that tables and chairs exist only in your mind, you are treating a figment of reason as a deeper and truer thing than the moments of life whose blind experience that reason has come to illumine. (LRI, p. 80)

Though this explains his describing material things as intelligible objects and so forth, the usage remains curious, especially when set beside his later (but already developing) sharp distinction between the Platonic realm of essence and the flux of physical existence. Still odder is the use of such terms as 'figment' and 'imaginary construction' which seem to carry the suggestion that material things are useful inventions rather than independent realities.

One might think that this interpretation is scouted by Santayana's dim view of the proposal that we confine the word 'real' to that which is immediately given. [5] Yet his defence of the 'reality' of material things seems to stress not so much their independent existence as their greater dignity as objects of thought than anything immediately given. He insists, in this connection, that one can only characterize most immediate experiences by reference to what they posit, so unseizable is the immediate considered as an existence in its own right.

Still, though his language is certainly confusing, and one cannot but wonder whether he did not at times waver in this opinion, it would seem that even then his considered position regarding the material world was a realistic one.

There is, however, one point on which there does seem to be a real difference in viewpoint between the earlier and the later writings. In *The Life of Reason* the view seems to be that what is immediately given is a flux of sensations and that the material world is posited to explain this flux. On the later view, of course, only eternal essences are given, and there is no question of physical facts being posited to explain mental facts, since the mental is no more given than the physical.

To say that material things are posited to explain sensations is one thing; to describe our conception of them is another, and some time is spent in *The Life of Reason* on the latter task. The nature of the conception is said to vary, but it is suggested that in perception our sensations are accompanied by an aura of images of different views of the object perceived and of qualities which it would present to different senses, together with a sense of all these as somehow constituting a single object to which, as a whole, certain responses are appropriate,[6] while in thought (which is not purely verbal) the same thing occurs without the sensation. It is true, says Santayana, that 'the practical burden' of that intellectual interpretation of one's sensation which is an essential part of seeing is:

assurance of eventual sensations. But as these sensations, in memory and expectation, are numerous and indefinitely variable, you are not able to hold them clearly before the mind; indeed, the realisation of all the potentialities which you vaguely feel to lie in the future is a task absolutely beyond imagination. Yet your present impressions, dependent as they are on your chance attitude and disposition and on a thousand trivial accidents, are far from representing adequately all that might be discovered or that is actually known about the object before you. This object, then, to your apprehension, is not identical with any of the sensations that reveal it, nor is it exhausted by all these sensations when they are added together; yet it contains nothing assignable but what they might conceivably reveal. As it lies in your fancy, then, this object, the reality, is a complex and elusive entity, the sum at once and the residuum of all particular impressions which, underlying the present one, have bequeathed to it their surviving linkage in discourse and consequently endowed it with a large part of its present character. With this hybrid object, sensuous in its materials and ideal in its locus, each particular glimpse is compared, and is recognised to be but a glimpse, an aspect which the object presents to a particular observer. Here are two identifications. In the first place various sensations and felt relations, which cannot be kept distinct in the mind, fall together into one term of discourse, represented by a sign, a word, or a more or less complete sensuous image. In the second place the new perception is referred to that ideal entity of which it is now called a manifestation and effect. (LRI, pp. 81-2)

The question how far such a complex of images supplies a true idea of the object as it really is, receives a primarily pragmatic answer in *The Life of Reason*, for it is said that since thought guided by such a conception is effective in helping us achieve our aims, it should only be abandoned in so far as other conceptions promise a greater success as do, for certain purposes, the conceptions of science.[7] Such a pragmatic evaluation of concepts is retained in the later ontology as the main criterion of symbolic truth, but is complemented, as it surely needs to be, by a recognition of the being of a literal truth, approximation to which may sometimes have, but certainly does not consist in, a pragmatic value as well.

2   Santayana's aims as philosopher of nature

It is time to turn to the views of the mature Santayana on these topics. These receive their principal statement in *The Realm of Matter*.

One might well ask Santayana what sort of task he conceives himself to be undertaking in this book. It is not intended primarily as a work of epistemology, concerned with the type of justification which attaches to our ordinary beliefs. What needed to be said regarding this is supposed to have been sufficiently covered in *Scepticism and Animal Faith*. One cannot say either that it is intended quite as a piece of conceptual analysis in the modern vein. Certainly it does not set out to analyse the language employed in common sense or scientific judgements regarding the natural world. Is its purpose then ontological, is it describing the real nature of material things? An unqualified affirmative would suggest that for Santayana there is a peculiarly philosophical method, distinct from the observational or scientific, of arriving at truths about Nature, yet this he firmly denies.[8] Philosophical reflection will show us how any system of beliefs must in the end, and from a transcendental point of view, hang in the air, inasmuch as in the last resort we simply feel confident that things are thus and so, without being able to offer any ultimate justification for our confidence other than one that begs the question, and that the scientist who puts his theories to the 'test of experience' must rely at every point upon his primitive animal faith. Still, this much granted, Santayana professes himself opposed to merely *a priori* theorizing about the constitution of nature, and holds that it is for the scientific imagination under the continual control of actual physical transactions with the subject matter of its enquiries to advance our physical knowledge.

One might think that Santayana was offering some account of his own aims when in the first chapter he describes the scope of natural philosophy. Yet his characterization of this virtually identifies it with natural science, or at least with an attempt to correlate all the sciences in a single picture of the evolution and destiny of the natural world. Half living in the ancient world as Santayana liked to do he had a strong sense for the thread of continuity running through Thales, Democritus, Ptolemy, Newton and Einstein and classifies them all under the old fashioned term of 'natural philosophers', a title to which he does not himself aspire. His own survey of the realm of matter he describes rather as 'merely transcendental', as concerned with the question how far we can suppose, on reflection, that any of the essences which we intuit in perception or thought correspond to the essences actually embodied in nature:

> In broaching this question I am not concerned with repeating, correcting, or forecasting the description which men of science may give of the world. I accept gladly any picture of nature honestly drawn by them, as I accept gladly any picture drawn by my own senses. Different circumstances or different faculties would certainly have produced different pictures. From Genesis to Thales, to Ptolemy, to Copernicus, to Newton, and to Einstein the landscape has pleasantly varied; and it may yet open other vistas. These variations and prospects show the plasticity of human thought. . . . Is it merely imagination that has become more laboured but no less fantastic? Or has the path of destiny been really cleared and the forces that control destiny been better understood? Within what limits does any description of nature, picturesque or scientific, retain its relevance to animal faith and its validity as knowledge of fact, and at what point does it become pure speculation and metaphor? That is the only question which I shall endeavour to answer. (RB, pp. 199–200)

Actually Santayana's description of his enterprise as merely transcendental is rather misleading, for he is not here (as he was in *The Life of Reason*) simply describing human ideas of matter in detachment from questions of external reference. On the contrary, he is asking how far human ideas, useful as they undoubtedly are for many practical purposes, reveal anything about the true nature of an independent reality.

We may well ask how Santayana proposes to get outside human ideas of matter to see how they relate to matter as it is in itself. The answer is in part that Santayana, just because he holds that this is impossible, concludes that we can never hope to grasp (or at least to do so knowingly) the true essence of things in the physical flux, and must be content to think of matter in terms of the essences it leads us to imagine (whether in perception or thought) and which (so we feel bound to believe) are usually symbolically or pragmatically true inasmuch as they constitute or express an appropriate psychic adjustment to the reality.

One might object to this that on Santayana's own account of knowledge there is no reason why we shouldn't claim to know that certain given essences are identical with the essences literally embodied in external things. He would reply, I take it, that not only is this identity not something in which I feel that compulsion to believe which I do in the existence of a material reality aptly symbolized by my ideas, but that it actually conflicts with beliefs prompted by practical investigation; moreover, it would be a remarkable coincidence with no antecedent probability if the essences evoked in intuition by states of my brain were identical with those which characterized their remote physical causes.

Still, Santayana can hardly mean to deny any element of literal truth to our ideas of matter, for he distinguishes certain highly abstract properties of matter without which it would not be matter, and in conceiving of these we presumably glimpse some part of the literal truth. In practice much of the book attempts to describe highly abstract features which we may ascribe to nature as it really is however different in its specific qualities it may be from anything we can imagine. Chief among these are the 'indispensable' and 'presumable' properties he discusses in chapters 2 and 3.

3 *Indispensable and presumable properties of substance*

Santayana lists five properties of substance (which, at this point, we need not distinguish from matter) which he describes as indispensable.

1 'Substance is external to the thought which posits it.'
2 'Substance has parts and constitutes a physical space.'
  'All the parts of substance are external to one another.'
3 'Substance is in flux and constitutes a physical time.'
4 'Substance is unequally distributed.'
5 'Substance composes a relative cosmos.'

(RB, p. 202)

We have already seen that for Santayana the first property must be ascribed to any existence we believe in and even supplies a minimal sense of the word in which every such existence must be a substance.[9] The indispensability of the remaining four properties turns, for Santayana, largely on their being essential requirements in a world in which the thinking subject is to be an active agent. We are told that since substance is 'posited in action, or in readiness for action' it must have the properties requisite in a 'field of action'.[10]

The general drift of Santayana's thought is clear enough but the precise sense in which these properties are indispensable to substance is somewhat elusive. The point does not seem wholly definitional, a substance which was not a 'field of action' is ruled out as *incredible* rather than self-contradictory or inconceivable. The point might be that since belief in substance exists *for the sake of* action it must be belief in a substance within which action is possible, but it is not clear how this teleological argument would fit in with Santayana's epiphenomenalism. Again Santayana might be saying that since belief or 'intent' expresses the active impulses of an animal organism it must be belief in a world giving these impulses scope, yet this is to take a point of view less transcendental than Santayana apparently adopts here. Perhaps Santayana means that since believing involves greeting given essences with the emotions of an agent, the world which one thereby takes them as characterizing must be one towards which such emotions would be appropriate. In any case, whatever the precise argument, Santayana certainly dismisses various metaphysical notions of substance on the grounds that thus conceived substance ceases to be a possible 'butt for action' and arrives, in this way, at his indispensable properties.

The general relevance of these considerations to propositions 2 and 3 is obvious enough. There could be no action if there were no contrast between the agent and the things in its environment, and if they were not in external relations one to another such as could change without the perishing of either term. We may note that Santayana does not list *permanence* as a radical property of substance only because he thinks that it is implied in the other properties, on the grounds, roughly, that one moment can only be the successor to another moment by containing the same objects transformed.[11] (The requirement he has in mind, is, however, not an absolute permanence of anything but the need for relatively enduring objects to link moment with moment.) The point of the fourth proposition is to insist that not all the parts of substance can be exactly alike in character, else action could effect no change in one's situation:

> it would defeat all action and art if all quarters were alike, and if
> I couldn't face a fact without turning my back on exactly the

same fact in the rear. . . . Action evidently would be objectless
in an infinite vacuum or a homogeneous plenum; and even the
notion or possibility of action would vanish if I, the agent, had
not distinguishable parts, so that at the least I might swim forward
rather than backward in that dense vacuity. (RB, p. 209)

Santayana is here distinguishing his idea of substance from various
metaphysical notions of a Parmenidean type. I think, perhaps, the
point is also related to the claim sometimes made in the Kantian
tradition (by Schopenhauer, for instance) that the category of number,
even of multiplicity, is not applicable to the noumenal reality behind
phenomena, for in discussing propositions 2 and 4 he has observed
that though the real essences exemplified by substance may be hidden
from us:

> whatever else its intrinsic essence may be, it is certainly complex,
> local and temporal. Its secret flux involves at least as many
> contrasts and variations as the course of nature shows on the
> surface. Otherwise the ultimate core of existence would not
> exist, and the causes of variation would not vary. But how shall
> that which puts on this specious essence here and not there, be in
> the same inner condition in both places? Or how shall that
> which explodes now, have been equally active before? (RB p. 207)

If the earlier propositions emphasize the multiplicity of substance,
proposition 5 may be seen as an acknowledgment of the modicum of
wisdom contained in monistic philosophies. (He refers to Spinoza in
this connection.) Santayana, however, explicitly denies that all things
must be in some relation to each other (leaving aside mere affinities
and contrasts in character) and insists only that one cannot recognize
the existence of things not belonging with oneself and each other in a
single cosmos. 'Since there is no occasion for positing any substance
save as an agent in the field of action, all recognizable substance must
lie in the same field in which the organism of the observer occupies a
relative centre' (RB, p. 203). But though one cannot believe in
the existence of things not directly or indirectly in 'dynamic relations'
with oneself, one can certainly acknowledge the possibility of things
belonging to a different relative cosmos, the events in which are
neither before nor after, nor in any spatial relations, to the events in
this one.[12]

The view that one can recognize a logical possibility in the actuality
of which one could not conceivably believe may seem strange, especially
to those philosophers who hold that every meaningful proposition is
one of which the truth-value could in principle be known. Yet it

does seem hard to deny that there might be universes whose contents are thus out of all relation to each other, and hard also to see how it would feel to *believe* in the existence of things so utterly detached from all that practically concerns one. That the essence of belief does involve some sense of things as liable to act upon oneself seems plausible, whether Santayana has adequately explained why this is so or not.

Two remaining points concerning Santayana's treatment of these indispensable properties of substance call for comment.

1 Santayana is surely right that there can be no action unless enduring things are able to change their relations to each other through time. However, this does not seem conclusively to establish the existence of external relations between things, relations which can change without alteration in the essence of the terms. It would do so if an enduring thing could not change its essence, even in the slightest, but this is never Santayana's position.[13] It is doubtless true that as action is ordinarily conceived I can, for instance, rearrange the furniture in a room without this turning logically on any alteration in the character of the individual pieces,[14] but it remains true that the denial of external relations does not rule out all alterations in the relations between things.

2 Santayana's discussion of these points is less clear than it might be because he often fails to distinguish the external relations between enduring things and those between facts, or phases of things. In both cases *external relations* are those which could be otherwise, but only in the case of things is it advisable to express this as the possibility of an alteration in the former without one in the latter. In the case of things there can be alteration in both internal and external relations, in the case of facts there can be alteration in neither. Santayana is not confused in his conclusions on this point, but his argument seems to exploit a certain unclarity here.

Santayana describes the support he gives to these propositions as in a certain sense 'transcendental', inasmuch as it turns on considerations concerning the nature and office of thought rather than of evidence drawn from the object. Clearly his use of this term derives ultimately from Kant, but whatever minor analogies and debts to Kant there may be, his total position is utterly different. Santayana believes that these propositions are true of reality in the most absolute sort of way; it is not merely that they somehow meet the mind's requirements. Certainly this belief of his is open to sceptical doubt but, so he insists, even the most transcendentalist or idealist philosopher has some beliefs which he holds in the same realistic spirit, and which are open to the same objection. The special status Santayana claims for these five propositions is that they are implicated in any sense that we have of our own animal needs, and that it is this sense which forces us to abandon scepticism.[15] Santayana seems on strong ground here.

Before passing on to other matters, we may note that in Chapter III these five indispensable properties of substance are supplemented by five 'presumable' properties of substance.

6. *Substance*, in diversifying the field of nature, *sometimes takes the form of animals in whom there are feelings, images, and thoughts. These mental facts are immaterial.* They offer no butt for action and exercise no physical influence on one another.

7. *The same mental facts are manifestations of substance;* in their occurrence they are parts of a total natural event which, on its substantial side, belongs to the plane of action. They are therefore significant and relevant to action as signs, being created and controlled by the flux of substance beneath.

8. Beneath the intermittence of phenomena, *the phases or modes through which substance flows are continuous.*

9. As far as action and calculation can extend, *the quantity of substance remains equivalent throughout.*

10. *Each phase or mode of substance, although not contained in its antecedents, is predetermined by them in its place and quality, and proportionate to them in extent and intensity.* An event will be repeated if ever the constellation of events which bred it should recur. This regularity in the genesis of modes or phases of substance is constantly verified in action on a small scale. To expect it in substance is the soul of science and art; but to expect it in phenomena is superstition. (RB, pp. 233–4)

Discussion of most of these points will be found elsewhere in this book.

4 *Space*

Chapter IV of *The Realm of Matter* has the appealing title 'Pictorial Space and Sentimental Time'. It contains some of Santayana's finest writing, presenting highly concentrated points in a flowing prose rich in delightful images. It is concerned mainly to characterize the specious space and time which are immediately given and to indicate their relation to the space and time of physical reality.[16] I shall concentrate attention here on space, and reserve time for a later chapter.

Santayana calls the space chiefly given to our consciousness pictorial space, but in spite of this name he does not think of it as merely visual in its character. All the essences given in perception and sensation (whatever their sensory modality) and those given in the imagination which extends that sense of our environment given in perception, are components in a single complex essence, the total pictorial space of that moment.

The chief characteristic of pictorial space that distinguishes it from the space of science or ontology is that such predicates as 'here', 'there', 'near' and 'far' apply to its various parts not because some point within it is chosen as an arbitrary reference point, but because it intrinsically has a centre, which is essentially here, and because its remaining components are ranged around this centre in concentric spheres, and each have their essential degree of farness or nearness. Although Santayana does not put it like this himself I think one might say that here, near, and far are *absolute* qualities of the various components of a certain pictorial space, and do not merely specify their relations to something else chosen arbitrarily as a reference point. (Possibly Santayana would say that they mark their relations to a reference point, but to one not chosen arbitrarily, namely the intrinsic centre of pictorial space. Yet, so far as I can see, the farness is no less a *quality* of the speciously far than the nearness of the speciously here.)

Here is normally the place of my own body, that is the specious essence or image of my body is at the centre of pictorial space. This quite special status of my body as represented in consciousness is the ideal symbol for my actual situation, since all action is, so to speak, from the real place of my body towards other places:

> *here*, in pictorial space, is a centre of occupied position and
> actual reference, the determinant of far and near, forward and
> back, up and down, right and left; animal categories imposed on
> the field of action by action itself, and impossible except in a
> perspective created by living intently in the act of looking,
> moving, or reaching out from an occupied centre in a particular
> direction. This direction could not be chosen, or even conceived,
> except in sympathy with some organic impulse; in pictorial space
> all structures and lines of cleavage crystallise about the axis of
> attention. (RB, p. 244)

Santayana does not tell us precisely what part of our body is at the centre of pictorial space, but I suppose he would think of it not as some *point*, but as some not very precise region varying with the kind of perception or action we are presently mainly engaged in. He suggests further that:

> Sometimes, as in deep thought, no image of one's own body
> figures at all in intuition. *Here* then means whatever point in
> imagined space is the centre of attention. *Here* may be the word
> on the page which I have reached in reading: or if my attention
> has passed from the words to the images awakened by them in

my fancy, *here* may be Dante's Purgatorio, rising solitary out of a glassy sea and lifting its clear-cut terraces in perfect circles, up to the fragrant wood at the summit, whence souls grown too pure for a mild happiness pass into the flame of heaven. *Here* is then at the antipodes of Jerusalem and Calvary. . . . But now, perhaps, someone knocks at my door and disturbs my reverie. *Here* is now, if still a purgatory, a purgatory of a very different sort; it is this room in this town where my body finds itself. I look out of the window, and now *here* is Paris; I notice on my table Baedeker's guidebooks and the *Indicateur des chemins de fer*, and I consider how easily *here* may be transferred to quite another geographical place. As to the *here* of a moment ago, it is not only not here, but it is nowhere. It belongs to Dante's imaginary world. It is a theme from the symphony of essence. (RB, p. 246)

Beautiful as this passage is, it seems to mark a confusion of *here* as naming the position in pictorial space which is the centre of attention and that which is the centre of the space. The centre from which one acts or looks out upon the world is seldom a chief object of attention. If I run towards the sea, the sea itself is the centre of attention, but *here*, in the sense first distinguished, is always where my body is. If in dream or deep thought the sense of my body is lost, here, in this first sense, will still be the point of view from which I regard and act upon the world, not that to which I chiefly attend. Ordinary usage contains aspects of each meaning. 'Here' as a demonstrative accompanied by a pointing finger corresponds to Santayana's second sense, but when we talk of ourselves as here on the land and our friends as there on that boat it is rather in the first, and for Santayana's purpose surely more important sense.

Pictorial space can be made the object of pure intuition and be enjoyed as an aesthetic object. Normally, however (on Santayana's view) a given pictorial space is the 'description' given to the animal, at the level of spirit, of the distribution of things in its environment and their relation to itself. Thus in intuiting a certain pictorial space with intent I am conscious of a portion of real space. The farness which is an intrinsic aspect of the specious essence of a certain bush is predicated of the bush itself. The bush is, for me, a far-off object in just the same way as it is a green object. Philosophical reflection may lead me to contrast these qualities which the tree has for me with the tree itself, but the contrast is not present to the ordinary unreflective percipient.

Santayana's account of specious space and of its contrast with real physical space is therefore very different from the account of private space and its contrast with public space sometimes developed by Russell and others.[17] For these latter philosophers a private space is a real region within which things happen, even if it be only the transition of a blue patch from one part of it to another. Public space had to be arrived at either by a construction or an inference therefrom. Sometimes the items within each have even been thought of as in spatial relation to each other within some over-arching six-dimensional space. For Santayana, on the contrary, a pictorial space is a certain eternal essence intuited at a particular time and taken as the character of the real physical environment within which the organism operates. It is the way an animal perceives or imagines real space, not itself a rival scene of action. Nothing happens within a pictorial space though it will normally contain a quality of change inasmuch as the same complex essence which is speciously spatial will also be speciously temporal, so that it will be a vision of things moving within a region.

One may note also that pictorial space is not essentially private. This can be explained more precisely if we make a distinction which Santayana's account presupposes, but which he fails to make explicitly, between the generic essence of pictorial space and the specific pictorial spaces which constitute its determinations. All specific pictorial spaces are specific cases of the former, share such properties as that of having a centre, and so forth. Generic pictorial space is the common possession of all ordinary percipients. Specific pictorial spaces are certain stretches of the physical world as they appear to individuals from time to time. There is no logical reason why we should not intuit precisely the same such space by occupying the same positions in turn, but in practice there may virtually always be slight differences, say, because things have changed or because our sense organs differ slightly.

Santayana does not think that pictorial space as so far considered is the only given spatial essence. The mathematician and scientist may envisage something more exact in its character but emotionally less rich described by Santayana as 'sublimated essences', or 'sensory essences washed clean'.[18] He seems to have in mind something rather like the pure spatial intuition of Kant – a sense, which is almost an image, of a mere vastness providing a determinate kind of room for objects which stretches out endlessly in all directions. But Santayana is far from Kantian in his attitude to geometry. The apparent self-evidence of Euclidean axioms represents for him a mode of imagination which has been built up by the experience of actual physical measurement, a process involving the juxtaposition of real physical thing with real physical thing.[19] Pictorial spaces, moreover, may be altogether vague in their geometrical character:

Pictorial spaces are pictorial in various degrees: they range from the simplest essence of extensity, through all images of motion, collapse, swiftness or scenic confusion; or they may culminate in a reposeful landscape, and in that essence of empty volume or immensity which, save for the absence of analysis, would fuse with the notion of geometrical space. Perfectly obvious, but not at all geometrical, is the space revealed by internal sensations, when in one's insides something is felt moving, it would be hard to say what, where, or in how many dimensions. In dizziness and dreams there are lapsing pictorial spaces; in semi-consciousness there are unmapped unrelated spaces waxing and vanishing. It is not only the latitude and longitude of visionary places that are unassignable, but their spatial quality that is unearthly: the talk about flatland and four dimensions is but a thin scientific parody of the uncertainty of animal sense. Even in rational human experience, the living intuition of space is endlessly qualified. (RB, pp. 249–50)

Space, then, may be envisaged in extraordinarily various ways, whether in perception or in conception, ranging from a vague but richly qualified extensity to a geometrically determinate vacancy. What distinguishes all these spaces from real physical space, however, is that the latter consists in the system of external relationships between certain ultimate physical facts which are complete in themselves while the elements within the former are internally related to one another in the manner I previously called holistic. In holding this view Santayana is faced with the obvious difficulty that the philosopher is somehow able to characterize a space which he cannot really imagine or encounter in any kind of intuition. Here, as elsewhere, Santayana can only reply that we do somehow have a sense of something appropriately depicted by the given but essentially unimaginable.[20]

Clearly there is a multitude of questions regarding space which Santayana leaves untouched, as is inevitable in a treatment so unmathematical. Still, the chapter is rich in acute phenomenological observation, and provides a splendid opportunity for Santayana to celebrate the glory of spirit in bringing the beauty of pictorial space into a world from which it would otherwise be lacking. At a more abstract level the most important theme in the chapter is the distinction drawn between spaces which have an intrinsic centre, an intrinsic here and there, forward and backward, up and down, and so forth, and those which do not. The recognition that different sorts of space could be classified upon this basis is not unique to Santayana,[21] but he puts the point with special persuasiveness.

What Santayana perhaps fails to grasp, or at least to say, is that the space, as one might put it, of everyday is at a point between these two extremes of a space without, and of one with, an intrinsic centre. The world as perceived, and as extended upon that basis, by imagination, certainly does have a centre, not indeed in a strictly geometric sense, but in the sense that it radiates out from that heart of things in all directions with no definite termination. Each person's perceptual world has a different centre, occupied by his own body. The real physical world, on the other hand, has no such centre (though, as Santayana points out, if it is finite it may have a centre in a totally different sense)[22] – a fact which is allowed for in the conception both of ontologist and scientist. I suggest that the conception of the world implicit in ordinary social intercourse is somewhere between these. For people who dwell in England, England possesses hereness and New Zealand thereness in a rich emotional sense having its roots in the quality of a perceptual centre, but which represents a move in the direction of the scientific conception, since we are no longer placing each his own body at the heart of things. Santayana does not explicitly distinguish any such social space from pictorial space, but I see an adumbration of it in the following where he seems to regard the Ptolemaic system as portraying a space somewhere between the geometrical and the pictorial:

> The dignity of being a centre comes to any point of space from the spirit, which some fatality has lodged there, to the exclusion, at least in its own view, of all other places. These other places appear in that view as removed, and ranged in concentric spheres at greater and greater distances. The cosmos of Ptolemy is the perfect model or systematisation of pictorial space. The choice of the earth for a centre, although arbitrary geometrically, was not arbitrary historically, because Ptolemy and all other human beings found themselves on the earth, and were natives of it. So the fatality which always lodges spirit at some one point in nature, and makes this its centre, is not arbitrary biologically; for wherever there is a living organism it becomes a centre for dramatic action and reaction, and thereby calls down spirit to assume that station, and make it a moving vehicle for one phase of its earthly fortunes. (RB, pp. 243–4)

5 Spirit's vision of the physical world

Santayana insists again and again that the knowledge we have of nature is symbolic rather than literal. We would only have literal knowledge of the physical facts we intend if the essences we intuited were the very essences they formally exemplified independently and in their aggregations and this we cannot suppose them to be. The essences we intuit in perception and thought may have a certain identity in structure with the real essences of physical situations but they are more or less wholly original in quality.

Santayana tells us that we should not think the originality of the essences it intuits a reproach to the spirit resident in us, to our consciousness. He sees it rather as a tribute to the creativity of the animal and human imagination that it actualizes the rich range of sensory and emotional essences, sound, colour, beauty, right, and wrong, which would otherwise have no home in nature.[23] Nor would literal knowledge of nature necessarily be more useful to us than the symbolic knowledge we possess which is capable of indefinite improvement so far as the practical utility of the psychic adjustment to nature which it expresses goes, though such improvement may go with a diminution in the charm of the essences intuited.

Santayana does not argue in much detail for the proposition that colour, tonality, beauty, shape as given, and so forth are not formally exemplified in the physical facts as they are in themselves. He tends rather to take it for granted and then to point out that there is equal reason to suppose that the essences conceived in scientific thought are original products of the human imagination useful for tracing the activity of substance without ever being its literal character. He does, however, refer to various fairly traditional arguments in this connection,[24] while emphasizing in any case that it would be a most remarkable coincidence with no antecedent probability if the essences exemplified in spirit and in the facts intended were identical in quality.[25] He emphasizes, in particular, that the essences given in perception, and in the imagination which extends it, are quite without the degree of internal differentiation which science bids us ascribe to the things intended in their real efficacious character, and are essentially bound up with the essences of pictorial space and sentimental time, such as those of the near and far, the now and then, which, though presented as their qualities, correspond not to the intended facts themselves but to their relation to a percipient (e.g. the specious essence of a tree is always of a tree at a certain distance). He is sometimes rather vague as to how far the reasons for rejecting specific given essences as the literal characteristics of physical facts are circumstantial (empirical, as one might put it roughly), and how far a priori, but his official doctrine would seem to be that, apart from 'moral' essences, all or most of these essences could have been exemplified in physical facts (though their intuition by spirit would even then constitute a numerically different exemplification of them). All these essences, however, including moral essences, are ordinarily taken by the psyche to be qualities of physical facts.

Santayana did not regard it as an absolute logical impossibility that science might reveal the real essence of physical facts but the supposition that it may ever actually do so appeared to him ever more and more absurd. [26] His positive view on this topic is insinuated rather than stated in *Realms of Being* but I think what it amounts to is that the essences intuited by the scientist consist either in strings of mathematical or verbal symbols which even if capable of some kinship in structure therewith would presumably never be put forward as essences actually embodied in physical facts, or are so evidently analogous to perceptual essences (as when one imagines the behaviour of an aggregate of atoms – or their individual structure) as hardly to be more plausible candidates for providing literal insight into matter, in anything but its most abstract quantitative aspect. (This last point would seem to require more argument; yet one must admit a certain implausibility in attributing to imperceptibles the qualities denied of the perceptibles in which we actually seem to encounter them.)

There is, of course, no question in Santayana's philosophy of physical facts in their independent actuality somehow lacking a fully concrete character, of their having quantity and structure without quality, of their consisting in systems of relationships between abstract nothings. [27] A fact which is not the actualization of a definite essence is a nonentity. [28] (If substance is sometimes said to lack character that is because substance here means not the whole fact, but its existence as opposed to its essence. See next chapter.) He is not guilty of treating physical facts as having that kind of vacuous actuality which Whitehead sees as their lot at the hands of philosophers for whom the ultimate constituents of matter do not have some sort of feeling of their own existence and derivation, such as our own experience provides us with some inkling of. [29] One might almost suggest that Being plays for Santayana the kind of role which Feeling does for Whitehead, and that the utter mystery of physical facts as they are in themselves is somewhat reduced for him by the sense that they are different determinations of that same pure Being of which all the essences we intuit are also determinations. The point which Whitehead (after Lotze and many others) is making that ultimately we cannot make sense of a thing existing *in itself* which does not somehow exist *for itself* is a persuasive one; the present author is more than half won over by it. It represents, in any case, the most respectable side of idealism (such as does not turn on that half-baked scepticism which Santayana so effectively demolishes in SAF), though as Whitehead shows it can be incorporated in a philosophy which can as appropriately be called realistic. Santayana was not insensitive to its blandishments [30] but insisted that since consciousness in any case confronts essences which contain no necessary reference to itself, e.g. shape,

145

colour, quantity and so forth it can conceive of these or other essences being actualized apart from it.

The claim that science does not reveal the real inner essence of matter seems to mean that science does not enable us to imagine things as they really are. Santayana's treatment of this issue may lead some modern readers to dismiss him as hopelessly 'imagist' in his account of thinking, and in particular of scientific thinking.

Santayana does not raise the question of the place of imagery in thought in quite the direct way of some recent discussions. What one can say, I think, is that for him thought, as a conscious process, must involve the presence to consciousness of some 'content', or essence as he would say, which functions as a symbol, but these essences need not be similar to those we would intuit in perceiving that of which we are thinking. Doubtless Santayana values most highly those richer manifestations of spirit in which it envisages the objects of its intent in vivid sensible form, but he often indicates that the only essences actually present to the mind may be strings of words, though he notes that what counts as the same word will really be a different essence according to the context, verbal and emotional, in which it is intuited. He seems to believe also in the intuitability of abstract structures without any determinate sensory quality. We may note also that though he does not make the point as such it is perfectly conformable to his theory to point out that the specious essences of perceived material objects (e.g. symbols on paper, my own throat movements and noises in speaking) may be the vehicles of thought.

If to hold that conscious thought consists in some manner of apprehending contents such as these is to be an imagist, then Santayana is an imagist. I confess, however, that I see no alternative to this view if the question be as to the nature of thought, conceived as a process in consciousness, while to deny that there is such a thing as thought in this sense seems to border on the insane.

What seems at first a more intelligent charge against him is that the point of science (and of other enquiries too) does not lie in the contents of the scientist's consciousness but in the production of statements (in particular, theories) which we know how to test and make use of in practice. But though Santayana contributes comparatively little to the development of this theme, his account of science, so far as it goes, is pretty similar thereto. From Santayana's point of view, however, the 'knowing how' involved here would be a largely physical disposition in the psyche, and he would remind us that all these basically physical facts only have value insofar as they affect directly or indirectly the quality of someone's consciousness. Thus if scientific knowledge has a value, besides the satisfying and useful control of the environment it provides, it must presumably lie in the essences which are from time to time present to the consciousness of him who possesses it and which supply some sort of vision, literal or symbolic, of how things are. This being so, it becomes relevant to say that the content of such a vision can be, at best, a fit rendering for the human mind of the character of physical facts and their interrelations, such as leaves the specific quality of these facts and manner of their interrelatedness mysterious, whatever identity in abstract structure it may bear to them.

On the general question of thought we may say that Santayana's position is neither that of the imagist who supposes that a rich envisagement of the objects of thought or speech floats constantly before us nor is it that of the brash modern who holds that the contents of consciousness are simply uninteresting adjuncts to the altered abilities for dealing with things (or for saying further things – which seems to be the heart of the matter for some linguistic philosophers) which are somehow being inaugurated. According to the system of values which Santayana for the most part espouses, all that can possibly matter in the end is the essences which come to spirit in all organisms from moment to moment, so that insofar as thought serves a purpose other than the merely instrumental (leading to situations which provide fresh perceptual essences) it must sometimes itself consist in the intuition of essences of some aesthetic, emotional, or formal richness (the better for being true, in some sense, because the world will then more readily sustain their intuition) but he is well aware that its actual state falls commonly far below this ideal. Whether one likes to put these points in terms of 'essences' or not I feel that Santayana is abundantly right in pressing this essentially simple message upon us.

VII

Substance

Santayana uses the words 'substance' and 'matter' in a number of rather different senses, which he distinguishes from time to time in a somewhat casual fashion. For the most part, I think, there is no greater difference between his use of the two words than that imposed by the grammatical permissibility of 'a substance', 'substances', and so forth as against the corresponding forms of 'matter'.[1] However, he does say at one point that the actual substance of the world (in sense 1 or 2 below) is properly called 'matter' because it is the source of phenomena (i.e. is that of which given essences are the appearance), is continuous and measurable, and in 'each transformation, though spontaneous in itself, is repeated whenever the same conditions recur'. On this definition, it would seem, there could have been, but, at least in our cosmos isn't, a substance not material (though it would not therefore be spiritual) but it is doubtful whether in practice his choice of one word rather than the other often reflects this distinction. (Cf. 'Matter is properly a name for the actual substance of the natural world, whatever that substance may be' (RB, p. 332).) The main senses in which he uses these terms may be distinguished thus.[2]

1   When one fact (i.e. particular phase of existence) passes into another, something transmits itself from the one to the other, which is usually called 'substance', but sometimes 'matter'. (As Santayana notes, it corresponds not to οὐσία (ousia) in Aristotle, but to ὑποκείμενον (hypokeimenon) or ὕλη (hyle) (see AFSL, pp. 144–5).) Temporal succession is constituted by this inheritance by one fact of the substance of another, which is therefore its predecessor. The spatial juxtaposition of facts, as opposed to the spatial relations between elements in complex essences which represent the world for us, are constituted by the lateral tensions between them which determine the kind of facts into which their substance is in the act of passing. Thus

facts would not form a common spatio-temporal world representable by specious space and time, if they were not related directly or indirectly each to each by substantial inheritance or mutual influence upon each other's issue; in fact, without this they would not be facts at all, distinct from their pure essences.

This is not to say, however, that all facts have substance for transmission to other facts, for a moment of spirit does not. For this reason, moments of spirit belong to the world of space and time only in an indirect way through the position therein of the physical facts which they arise from and express. They arise from these facts in a manner which does not involve the transmission of substance, but all the other external relations in which they stand turn on their being rooted in facts which do contain substance.

In virtue of containing substance a fact is not only a complete something in itself but a potentiality for other somethings, since its substance is in the very act of passing on to form some new fact under the pressure of its own internal drive conjointly with the influence ('the lateral tensions' to which it is subject) of the substance in other facts. Indeed, Santayana seems to suggest sometimes that substance, in the present sense, simply is the potentiality within a fact for passing into other facts, and influencing the passing of other facts into each other. [3]

Substance, in this sense, should not be thought of as something without character. The substance at every point in the world must take on a quite definite character and stand in definite relations to the substance at all other points. Yet it is something more than that character, inasmuch as it will pass on into another fact in which it may have a different character, and inasmuch as it has no character which is fully and once for all its own but is condemned to capture and desert one essence after another like a Don Juan with nothing to offer the ravished but the characterless and momentary throb of existence.

Substance, or Matter, in this sense, is said to be the one efficacious reality. The ultimate explanation of every fact is that substance, as a matter of absolutely contingent and inexplicable fact, adopted that essence at that point.

Santayana is wont to speak of substance or matter, in this connection, as having a kind of inner spontaneity and creativity. He even seems to suggest that our sense of freedom and self-determination is a sense of this aspect to the physical forces which are at work in us. [4] The free-willist is not absolutely wrong in his rejection of determinism, if he is insisting that no law of nature or power alien to his own substance compels his choices and behaviour. No event, human action or otherwise, is ultimately explained by a law of nature, by the fact that events of that kind always occur in these circumstances, for it is the contingent as-it-were decision of each phase of substance to transform itself into a determinate next phase which preserves the truth of the generalization, not the converse.

There is a certain similarity here to the familiar insistence of philosophers such as Hume and Schlick that the popular dismay at determinism arises from the misconception that laws of nature are compelling forces. This receives, however, a special twist in Santayana's thought from his insistence that the *spontaneity* and *creativity* of each node of physical existence therefore offers the fundamental explanation of change. Perhaps one can best understand such expressions as representing a rhetorical reversal of the languages of idealism and of Platonism, ascribing to Matter, and even uniquely to Matter, those attributes regarded there as the peculiar prerogative of spirit, or of the Ideas.[5] These terms are well chosen insofar as the attitude they express to matter – or, as one might say, nature – is more appropriate than is that of the idealists, Platonists or spiritual aspirants who have described matter as 'stupid' or 'passive'. It serves also, from Santayana's point of view, to allow the true glory of spirit, as the focus for an intense actualization of essence, to shine out the more clearly, by stripping it of such gross, adventitious and unspiritual honours as go with mere power, as are allotted to things for what they do rather than what they are. The moments of spirit have, indeed, the spontaneity of fresh facts with a character undeducible from anything outside them, but they are not the states of a substance even now actively and 'freely' transforming itself into another state beyond.

Though this language is chosen in part to convey a certain 'attitude' it also implies claims susceptible of a quite prosaic assessment such as we shall be considering later in this chapter.

2 (a) By 'a substance' is often meant an individual existence the persistence of which through time is constituted by the fact that a sequence of facts inherit each other's substance and exemplify much the same essence, or gradually shift in character according to some recognized 'life cycle'. Since there are alternative essences which can be taken as marking off individual substances in this sense, and since the degree of identity of essence required can hardly be definitively fixed, it is to quite an extent a matter of convention just where we mark the beginning and end of a substance in this sense.[6] Note that a man is a substance in this sense, but the spirit 'within' him is not.

When philosophers of the early twentieth century, most notably Whitehead, attacked a 'substance' ontology, and proposed to replace it with an 'event' ontology, they were concerned mainly to attack an ontology for which individual trees, stones and men (Aristotle's primary substances) were the most basic realities. In this sense Santayana's is really no more a substance ontology than Whitehead's, since these substances have a status derivative from that of facts (equivalent to Whitehead's or Broad's events), essences, and substance in sense 1.

(b) The substance or matter of an existence may mean the stuff or stuffs out of which it is made, where these stuffs have an identity over a certain period of time in a manner not fundamentally dissimilar (so Santayana argues) from that possessed by substances of the previous type.[7] The difference, he ought to have pointed out, is that the identifying essence is not an overall form or structure but a characteristic exhibited, at least down to a certain level, by every part of the stuff. The flour in a cake is a substance in this sense, while the cake is a substance in the previous sense. That the cake becomes substance in this second sense when it is subsequently used in a pudding lends support to Santayana's denial of any very fundamental distinction between the two.

Santayana does not seem to distinguish between the sense in which that particular pound of flour was part of the substance of that cake, and the sense in which flour in general is a substance. It is not very clear what he would say about the latter, but perhaps he would regard it, as some other philosophers have done, as a curious kind of individual composed of all the flour in the world, of all that substance, in sense 1, exemplifying the essence flour at the time in question.

3   The realm of matter is the sum total of all material existences (substances in senses 2a and 2b). Santayana seems sometimes to use 'substance' to name the whole material world considered as a single thing, and sometimes as applying to each part of it rather as a mass term like 'water' applies to each drop of water. In other words it is a kind of mass term for all actual substances or stuff (or for all of it in our relative cosmos) in the sense of 1, considered as characterized by the essences it exemplifies, rather than in abstraction from them. (As such it does not really name anything different from the substance of 1, but invites its consideration in whatever character it has actually taken on rather than as the unintelligible something more or less than any character it exemplifies.)

4   Santayana also points out a sense in which every existence (including under this head every occurrence) is a substance, inasmuch as it is external to any thought about it, and does not depend upon such thought for its existence.[8] In this sense every physical fact is an individual substance, and so even are moments of spirit, the unsubstantiality of which in every other sense is one of Santayana's favourite themes. The point of this rather untypical (for Santayana) sense of the word is that it brings out how some of those characteristics which certain philosophers have taken as disqualifying substance in various other senses as a reality to be reckoned with belong even to such items as are found in the most ethereal ontology.

In this chapter I shall consider the important role which Santayana ascribes to *substance* in the first sense as essential to the relatedness one to another of those basic physical facts which make up the material world, and it is in this first sense that 'substance' will be taken throughout it.

We have already seen Santayana maintain that there is a radical difference between the specious temporal relations present to intuition and the real temporal relations which they symbolize for intent. In the former case the earlier and later phase of a change are essentially components in a single complex essence, and have no reality except as such components; in the latter case there is a complete absence of togetherness between the facts which follow on each other's heels, each is complete in itself, and has its own independent essence. The same sort of contrast holds between specious space and real space. The elements of a given pictorial space have being only as components of that single total essence, but the real spatial region of the world represented thereby is a complex of individual facts each of which has its own independent essence.

In thus characterizing real space and time one might seem to have so emphasized the apartness of their ultimate constituents that it is impossible to see how they can belong together at all. Santayana does in a manner admit this; we cannot 'see' how they belong together, but still, we only believe in their existence as elements which do somehow belong together, and, so he argues, if we try to clarify our sense of the way in which they do belong together, without, like the elements of specious space and time, merely being abstractions from the totalities to which they belong, we find ourselves using the concept of substance (in the first of the senses distinguished in the last section), and saying that real time consists in the way in which one fact 'inherits' the substance of another fact and real space consists in facts which are collateral in virtue of the 'lateral tensions' between them.[9]

In developing the temporal aspect of this thesis Santayana is very effective in showing the inadequacy of various conceptions of endurance through time which try to dispense with the notion of substance.[10] One such view tries to reduce the metaphysical idea of a substance of things which endures throughout their successive phases to the observable fact of continuity in the character of what fills successive moments. What this comes to is that each moment of time contains a world the character of which is a slightly modified version of that of the previous moment and which contains constituents that can be regarded as the continuation each of a specific constituent in the previous world on account of their similarity in character and environment. Santayana is right, it seems, in arguing that this is to replace the notion of substance by the much less acceptable metaphysical idea that there is a series of moments of absolute time to which facts belong and which order them without, so to speak, their having to contribute anything to this themselves. Such a view is not of course explicitly proclaimed by philosophers in the Humean tradition but it is not easy to make sense of their outlook without it. Santayana maintains, on the contrary, that one state of things only comes after another because it contains the substance of the previous one transformed.

The empiricist view may turn under attack to one associated rather with absolute idealism, namely that one moment is successor to another only because the character of its filling is continuous with that of the other (whereas for the empiricist the survival of individuals from moment to moment, but not the very fact of time itself, consists in such purely internal relations between qualities). This goes most typically with a view for which ordinary facts have no status except as objects of mental acts:

> If we could compare these scattered spiritual acts – as the idealist
> is always doing, although on his principles it would be impossible
> – we should see correspondences, developments and contradictions
> in their objects. A feature central in one view might be recognized
> as the same as a feature quite marginal and faint in another view:
> the pictured future there might be the living present here, and
> the pictured past here, in some measure, the present there.
> Comparing and, as it were, matching these pictures by their rims,
> we might compose a tolerably continuous landscape; and by
> identifying the original states of spirit, actually existing each for
> itself, with those ideal elements which they supplied to this
> panorama – another illegitimate habit of idealists – we might
> attribute to those existing states the dates of their objects, as these
> reappear in our own synthesis. Thus we think to cast specious
> time, like a butterfly-net, over spirits freely fluttering and dateless
> in themselves, which altogether escape it: they are not rendered
> successive by the fact that some of them may repeat the beginning
> and some the end of what, in our survey, seems a single story.
> (RB, p. 271)

Santayana rejects any view for which the temporal relations, either between individual facts or total states of the world, consist in ideal relations between their characters, on the ground that this robs the world of any of that real change and transition which the whole sense of being an active agent involves belief in. We may note as a further objection to such views that they would find something basically perplexing in the essentially quite straightforward idea of the world running through the same phase twice; and even of a thing running through the same phase twice, if individual events are taken as distinct realities in their own right (and not as mere abstractions from a larger spatial whole) temporally positioned by their own ideal relations of a contrastive sort.

I have claimed that Santayana's discussion of various issues would be clearer had he distinguished explicitly between the two quite different sorts of internal relation I have called contrastive and holistic respectively. Since specious temporal and spatial relations are internal in the latter way, it might have been helpful if Santayana had argued against this being the character of real spatial and temporal relations at the same time as he argued against the views just considered. The reasons which he in fact had for rejecting any such notion that items in temporal or spatial relations are mere abstractions from a more comprehensive whole will emerge when we discuss his postulation of 'natural moments'.

Sometimes Santayana's allegiance to the notion of substance seems to be mainly negative in its content, to represent a rejection of the various accounts of change and persistence which set out to avoid it and an insistence that the essential mysteriousness of the way in which one fact takes over from another is better suggested when we use traditional metaphysical language and say that one fact inherits the substance of the former, is that same substance transformed, than when we try to reduce this aspect of reality to one more perspicuous to intuition:

> The classic expedient is to analyse existence into matter and form, the matter being transmissible and serving to connect moment with moment and to render the later the offspring of the earlier, while the form serves to characterise each moment and give it individuality and limits. This is a correct and – as might be seen by reviewing the alternatives – an inevitable way of expressing the nature of change in rhetorical terms. . . . Yet these categories, being logical or poetical, are not important to the naturalist. (RB, p. 279)

The meaning of this might seem to be that though this 'classic expedient' represents the only practicable way of looking at things in ordinary life the scientist or philosopher must strive after a more fundamental account, which will not make use of the notion of substance. There are indications, however, that Santayana supposes that 'substance' can be used in a more recondite sense to name some obscure inner stress which passes through one fact to another and that as such it is not merely 'logical or poetical' (the two go together for Santayana as signifying what has status only as an object for consciousness and does not figure in the inmost texture of existence). These opposite interpretations are largely reconciled, however, when we realize that for Santayana the essences present to our minds when we speak of substance can never bring complete understanding of the togetherness in separation of facts which succeed one another, but that the essences suggested by some locutions give us a better inkling of the reality than others.

It is for words which will convey some such inkling, and not for formulations which will be true or false in some strictly yes or no manner, that Santayana is striving when he speaks of each ultimate fact or 'natural moment' as containing a 'forward tension', or when insisting that each ultimate fact is somehow both an independent item with its own character ('a distinct and separate existence' as Hume would say) and yet also 'an indivisible beat between states of existence which are not itself yet are its closest kin', he asks in what this 'kinship' or 'derivation' consists and answers that, as it can consist neither in mere similarity nor in 'mere juxtaposition, since we have seen that there is no prior medium in which such juxtaposition can occur', we must conceive the individual fact as somehow 'like a valve' containing 'a reference to the direction in which matter may pass through it'.[11]

When Santayana indicates further that it is of the essence of a fact, of 'elements of *existence* (not mathematical or dialectical patterns which analysis might discover there)' (RB, p. 283), that 'it overlooks its neighbours on either hand without trespassing on their ground' we may well feel this contradicts Santayana's insistence on the possession by each of its independent essence. It almost looks at times as though Santayana is attributing to each basic physical fact two essences, first its own individual essence, and, second, the essence of existence or factuality without which 'it would be simply its essence, and not the act of reaching and dropping that essence' and somehow reaching out to essences actualized in acts beyond itself; but though this would parallel the two essences attributed to each moment of spirit[12] it is not worked out explicitly.

There is no denying the obscurity in which Santayana leaves this topic, but this is hardly in itself a ground of complaint, since it is a chief part of his thesis that this is inevitable, that real temporal transition cannot be imagined in its true character. I myself see no way round this conclusion except in directions which will take us much further away from common sense than does Santayana; certainly Santayana disposes of the more usual alternatives to 'substantial inheritance' in a highly effective way.

Just as a temporal sequence, a history, is constituted by the transmission of substance from fact to fact so, according to Santayana, is a region of space constituted by a collection of facts which are neighbours, not in virtue of their position in pure space conceived as some receptacle containing them or because they are juxtaposed in some common medium, but in virtue of the 'lateral tensions' holding between them. There is the same difficulty in understanding the real nature of adjacency in space as there is in understanding the real nature of temporal continuity. The ultimate parts of an extended object are complete items in their own right, not mere abstractions from the whole as are the elements of any essence which represents it in pictorial space. The whole extended object lacks the kind of unity possessed by an essence or by its ultimate parts, yet all the same its elements must obviously have some sort of togetherness. Santayana again claims that this can only be provided by substance, but he spends much less time in justifying this than he does the case of temporal sequence.

Real space, he maintains, is constituted by the system of lateral tensions holding between the substance in collateral facts. Facts are collateral if their substance has been partly inherited from, or is partly to be transmitted to, some one and the same fact, whether mediately or immediately.[13] (In his discussion of substantial inheritance Santayana's language tends to suggest that each fact transmits its whole substance to just one successor, but it is evident from what he says in the present context that facts must be supposed capable of sharing 'heirs' and 'benefactors'.) Such collateral facts are not necessarily simultaneous, but I take it that it is meant to be a necessary condition of simultaneity, a concept which Santayana does not analyse further. It would have fitted in with some aspects of Santayana's view of space and time to hold, like Whitehead,[14] that simultaneous facts are those which are causally independent of each other, though having common sources and results, but such is apparently not his view, for he holds that collateral facts are immediate neighbours in space if and only if lateral tensions hold between them, and this seems to mean that they influence the destiny of the substance within each other, help determine what sort of fact it will pass into next. (One wonders, however, whether such mutual influence could be reduced to their transmitting substance to the same fact.) All this is very vague as to details but it points to a general idea which, if intelligibility be granted to the notion of lateral tension, is clear enough, namely that a region of space at a given moment is a system of facts, linked directly or indirectly by lateral tensions, which is in the process of passing into another system of facts in lateral tension. (This view, incidentally, seems to be, and is meant to be, compatible with the possibility of alternative blocks of facts counting as simultaneous according to the point of view.)[15]

The aspect of Santayana's treatment of space and time which may seem most contentious lies in his conviction that physical things and successions have ultimate components such as he calls 'natural moments', not meaning 'instants or cross-sections of the whole flux, where everything is supposed simultaneous', but 'rather any concrete but ultimate elements in the web of existence, within which there is no change or variation of essence, yet which are not merely their essences, but events exemplifying those essences, facts generated and dated in a general flux that outruns them on every side'.[16] Some readers may say that this is incompatible with the very essence of space and time either as it presents itself to our senses or our thought. I think there are two considerations which should remove this objection.

1 Although Santayana does not make the point himself, he might well have taken over from Whitehead, whose 'actual entities' are in many respects similar to Santayana's 'natural moments', the point that time and space may be infinitely divisible without being infinitely divided.[17] The distinction here meant is not merely one between matter operated on by man in some manner and not thus operated on, but between actuality and potentiality. A given region of space consists for Whitehead, as for Santayana, of a determinate number of ultimate components in relation to each other, but it is infinitely divisible in the sense that the position in the system of spatial relations actually occupied by one such component might have been occupied instead by any number of such components. In short there is no limit to the number of actual entities which can compose a region of a certain size, as measured in some standard way.

2 Whitehead, of course, has a theory of space and time worked out in mathematical detail, while Santayana pretends to do no more than give a general impression of reality. Had Santayana had the mathematical interest or ability, he might have made this general impression more exact on lines close to Whitehead's without taking over the parts of Whitehead's philosophy, in particular his animism, which clash with it. Yet it is not clear that he would have thought this appropriate, for on the whole his position seems to be that detailed scientific work must use the conceptions of space and time which are most useful for calculation and prediction and that these need not coincide with what the ontologist conceives as being the nearest to their real character he can get. Santayana's reflections upon space and time are therefore no more supposed to contain recommendations as to how scientists should conceive them than as to how people in general ought to perceive them; they represent an attempt to glimpse what lies behind the sensuous and conceptual scenery of practical life, not an attempt to change it.

But even if there is no positive objection to the postulation of these ultimate elements in existence it may still be felt that there is no positive reason in its favour. There is, however, a line of argument which hovers in the background of Santayana's statements regarding natural moments which I shall try now to develop in a somewhat more formal manner.

We have already noted Santayana's view that an essence which is essentially an element in a more comprehensive essence is not strictly the same essence as one which is complete in itself. If it were possible to imagine either a square or a cube all on its own one would be intuiting an essence different from that intuited when one imagines it in a certain setting. It is only the same point being pursued a little further if we say that if one supposes that the very essences intuited in each case are actualized outside consciousness, one must suppose that they are actualized in different existences. If cubeness, for instance, can be thus actualized the instance of the cubeness which is complete in itself could not be the same particular as the instance of the cubeness which is essentially an element in a larger whole. An existence which actualizes cubeness taken as a complete essence in itself must somehow, if Santayana is right, be capable of being related to other existences, but it cannot be so by exemplifying that other sort of cubeness which is essentially a mere element or aspect in a more comprehensive essence.

The kind of specious cubeness here in question, something visual or tangible in its quality, is not thought of by Santayana as being actualized outside consciousness (though upon the whole he would seem to think of its being so as a logical possibility). However, the same essential considerations must apply to whatever essences are actualized outside consciousness. An existence which is the actualization of an essence complete in itself in the sort of way in which the total essence I intuit at any moment is complete, that is, which is not essentially a detail in, or aspect of, some more comprehensive essence, cannot be related to other things by also being the actualization of an essence which is essentially a component in some more comprehensive essence, since that could only be actualized by something essentially incomplete. Its relation to other things must be of that external sort of which we have already considered the essential unimaginability.

By a natural moment Santayana means, in effect, the actualization of an essence which is complete in itself. Such a natural moment may have any amount of complexity, but all its elements will be essentially components in it, not existences having their own independent character. Santayana leaves it somewhat unclear as to whether a natural moment could ever properly be said to have parts. In fact I believe there is little real difference in saying that its character or essence may be complex but that it does not have existing parts, and saying that it may have existing parts, but that it is of the very essence of each such part to belong to that whole.

Granted Santayana's view that existence involves the being in external relations it is evident that at least two natural moments must exist, if any do, since there are no external relations within a natural moment.

Moreover, even without invoking this definition of existence in general Santayana can argue that a single natural moment could not provide a real temporal succession since this requires a series of different natural moments which take over from each other. He does indeed hold that there is a kind of before and after within a natural moment distinguishing its beginning from its end, but this internal temporality has the same sort of status as the specious temporality of intuition in which there is no real replacement of one state of things by another, only contrasting aspects of a single totality.

To the idea that there might be no natural moments whatever Santayana would reply, I think, that there would then be nothing for external relations to hold between. Existence requires the actualization of definite essences, and evidently some of these essences could not be elements within more comprehensive essences without others of them being the total essences to which these belong. This is not an insistence that the world must be of a finite size (for a possible infinity of natural moments is not denied) but an insistence that that from which one essence is a mere abstraction cannot itself be a mere abstraction. If real change demands that a fact with one character give way to a fact with another character, it demands that there really are facts with characters, but no characters or essences could be exemplified at all if no character not a mere abstraction from some more comprehensive character, were exemplified.

Once granted, on these general metaphysical grounds, that the world must consist of natural moments in external relations to each other, Santayana's contention that these are on a very small scale seems far the most plausible hypothesis. It would be odd, for instance, if the many organisms which give rise to distinct moments of spirit with the individuality of natural moments, as they evidently do, were at a given time mere abstractions from a simple over-arching natural moment; the region of the world including them both must consist, at each 'moment of time', then, of many collateral natural moments. It seems, moreover (though perhaps the point requires more argument than Santayana gives it or I have space for) that the division of the world into natural moments can hardly be grosser than the most fundamental division into efficacious units that science requires for its purposes. Santayana does not, however, like Whitehead, try to identify natural moments with any happenings empirically distinguished by science, and I think he would regard any such identification as unverifiable.

It is difficult not to believe that natural moments are conceived by Santayana on the analogy of moments of spirit. These surely are unities of the sort in question, complete all at once exemplifications of essences however complex, even if he prefers to reserve the term 'natural moments' for those fundamental actualities of the realm of matter, which possess an analogous intensive unity. 'It is certain that consciousness comes in stretches, in breaths: all its data are aesthetic wholes, like visions or snatches of melody; and we should never be aware of anything were we not aware of something all at once' (WD, pp. 79–80). Surely we have here the very type of entities such that all their parts are essentially qualified by being parts of just that whole, while they themselves could not belong in this same manner to any larger whole.

But though he does sometimes make use of this analogy,[18] he is inclined, upon the whole, to play it down, as in fact his account of spirit compels him to do. We must remember that moments of spirit are not themselves given, on his account, and are by no means for him, as they are for some philosophers, the realities with which we are most intimately acquainted and in terms of which we must conceive other things. Comparison is complicated also by the view that the complex essence, with its before and after, present to a moment of spirit is not its own character as is the essence actualized by a natural moment its own character. Above all, we must bear in mind that for Santayana moments of spirit do not hand on the burden of existence to each other as do natural moments, there being no substantial inheritance within the realm of spirit.

But though Santayana cannot officially acknowledge moments of spirit as the model in terms of which he conceives the fundamental constituents of the physical world, one may still suspect that they really are such. I am the more inclined to do so because I am, in any case, dissatisfied with those elements of his characterization of spirit which count against this. Surely moments of spirit do inherit the burden of existence from each other in very much the way Santayana thinks of natural moments as doing (though on the face of it different mental sequences do not flow into each other as the physical ones must do) and surely moments of spirit if not exactly 'given' can properly be said to be experienced. Paradoxical as the expression may seem, Bradley's claim that immediate experience is a 'knowing and being in one'[19] seems more apt to the facts than Santayana's formally more satisfactory insistence that experience is no object of experience. To say this is neither to embrace panpsychism, nor to say that moments of spirit are certain physical facts experienced from the inside, but only to say that moments of spirit supply us with a familiar instance of certain formal requirements which must also be met somehow by the ultimate constituents of matter.

Apart from this, I find Santayana's treatment of natural moments very compelling. It is not as though he fails to do justice to the fact that the division of the world into units on the scale at which we actually encounter it is relative to our interests and hence variable (suggesting, however, that such 'conventional moments' are conceived as though they had the kind of unity which really only belongs to natural moments).[20] Many philosophers would probably maintain that all units are conventional in this sense, but the case for the necessity of intensive non-conventional units, on some scale, seems unanswerable; though none too easy to make clear to those not used to this way of thinking. Unless something exists in the all at once way ascribed to a natural moment it seems that nothing would really exist at all.

There is, indeed, one alternative to Santayana's view which I would not dismiss too lightly, the view namely that there is, so to speak, just one natural moment, the universe as a whole. Such a position (as found for instance in Bradley's metaphysic) dispenses with the grave problem of the external relations which Santayana insists on, though finding them unimaginable. If the only relations we can clearly conceive are those which exhibit their terms as mere abstractions from a more comprehensive whole, we will certainly render the universe in a manner more intelligible by conceiving the mutual relatedness of its contents as entirely of this sort. Santayana would by-pass this claim by appeal to the meaning of 'exists' but like most such appeals this seems largely to beg the question. The greatest difficulty for such a monism lies in the evident separateness of moments of consciousness from one another and the apparent impossibility of their being mere abstractions from an over-arching totality, an impossibility which seems to extend to their physical basis, if the reality of this be once granted. This is to put the emphasis in a different place from Santayana, but it leads to the same result, the conception of a world containing a multiplicity of intensive unities. The obscurities of 'substantial inheritance' and 'lateral tensions' are then forced on us if they are not to be left in a monadic isolation one from another such as would make nonsense of that compulsive belief in a world environing the self which alone makes scepticism an impossible stance. There seems no theory of these matters which does not leave perplexities. One can say at least that Santayana's is among the more plausible.

It is evident that Santayana's whole treatment of substance and natural moments is rooted in reflections upon a wide range of metaphysical systems. The diversity both of sources and of unsatisfactory positions to which he was deliberately seeking alternatives, is so wide that one could only find time to discuss it in a work which, assuming familiarity with Santayana's positions, attempted to chart the forces which had moulded them. Here it is only practicable to note that Aristotle, Leibniz and Spinoza have all acted at points as positive influences, while idealistic monists (such as Lotze, Royce and Bradley)

have greatly influenced the manner in which he conceives his problems. [21]
The upshot in its total character is, I believe, decidedly original. He is
closer to Whitehead than to any other philosophers of his time (which,
considering that Whitehead represents himself as the great opponent
of substance, only goes to show how treacherous it is to classify philosophers by their attitude to some traditional term); both develop
their views on the basis of a rich grasp of the difficulties which have
forced some of the great philosophers into such *prima facie* bizarre
extremes as monadism and monism.

We should note, perhaps, the enormous contrast between Santayana's
position and that of any Kantian view for which substance is merely an
inevitable category in terms of which we construct the phenomenal
world while the transcendental unity of apperception is the true source
of connectedness. For Santayana such a view simply leaves the multiplicity of moments of spirit (within which alone anything describable
as the synthetic unity of consciousness holds) in an utter isolation from
one another which it makes no serious attempt to bridge. Spirit does
synthesize things, indeed, but only in the sense that at each distinct
moment of its existence a single complex essence supplies its vision, its
unitary phenomenal rendering, of an ununified flux of individual
facts. Santayana's claim is that, unless we take the notion of substance
as somehow having a genuinely transcendent application to these
facts as they are in themselves, we will be lost not only as to how
physical facts, but even mental facts, in any way belong together.

VIII

Truth

When Santayana first projected a book on Realms of Being, the realms were three. The realm of truth joined the ontological UN only at a later date.[1] Its status is in one way peculiar, for it is explicitly described as a certain segment of one of the other realms, namely the realm of essence. Its right to be regarded as a realm in its own right lies in the peculiar interest which attaches, for us frightened animals, 'to this tragic segment of the realm of essence', and in the fact that the boundaries of this segment are settled not by anything within the realm of essence itself, but by the two existential realms, those of matter and those of spirit. The realm of truth is not itself an existential realm. Truth does not exist. It has an eternity such as existence cannot have. Santayana has some inclination to say that it *subsists* (a term which he regards as misleading when applied to essences) but this term is not central to his thought as are 'existence' and 'being' and he usually says of Truth, as of Essence, that it has being but not existence.

The truth, as Santayana conceives it, is to be distinguished from any 'opinion, even an ideally true one'[2] and holds whether anyone has knowledge of it or not. One might almost say that its depsychologizing is the main aim of his theory of truth, a task which seemed especially necessary in the light of the treatment truth had received at the hands of William James and Josiah Royce, for the first of whom it consisted in an efficacious personal adjustment and for the latter of whom it consisted in an over-arching divine thought.[3]

The pragmatists were at fault, for him, both in confusing an elucidation of *true* and of *truth* and in what they said about either. In insisting on the distinction Santayana is, apparently, not merely contrasting a predicate with that to which it applies but denying that this is how the two are related. It is opinions or beliefs which are or are not true, yet the truth is not the sum total of true opinions but that which, independent in its being of the existence of any opinions whatever, determines whether an opinion is or is not true. It seems then that the Truth is not true, is not something to which this predicate applies. But what of a *truth*? Is not this something to which *true* applies, and is it not also something of the non-psychological sort Santayana favours, a proposition which has being whether opined or not, and such as may be opined by many different minds while remaining one and the same? It is difficult to know quite how Santayana would view this claim. He says very little about propositions, and when he does use the word it is unclear what he means by it. [4] One cannot say that he was positively opposed to propositions as conceived, say, by G. E. Moore, but his theory makes little or no use of anything having this sort of status and centres mainly round the contrast between individual acts of judgement, which he usually calls opinions, on the one hand, and *the Truth*, or alternatively *the truth* (not *a* truth) *about a fact* on the other. Let us consider the significance of these two latter terms.

The notion of the truth about a fact is explained as follows:

> Opinions are true or false by repeating or contradicting some
> part of the truth about the facts which they envisage; and this
> truth about the facts is the standard comprehensive description
> of them – something in the realm of essence, but more than the
> essence of any fact present within the limits of time and space
> which that fact occupies; for a comprehensive description includes
> also all the radiations of that fact – I mean, all that perspective of
> the world of facts and of the realm of essence which is obtained
> by taking this fact as a centre and viewing everything else only
> in relation with it. The truth about any fact is therefore infinitely
> extended, although it grows thinner, so to speak, as you travel
> from it to further and further facts, or to less and less relevant
> ideas. It is the splash any fact makes, or the penumbra it
> spreads, by dropping through the realm of essence. Evidently no
> opinion can embrace it all, or identify itself with it; nor can it be
> identified with the facts to which it relates, since they are in flux,
> and it is eternal. (SAF, pp. 267–8)

I think we may elucidate this further by saying that every fact (whether it be past, present, or future from our point of view) has its own essence, and that every larger situation to which it belongs has its own essence (which will include the essence of that fact as an element in a certain position therein) and that the complete set of all these essences is the truth about that fact. These essences are all regarded as parts of the 'comprehensive description' of that fact, not in any sense in which descriptions are composed of words, but in the sense that even the most omniscient spirit could know no more of that fact than that it exemplified those essences. The word 'standard', I take it, serves only to point out that the comprehensive description of a fact supplies the standard of correctness in opinions about that fact, so that they are true to the extent that they reproduce or aptly symbolize some part of it.

Santayana does not altogether dispense with the notion of *a* truth about a fact, for he so describes any component of the truth about it. But this highlights a peculiarity already present in his theory of which he seems hardly aware, namely that there is really no such item for him as a truth simply, but only essences each of which is a truth or the truth about some fact. He ought to hold that when a man knows a truth, even if miraculously it is a quite literal one, there is nothing present to his mind such that any other man to whose mind it became present would *ipso facto* know a truth, for every such essence would be a truth about one fact and not about others, and only the man who, in virtue of matters lying partly outside his consciousness, intended the right fact would be in possession of a truth. Sometimes Santayana seems well aware of this, but at other times (especially in *The Realm of Truth* where the eternity of truth is a chief theme) he seems to think of there being essences such that all who intuit them are in possession of the same truth. (Evidently this is related to his ambivalence as to the manner in which particulars are identified by consciousness.) He does, indeed, always insist that truth is truth about something, but sometimes he seems to think of this as meaning only that it is true in virtue of something lying outside the realm of essence, and not as meaning also that the same essence may be both true and false according to the intention which accompanies its intuition.

A strong holistic tendency is evident in Santayana's treatment of truth[5] (which seems to be influenced, for good or ill, in this one respect by the absolute idealism to which he is otherwise so opposed). A truth about a fact is conceived of as merely a component in the truth about it, and the truth about a fact tends to collapse into the total truth about the world, considered with a certain peculiarity of emphasis. (Maybe Santayana means something more than a difference in emphasis when he talks of a difference in perspective, but it is not clear what.)

But what exactly is the Truth? On the whole, Santayana seems to conceive it not as a mere collection of essences but as a single inconceivably complex essence exemplified by the world as a whole (though we may point out that if this whole comprises more than one distinct relative cosmos its character will hardly be that of a whole in any ordinary sense). If we consider this in connection with other aspects of Santayana's thought it raises problems of which he does not seem sufficiently conscious.

It might be asked, first, whether the Truth, considered as the total complex essence of the whole universe, is true simply of that whole, or whether it is true of that whole only insofar as each of its component essences is ascribed to the right part of that whole. We could ask, similarly, of any essence of a complex of facts, whether to know it as belonging to the truth about that complex one must simply intend the right totality when intuiting it, or whether it is also required that the right sub-intendings, so to speak, accompany each of the component essences. I raise this question as one which will occur to philosophers in the Russellian tradition. Santayana does not himself raise it in so many words, but it would be in the spirit of much that he does say, to answer that when one is intending the whole, the parts are identified only as those contributing a certain aspect to its overall character, and that no further identification can meaningfully be required when the whole, rather than any part, is the object of thought. This answer has the advantage that the character of some historical individual's life (or other historic fact) can always figure among the truths I know without my needing to intend him (or it) separately, since I may envisage this character as a specific and emphasized element in the general mosaic of history.[6] This fits in with that very holistic tendency of Santayana's we are discussing, according to which the truth about an individual is essentially only an element in the Truth.

But there is a related difficulty of a more serious kind. Santayana thinks of all true essences as belonging to, as components of, the Truth. If, however, the Truth is the complex essence of the whole universe the essences of lesser entities, the character each possesses within its own boundaries, will indeed correspond to (be *virtually* identical with) some element in that complex, but they will not strictly *be* such elements. In saying this I am not foisting a needless subtlety on Santayana, but raising a point, which, if he is right in his account of complex essences, is of the first importance.[7] No element in the character of a whole is, on that view, identical with the character of any part of that whole, e.g. the character a door has considered in itself is not identical with the contribution it makes to the complex essence of a building. It would seem to follow that the other members of the realm of truth are not all properly mere elements in *the Truth* but essences each actualized in its own right by something less than the whole world. Such seems to be the view that Santayana should have held, granted his own main premises. But though this fits in with his speaking of a realm of truth with many members better than a view for which it consists solely of that single complex essence, the total Truth, and the essential components thereof, it clashes with this other more holistic strain in his thought. He could continue, indeed, to think of the Truth as a single inconceivably complex essence exemplified by the universe as a whole, but the truth about, or standard comprehensive description of, a fact certainly would have to be, not a complex essence, but a set of essences (of which the essence it exemplified within its own boundaries would be one and the essence of the whole world considered with emphasis on the contribution made thereto by this fact would be another) each true of that fact and not so, or rather not so in all cases, merely as essential elements in a more comprehensive essence true of it. From one point of view, indeed, it is rather a pity to foist on Santayana the view that the truth about a fact is *a set* of essences, since otherwise he manages to develop his ontology without resort to the rather unsatisfactory category of sets or classes. Not that he expresses any view at all as to the ontological status of sets, but I can hardly conceive of him accepting that they form any genuine realm of being in their own right.[8] It is true that the various realms of being could themselves be thought of as the sets of their members, but it would seem more proper to think of the whole language of realms as a playful way of distinguishing various different modes of being, so that to describe something as belonging to the realm of essence or spirit (say) is simply to indicate the sort of reality it is. There seems no reason, in any case, why he should put such emphasis upon the total truth about a fact, as opposed to mere truths about it, beyond a certain hankering after totality hardly suited to his system.

However Santayana might have resolved some of these questions had they been pressed on him, it appears that a certain unclarity surrounds the precise meanings he gives to such key terms in his discussion of the realm of truth as 'the truth about a fact', 'the Truth', and 'a truth'. All the same, the general upshot of his theory is reasonably clear and may now be summarized thus: Every fact has its own definite character and makes its own contribution to the definite character of various larger wholes and ultimately to the whole scheme of things. One who intuited any of these characters (and – if one of the latter – intuited it with a special degree of interest in the component contributed by that fact) while intending this fact, or the relevant larger whole, would be in possession of some part of the literal truth about that fact. Truth, however, has being whether anyone is in possession of it or not, in the sense that these essences really are exemplified by facts and can be called the truth about them. (It would seem, however, that unless one can talk of *emphasis* in the realm of essence, the essence exemplified by a whole is no more in itself a truth about one part thereof than another and becomes so only in the light of human interests.)

The possession by man (and Santayana believes in no conscious being in better case) of such literal truth is rare or nonexistent, but he has some sense of there being such a reality, and may ascribe this status to much that he does possess. If the philosopher has to discountenance this claim and regard all or most intuited essences as at best apt substitutes for the essences literally true of things, he should at least retain his sense that there is a literal truth about things, that the world and all that is in it has a real and definite character irrespective of any consciousness thereof, which can be reverenced as a kind of judge of all our cognitive and other strivings, in however murky a form its judgements reach us. Santayana detested pragmatist, and to a lesser extent coherence, views of truth as removing man's humble acceptance that there is *a way things are* independent of any knowledge thereof and substituting the insane notion that our cognitive activity should feel free of all external constraint. This is one aspect of the *egotism* that he found so typical of modern philosophy; a presumptuous claim to independence on the part of mind, universal or individual, from all realities not of its own spontaneous creation.[9]

There is a good deal of criticism in Santayana's writings of the coherence theory and of pragmatism. He says that the more coherent a dream is, the more unlikely it may seem that it is a mere dream, but the more delusive it is if this is what in fact it is, as it always may be.[10] It will be noted that what he attacks here is the more serious version of this theory in which the coherence in question is between judgements actually made and not merely between propositions formulated as obviously false or not formulated at all. In his criticisms of pragmatism he goes more to the heart of the theory than do many of its opponents, and says, suggestively, that the theory confuses the conditions under which something becomes a sign or symbol for a reality (which is when it can mediate a prosperous adjustment thereto) with the question of truth.[11] In fact Santayana's notion of the symbolic truth, which is all that, for the most part, we possess, is not far removed from the truth of the pragmatists.[12] Such truth belongs to the essences we ascribe to intended facts to the extent that their intuition expresses a successful adjustment thereto, though he also supposes that this goes together with some kinship in structure or other affinity which they bear to the literal truth. It is in his insistence that there is such a literal truth, and that we should retain our sense of its reality, however indirect our relation to it, which sets him apart, surely to his advantage, from the pragmatists.

Philosophic textbooks usually list a third standard theory of truth, known as the 'correspondence theory', though the expression covers some pretty various theories. One could hardly call Santayana's account of truth a correspondence theory, since the truth about a thing is, for him, rather its actual character than something corresponding to anything else. One might, however, call his theory of *the true judgement* a correspondence theory, since such a judgement or opinion is one which corresponds to the intended fact even to the point of an identity in the essence each exemplifies, should it be a case of literal knowledge.

The main peculiarity of his theory is the absence of any item which is simply a truth, and not merely true of, or a truth about, something.

As Santayana intends it this view is not so odd as it may at first seem. One might take it, for instance, as implying that there is no such thing as the truth that Julius Caesar was dictator of Rome, only the essence 'dictator of Rome' which is true of Julius Caesar at a certain phase of his life. I think, however, that, like Bradley, Santayana (though only by implication) takes the whole sentence 'Julius Caesar was dictator of Rome' as summoning up (or even as itself being) an essence which does duty for the character of a total situation, comprising Caesar and the Romans; the former being a symbolic truth, the latter a literal truth, about the world at that juncture, so that a truth, though an essence exemplified by a fact, comprises an element corresponding to the subject as much as to the predicate of a sentence. (A faint analogy may be felt between such truths, symbolic or literal, and the sense of a sentence in Frege, with the world, or the relevant part of the world, taking the place of the reference.)

This seems to be the best way of taking Santayana's not very clear intentions on this score. One might even see it as a strength in Santayana's theory that it avoids the troublesome notion of a proposition conceived as a peculiar complex of universals and particulars capable of reflecting, without being identical with, their combination in the world. There is, however, no indication that consciousness of these difficulties influenced Santayana.

His view would not have struck so strangely had he identified truths with true judgements. It is the combination of a depsychologizing of truth and the absence of anything akin to the proposition which is odd, though the oddity is largely terminological. How far the clash is with ordinary language in its more reflective modes and how far with a terminology ingrained in all those in the Moore-Russell tradition is not so clear. The notion of a stack of truths and falsehoods, which become objects in judgement, is not so obviously nearer to ordinary language than that of a truth about the world which our thoughts reproduce with more or less success. Santayana is, at any rate, closer to ordinary modes of thought in not treating falsehood as a reality on a par with truth.[13] 'False', 'untrue', 'incorrect' are epithets for him applicable to opinions which fail in various ways to seize the truth about their objects, but there is nothing outside consciousness which deserves to be called false of anything, or the False, since when not attributed to a thing in the world by a thinker the essences it does not exemplify are simply irrelevant to it.

One crying weakness in Santayana's theory is that it is directed almost exclusively to truths about particular matters of fact. I can only see one way in which it could cope with general truths such as laws of nature, and that is to take it that these are aspects of the essence exemplified by our relative cosmos as a whole, and known as such by one who conceives them either by direct intuition or through symbolic intermediary, while intending, that is somehow adjusting to, the realm of nature as a whole. There are faint indications of such a view in some of his remarks.[14]

It would be inappropriate to carry any further an attempt to develop Santayana's theory of truth beyond what it receives at his hands. Upon the whole it is the vaguest and least satisfactory part of his ontology (though this is certainly a pronouncement which would have surprised him).[15] Still, despite these deficiencies, there is a good deal of sound sense in his treatment of truth. Surely he is right to insist, as against so many more elaborate theories, that every part of the world, every event, every state of affairs, has its own real definite character, and that our knowledge approaches literalness only to the extent that we enjoy some sort of intuitive acquaintance with this real character of that with which we are concerned.

The actual book, *The Realm of Truth*, is concerned much less with the clarification of the general nature of truth than with various specific human relations to and attitudes to truth, and with the kind of way in which the human vision of things departs from the literal truth – not entirely to its disadvantage. We shall here largely pass these matters by. We may note briefly that there are chapters on Conventional Truth and Dramatic Truth (essences which take the place of the real characters of things in human consciousness), which develop, somewhat vaguely, the idea of symbolic truth or knowledge on which we have already touched from time to time. There are, however, three further aspects to Santayana's account of truth which demand attention, namely: 1 the sense in which truths are exemplified by facts; 2 the contingency of truth; 3 truth and time, which last is the topic of the following chapter.

1 If a truth about a fact is an essence exemplified thereby and a fact is an essence exemplified (and both these are statements made by Santayana), it might seem that a fact comes perilously close to being a truth about itself. Such an idea is both fantastic in itself and one which, without recognizing it as a conclusion someone might draw from his own theory, Santayana deliberately rejects.[16]

Actually, we may absolve the theory from any such implication. The fact is a character become a constituent in the flux of existence, thrown into external relations, and tied down to a particular time and place. That same character, considered as an eternally available object of intuition ascribable to that fact by anyone at any time who can intend it, is a truth, as is also any distinguishable and separately intuitable element thereof.

Another more recondite contrast appears to hold for Santayana between essences as truths and essences as what facts in themselves are when their substance and external relations are discounted, namely that most essences which play the former role do not play the latter at all. This is a clear consequence of Santayana's principles and one to which he directs attention from time to time in his usual informal way.[17]

A fact may either be a natural moment or it may be an aggregate or sequence of natural moments. In either case it has a character or essence, but its relation thereto would seem to be somewhat different according as to which it is. The natural moment is the all at once actualization of a single essence, and any complexity it possesses is the complexity of that essence itself, so that its elements are internally related one to another, are mere abstractions from a totality which alone is a concrete reality. This cannot be true of a fact composed of many natural moments, for this has parts in external relations one to another, although the relations between the elements of the complex essence which is its character are all internal. We must remember here that even if one cannot actually intuit the real essence of a fact, that real essence, as opposed to the fact itself, is always conceived of as something intuitable in principle, and as being an intensive individual unity, whose elements are mere abstractions therefrom, in just the way in which the essences we do intuit are, not as something with the essential opaqueness to mind of anything involving external relations. It seems to follow that a complex fact stands in a much stronger contrast to its complete character considered as a whole than does a natural moment. Santayana tends to express this point by saying that the former is a *truth about* some part of the world, or 'illustrated' therein, but is not ever actually 'embodied' in existence, and it seems that by 'truths' he means mainly or even exclusively essences thus illustrated without being embodied or actualized in any single node of existence.

It might have been clearer if he had distinguished two sorts of exemplification (other than those already distinguished) – that where the flux of existence assumes a certain essence all at once in a natural moment, and that where some part of the world, which is no real intensive unity in itself, conforms to some pattern such as might be intuited as a unity by an appropriately endowed mind.[18] In spite of the elusive manner in which he expresses it, I have no doubt that this essentially is Santayana's view, and once it is grasped the importance he attached to the realm of truth becomes a good deal clearer, for without it nothing much would be added to his general account of things by the addition of this realm to the other three. The essences he thinks of as truths, even as quite literal truths, are not primarily (and possibly not at all) those exemplified by natural moments but those 'illustrated' by complex facts. These have status only as truths about things and are never what any existent actually *is*.

There are, in fact, two barriers which stand between mind and the real flux of existence. First is the logical point that even if it knew the literal truth about the facts it intends, every truth, being a unitary essence, would be distinct in kind from the hopelessly ununified flux of existence itself. Second is the matter of fact that actual mind must be content with essences which are not literal truths at all, but merely suitable renderings for an animal consciousness of the world on which its existence depends.

This, incidentally, makes more intelligible Santayana's tendency to contrast knowledge of existence with awareness of truth, the former representing the stock a worried animal takes of its environment, the latter a state of contemplative detachment nearer to pure intuition. The first involves a formless and inarticulate sense of bustle (such as he identifies sometimes with the feeling of intent) which represents the unintelligible flux of existence so far as this can be represented in consciousness. The second involves a concentration on clearly articulated complex essences such as can be taken in as wholes only to the extent that the bustle of life (or 'intent') recedes. Thus the apprehension of truth has the curious property that it demands a minimum of intent to distinguish it from pure intuition but is destroyed if this becomes too strong.

Be this as it may, I believe that the claim that there are essences 'illustrated' in the facts, without exactly being exemplified in them, is the most important aspect of Santayana's theory of truth, though it might have been better presented under a different heading. Whether Santayana is right in what he says or not (and in any case he leaves many relevant questions unanswered) the issues raised by this assertion are of the first importance and are seldom appreciated except by those driven thereby to a desperate extremity of monism. The question how it is that many different facts, each possessed of a genuine individuality in its own right, can still somehow belong to a totality which has its own character ought to puzzle all those who are not prepared to solve it by the simple expedient of denying the many different facts. A totality composed of such facts can hardly be an individual in the same sense as its ultimate elements, yet it must surely somehow have a character. Perhaps Santayana does little more than point out the problem, but that is a worthy service.

2   The first three chapters of *The Realm of Truth* are spent in arguing that all truth is contingent. Before considering a claim obviously so important to any account of truth it may be as well to notice, rather

briefly, the upshot of two chapters (VI and VII) on 'Implication' and 'The Basis of Dialectic' in *The Realm of Essence*.

Santayana's concern here is to establish that the order in which essences pass before the mind of a reasoner (whether they are intuited or intended) cannot be explained by appeal to the essential relations between them, namely the internal relations we have called contrastive. Indeed some of his remarks, taken in isolation, look like a denial of there being such relations and have been taken as being therefore inconsistent with the views he advocates elsewhere.[19] A more careful reading shows, however, that he is even insistent upon there being some significant way in which each essence relates essentially to its predecessor, perhaps as an element within it detached for separate consideration, perhaps as a larger whole including it as an element, perhaps as possessed of some specific affinity or contrast thereto, holding that otherwise there would be no reasoning at all. The point he is concerned to make, however, is that the holding of these relations does not explain the mind's wandering along this particular path through the realm of essence, and this results, in fact, from the obscure physical processes, teleological only in the nonspiritual sense, underlying intuition.

The main object of attack, here, is presumably the Hegelian dialectic and related views, for which concepts have a vitality of their own and pass into each other on their own initiative. Santayana was somewhat 'out of date' in spending so much time attacking this theory, but living in retirement the powers of his youth were more present to him than the fashions of the present. As the time has even now not quite arrived again when these discussions can be of interest as criticisms of current orthodoxies I shall pursue the point no further, though I may note, without exploring, a certain relevance his discussion has to the Wittgensteinian question as to our readiness to continue series in a corresponding manner. So let us turn to the 'contingency of truth'.

Since a truth is (for Santayana) an essence 'illustrated' in some existent state of affairs (past, present, or future) the claim that truth is contingent is the claim that there is no essence which had to be thus illustrated in view of its own intrinsic nature. There is nothing within the realm of essence, considered merely as such, to show which essences possess this status. The general spirit of such a claim is so familiar to all philosophical readers today that we may confine discussion to two specific points.

1   Santayana claims that the very being or subsistence of any truth at all is contingent. No essence whatever need have been illustrated in an existential flux, so that there might have been no truth at all.[20]

This is an almost inevitable contention granted the sense Santayana attaches to 'truth' but one might well think it pointed the need for understanding the word otherwise. For should not we be able to express the possibility Santayana has in mind by saying that the truth might have been that nothing whatever existed? It is remarkable that Santayana never considers this objection in *Realms of Being* although he had himself invoked the very same idea in *The Life of Reason* as showing the inevitability of the subsistence of truth. [21]

We may suggest, on his behalf, that the objection is less powerful than it seems at first. Does it really seem appropriate to say that there would still have been the truth that nothing existed if nothing had existed? It is certainly plausible to contend that the truth that no things of a certain sort exist is always understood as providing information about their absence from some part of the world, or from the world as a whole, and that without a world from which things can be absent there could be no negative existential truths. But the whole notion of the nonexistence of anything at all is so perplexing that it is hard to know what to say about such a hypothetical situation, and the very fact that we find ourselves using the word 'situation' here shows how readily we misconceive the issue.

Upon the whole I would conclude that the implication that there would have been no truth at all, had there been nothing to possess any character positive or negative, requires further discussion than Santayana ever gave it, but is not a very serious objection to his account.

2   A more important question concerns Santayana's treatment of commonly recognized necessary truths, such as $7 + 5 = 12$, to take a classic example.

We have seen that, for Santayana, internal relations (of a kind we have called *contrastive*) hold between independent essences. He refuses, however, to admit that this constitutes a truth, and says that the holding of such a relation is simply another essence which can be made an object of contemplation. This seems to mean that one who recognizes in abstraction from all matters of fact that $7 + 5 = 12$, or that a certain colour is of the same intensity as another, intuits (or intends) a comprehensive essence, the equality of $7 + 5$ and 12, or the correspondence in intensity of two colours.

He contends that these essences are not truths in themselves but that they are truths if there is some field of existence in which they are 'illustrated'. (He adds, for good measure, that there would be no such truth as the contingency of truth were truth not an exemplified category.) [22] Thus in a world containing a sufficient number of discrete entities every group of twelve illustrates the equivalence of 12 and $7 + 5$ and every coupling of those colours illustrates the relationship of those essences. Even essences unexemplified are dragged into the realm of truth in this manner since their precise differences from exemplified essences become truths about the instances of the latter, just as it is a truth about a group of three that it is four off seven. (Santayana discusses all this at some length but in a highly abstract way without developing his examples even so far as I have done.)

We may comment as follows:

1 Certainly the mere holding of essential relations between essences is something radically different from any truth about the actual world, and it is arguable that it is misleading to use the same word 'truth' in each case. Santayana seems himself to admit an element of considered departure from ordinary language in his terminology here.[23] If this is all there is to it, Santayana is not really in disagreement with a fair number of those who believe in necessary truths.

2 The position is, in any case, complicated by the fact that all such essential relationships are, as he himself insists,[24] actually dragged into the realm of truth, in his sense, by their relation to some actualized essence. Every essence together with all its essential relationships with all other essences adds to the truth about any existence, since this latter's essence is bound to stand in some definite relationship of contrast or affinity with that original one. The point, presumably, on which Santayana means to insist is that one is not taking these relationships as truths unless one finds in them some revelation regarding the existing world and its constituents, so that, for instance, an exploration of some eccentric geometry is a discovery of truth only so far as it illuminates the structure of the actually existing world. As a terminological recommendation this seems rather sensible.

3 What is really unsatisfactory is the claim that the holding of an essential relation between essences is itself an essence. One may admit that a special content is present to a mind which intuitively grasps the relations between two given figures, but on Santayana's own showing these figures are not strictly identical with any figures outside that (eternally repeatable) content. Since the relation between the figures inside and those outside this content must itself be an essential one, an infinite regress of a vicious kind ensues. There is also the question whether kindred figures may not belong to a complex essence in which they are related in some opposite and incompatible way. Santayana sometimes seems to hold that this is always actually so and that the necessary relations *we* find between essences are balanced by opposing necessary relations which other minds, intuiting them within different complexes, might find between virtually the same essences.[25] There are adumbrations (but unfortunately no more) here of a challenging view. However, I see no satisfactory solution, not requiring a radical break from some of his pronouncements, to the Bradleyan question how essential relations manage to lie 'between' essences which are not components in a single complex.

IX

Truth and Time

Santayana insists again and again that Truth is super-temporal or eternal, and contrasts therein with that restless flux of existence concerning which it is the truth. All things pass away, but the truth about them neither entered being at their birth nor departs with their cessation.[1]

To assert the eternity of truth, as Santayana asserts it, is to do more than merely remind us that truths are essences, and that essences are eternal, for the point is not merely that the character of my life is an eternal essence, but that there is no time at which it acquires or loses the status of a truth. Although on occasion Santayana seems to overlook this and to rest the eternity of truth simply on its status as an essence, he does provide reasons of a more relevant kind.

Ever since Aristotle, but with renewed enthusiasm in our own philosophical day, it has been debated whether the truth about the future is determinate in every detail. Santayana is firmly with those who oppose Aristotle in saying that it is so. His dismissal of the idea that truth changes is somewhat similar in tone to that of those analytic philosophers who have distinguished the essential content asserted by a statement from the implications it carries as to the temporal point of view from which it is made:[2]

It might seem, for instance, that the truth changes as fast as the facts which it describes. On a day before the Ides of March it was true that Julius Caesar was alive: on the day after that Ides of March it had *become true* that he was dead. A mind that would keep up with the truth must therefore be as nimble as the flux of existence. It must be a newspaper mind.

This, on the surface, is an innocent sophism, if not a bit of satire, mocking the inconstancy of things. Idiomatically we might

176

as properly say, 'It was then true that Caesar was living', as we might say, 'The truth is that Caesar was then living'. In using the former phrase we have no thought of denying the latter. If Julius Caesar was alive at a certain date, it was then true, it had been true before, and will be true always that at that date he was or would be or had been alive. These three assertions, in their deliverance, are identical; and in order to be identical in their deliverance, they have to be different in form, because the report is made in each case from a different point in time, so that the temporal perspectives of the same fact, Caesar's death on the Ides of March, require different tenses of the verb. This is a proof of instability in knowledge in contrast to the fixity of truth. For the whispered oracle, *Beware the Ides of March*, the tragic event was future; for the Senators crowding round Pompey's statue it was present; for the historian it is past: and the truth of these several perspectives, each from its own point of origin, is a part of the eternal truth about that event. (RB, p. 489)

For Santayana, however, the claim that truth is unchanging or eternal rests rather upon an ontological insight which purports to go somewhat beyond our most usual way of looking at things than on such considerations of the proper ordinary use of the word 'truth' as seem all important to many philosophers today. Such ontological insight would seem to concern the realm of matter (and spirit) as much as that of truth, for it turns on the nature of time as a physical reality. Granted his view that truth is always truth about something, Santayana could not hold that there is a determinate truth about the future unless he held that future facts are as much realities in their own right as are present facts. One might think likewise that if past facts have utterly ceased to be, then there would be nothing to distinguish those essences true of them from those not belonging to the truth at all. In fact the conception of truth as eternal developed in *The Realm of Truth* is inseparable from the conception of all moments of time as intrinsically present developed also in *The Realm of Matter*. Past facts, he maintains, though they certainly do not exist now, are as much parts of reality as are present facts. Moreover, they are not distinguished from present facts by some special quality of pastness. In itself every natural moment or moment of spirit, of whatever date, is a living present reality, though every one (except for those at the beginning and end of cosmic history if such there be) is past or future in relation to indefinitely many other moments.

Although this thesis concerns the status of past and future *existence*, and not merely the realm of truth in isolation, it is especially connected with the latter inasmuch as Santayana seems to arrive at it as an inference from the complete determinateness of the truth about the past and future. If, for instance, a past fact only had status as something conceived in the present and was not a living reality in itself in just the same way as is any present fact, there would be no sense in which our beliefs could approximate more or less to the precise essences literally true of it, while the denial that there is such an absolute truth about it is tantamount to abandoning the very idea of a real past.

Santayana recognizes that the status of future facts as living present realities in themselves will be less readily granted, since it is not so readily admitted that there is a determinate truth about the future as that there is about the past. He points out, however, that the issue here is liable to become confused by a failure to distinguish the question whether the future is determinate from the quite different question whether it is determined (by what has happened so far).[3] He has no dogmatic view on the issue of determinism (though he certainly thinks its denial in the interests of human freedom a futile confusion) but he is quite sure that unless future facts are determinate realities in their own right, however loose the laws which bind them to earlier times, it makes no sense even to wonder what will happen.

We may note that the confusion here, which Santayana brings out so well, is still with us and vexes discussion as to the truth-value of propositions about the future.[4] What Santayana does not bring out as clearly as he might have done (though he evidently has it in mind) is that the determinateness of the future is already implicated in the more readily granted determinateness of the past, since if past facts are present living realities in themselves, as they must be if there is to be a determinate truth about them, we have the example in our own present of a fact which is both future from the point of view of other facts intrinsically present, and intrinsically present in itself. If I say that the future beyond the present date in history (20 June 1972) is somehow intrinsically open, we must suppose that the man of 1066 would have spoken truly who said that the future was fixed up until 20 June 1972 but 'open' beyond that – an obvious absurdity to which my future reader can give the lie direct.

All this may look like the denial of a real flux. 'Since all moments of physical time are intrinsically present, it might seem that real existence was not changeful at all but only, perhaps, asymmetrical, like a frieze of sculptured arrows, all pointing one way, or a file of halted soldiers lifting one foot for ever, as if they had meant to march.' Sometimes it is thought that the real flux is not from one physical event to another but from one act of awareness to another, so that the history of the physical world is all there in one changeless block, though consciousness is aware of its constituents only successively.[5] Santayana dismisses this view as an absurdity, pointing out that one could never then explain the transition from one mental act to another by reference to a physical cause.[6] A saner view would attribute the same changeless status to acts of consciousness as well, but Santayana is concerned to distinguish his own position from that of any which seems to deny the reality of change. Santayana's vision of the hopeless flux of the natural world is, after all, close to the Platonic one for which such things become but never properly are.

What this insistence on the reality of the flux principally amounts to is that it is of the essence of every natural moment, *qua* natural moment, to be in transition to other natural moments. Santayana would, I think, reject the suggestion that he has made every moment *eternally present* as carrying a misleading implication of stillness and peace. (It would, of course, be still more misleading to say that it was present for ever, i.e. at all times.) Each moment is indeed in its own internal nature present, but it is 'unstably present, or in the act of elapsing' (RB, p. 264). It is hard not to believe that Santayana often thinks of this as equally applicable to 'moments of spirit', in spite of the fact that he also sometimes maintains that these are not properly speaking in flux.

One might think, nonetheless, that Santayana somewhat misrepresents his position when he makes eternity an attribute of Truth but never of anything in the realms of existence to which the Truth applies. Is not the truth about the world eternal simply because the world itself, understood as the actual system of all events in our space and time, is an eternal unchanging being?

Apart from the general wish to avoid language which reduces our sense of the flux of existence, Santayana would seem to object to the implication that there are such things as spatio-temporal chunks of the world. An existence is something which can exist all at once with an essence not exemplified in a merely piecemeal fashion.[7] Strictly only natural or spiritual moments exist in this sense, but in a weaker if more normal sense a system of contiguous collateral moments may be said to exist, as also any persistent but changing individual whose presence as a whole at any one time consists in the exemplification of an essence by collateral natural moment (or by some one such). In a certain sense, then, the truth about the world's whole history, and similarly about the history of any lesser individual, though certainly exemplified in its own piecemeal fashion, is not exemplified by any *something* describable as eternal or otherwise.

In part these contentions amount to linguistic preferences on the part of Santayana which cannot be binding on others. Certainly they do not affect the point that the thesis of truth's eternity is bound up with a theory of time considered as a physical reality and which concerns therefore the realm of matter as much as that of truth. What I think we

may grant Santayana is that there is a real difference between his insistence that: 'In itself, by virtue of its emergence in a world of change,
each moment is unstably present, or in the act of elapsing; and by
virtue of its position in the order of generation, both pastness and
futurity pervade it eternally', and the kind of view which spatializes
time by assimilating the lapse of one phase of existence into another
to the contiguity of things in space and substituting unchanging four-
dimensional spatio-temporal objects for the changing things of ordinary thought. For Santayana, on the contrary, it is only the latter
which really exists, since only they are ever all there at any one node
of existence. (On a stricter view, however, this would not be true
even of them unless their temporal phases were each a single natural
moment.)

There is another way in which Santayana's position differs from
that typical of many philosophers who have laid emphasis on the relativity of pastness and futurity to the point of view. Such philosophers
have tended to equate the meaning of 'Caesar's death lies in the past'
with 'Caesar's death is earlier than *this event*' where the latter expression
refers to something directly indicated or to the act of speaking itself.[8]
(To use McTaggart's terminology, they reduce the A series to the B
series.)[9] This is not quite Santayana's view.[10] He would allow, indeed,
that this is all I could mean by calling an event past when, in rare
moments, my ideas approximate to a vision of the world in its literal
truth, but as a general rule past and future present themselves to me
under a quite different aspect from each other and from the present,
and it is these aspects, these 'sentimental' or specious temporal essences,
which are signified by such expressions as 'then', 'long ago', 'once
upon a time', 'not yet', or 'soon':

> The notion that there is and can be but one time, and that half of
> it is always intrinsically past and the other half always intrinsically
> future, belongs to the normal pathology of an animal mind: it
> marks the egotistical outlook of an active being endowed with
> imagination. Such a being will project the moral contrast
> produced by his momentary absorption in action upon the
> conditions and history of that action, and upon the universe at
> large. A perspective of hope and one of reminiscence
> continually divide for him a specious eternity; and for him the
> dramatic centre of existence, though always at a different point in
> physical time, will always be precisely in himself. (RB, p. 253)

His position, then, is not so much that past and future are analysable
away in terms of the earlier-later relation as that they are specious or
sentimental essences having symbolic or dramatic truth as descriptions
of a real temporal succession in the literal truth of which they have no

place. 'In the romantic guise of what is not yet or what is no longer, the fleeting moment is able to recognize outlying existences, and to indicate to its own spirit the direction in which they lie' (RB, p. 257). We live through a flux of events which being unsynthesizable in consciousness as what it really is 'a steady procession of realities, all equally vivid and complete' must be represented for the psyche at each moment by a single essence in which the emotional contrast between what is over and done with and what is yet to come are qualities, of the events as envisaged, aptly rendering the contrary relations of generation in which it is then standing to each. But though the qualities of past and future belong for Santayana to appearance rather than to reality (as an Idealist might put it) we must remember that he also eschews any vision of the world as a changeless *Nunc Stans*; events are not present *for ever*, rather it is eternally of the essence of each to be ephemeral, to be in hopelessly unhaltable passage into one another.

How far is this account satisfactory?

We have already suggested that Santayana seems to assimilate unduly two distinct aspects of specious time, namely the before-after relation as it holds between the elements of a change experienced as a whole and the difference in the felt quality of an envisaged event according as to whether it is regarded as past or future.[11] In the discussion of 'sentimental time' on which we are drawing[12] he tends to represent the conceived past as continuous in quality with the fading aspect of the specious present, but one may well feel that the emotional or 'moral' quality of the former is something different in kind from the mode in which we experience the latter. Another distinction which should also have been made much more clear is that between *now* as a specious essence (the way in which contemporary events are perceived or otherwise envisaged) on a level with specious pastness and futurity, and *now* as a certain quality of 'livingness' which belongs to the intrinsic nature of every ultimate fact. These are, of course, points of detail which do not call the main thesis in question.

One might object, further, that there is anyway no single specious essence of pastness (or futurity) but only an infinity of different emotional colourings which qualify our envisagement of what is over (or to come) the 'mix' of which must vary greatly from person to person. This criticism would not, perhaps, disturb Santayana greatly, since he holds in any case that the decision to call different essences *the same* is always optional and relative to a purpose.

Many contemporary philosophers would make a much more fundamental criticism of Santayana's thesis and insist that the feelings with which we envisage past or future events (or rather the emotional quality of our vision thereof) have little or nothing to do with the meaning of statements of temporal fact, which make straightforward

181

claims the character of which can be explicated without reference to anything so subjective and irrelevantly variable.

Yet the clash here is less than head on. Santayana's position is not set out as an analysis of temporal propositions in the modern, or recently modern, vein. He is intent rather to contrast our usual envisagement of temporal facts with their actual character so far as the philosopher can grasp it. Still, he does imply that these specious essences somehow belong to the usual meaning of temporal expressions.

In this I think he is importantly right, not in every detail, but in the main point. Granted the meaning of 'meaning' is notoriously variable, it is a pretty limited conception thereof which ignores the immense difference in the way we feel about the past and future, the sharply contrasting sort of reality they seem to have for us, when explaining the meaning of tenses and temporal expressions. These differences cannot be tied down in cut and dried formulae, and it is only language of an essentially literary sort (essentially Santayana's 'literary psychology') which can bring them before our reflective consciousness. This is what Santayana calls 'literary psychology' and is what 'phenomenology' at least *ought* to be about. Some of Santayana's own discussion belongs to this category.

But if an adequate philosophical discussion of time should not ignore the points on which Santayana is so insistent it would, of course, have to deal with many issues on which he barely touches, including those which concern the practical procedures by which events are dated relatively to one another and times are measured, at various levels of enquiry. The sense of a vast unexplored gap between real Time in its most general character so far as the pure philosopher can grasp it, and Time as immediately presented to our consciousness at its least analytical and scientific, lends a certain unreality to Santayana's discussion. Still, Santayana makes no profession of completeness of treatment and there appears to be a good deal of sound sense in what he does say. It may be as well to bring this out more fully by a comparison with some other philosophical treatments of Time.

Philosophies of Time may be divided first into those which regard future, past, and present as essentially of the same ontological status and those which do not. Theories of the former type usually affirm that the past is simply what is earlier and the future what is later than the time of speaking or thinking, and that the truth or falsehood of our beliefs about either lies equally in some sort of correspondence with the facts they would normally be taken to concern. The main defect of such views is the suggestion they tend to carry, in spite of denials, that temporal flux is somehow unreal and that the events of all times really lie side by side in a changeless universe. As was noted by McTaggart[13] there is a real kinship between such views and those which assert that Time is unreal; it is, indeed, one of the oddities of the subject that the more we emphasize, as against sceptics, the reality of the past or future, the more we make Time itself seem an illusion. Santayana's theory certainly belongs to this first division, but he makes valiant efforts to free it of these implications of changelessness, efforts which seem at least to point in the right direction.

Among the possibilities implied in our second division of theories would seem to be one for which the future and the past are alike in status, but stand in contrast with the present. This might be exemplified in the thesis that only the present is real.[14] Though some such thesis appeals to one aspect of 'common sense' and may sometimes be implicit in philosophical theorizing, it is difficult to take such a position seriously, since it rules out any real temporal sequences from reality, comprised as these must be of terms from different times. Pragmatist and positivist views for which the truth-conditions of statements about the past lie in the correctness of the expectations they arouse may be associated with some such idea in their authors' minds but their logical implication is rather that the future has a reality denied of the past.[15] In any case these views are palpably absurd requiring, as they do, the breakfaster to accept that it is the day after tomorrow, and not his present munching, which will determine the truth of tomorrow's beliefs about the meal. The inspiration behind such ideas (still active in discussions of memory among the Wittgensteinians) is perhaps adequately dealt with by Santayana in the following passage:

> Empiricism used to mean reliance on the past; now apparently all
> empirical truth regards only the future, since truth is said to
> arise by the verification of some presumption. Presumptions
> about the past can evidently never be verified; at best they may
> be corroborated by fresh presumptions about the past, equally
> dependent for their truth on a verification which in the nature of
> the case is impossible. At this point the truly courageous
> empiricist will perhaps say that the real past only means the ideas
> of the past which we shall form in the future. Consistency is a
> jewel; and, as in the case of other jewels, we may marvel at the
> price that some people will pay for it. In any case, we are led to
> this curious result: that radical empiricism ought to deny that
> any idea of the past can be true at all. (COUS, p. 160)

Less wild is the main representative of views for which past, present, and future each have a radically different status, namely that version of the theory of 'Absolute Becoming' for which past and present both belong to reality in different ways but the future simply is not.[16] Although never discussed in these terms by Santayana it will be useful to compare it with his theory.

The main idea of the theory I have in mind may be indicated in a rough and ready manner by saying that reality for it is a spatio-temporal totality, containing the whole past, and (whether bounded in other directions or not) bounded in one plane by *the present*, a surface 'for ever' being covered by new matter such as possesses a unique kind of liveliness for just the one 'moment' that it remains upon the surface. (Whether the present would be strictly the surface, or rather matter of some temporal thickness 'on' the surface, need not concern us here.) In short, future events are utterly unreal, but once entered into reality by being momentarily present they always remain a part of reality. The one great alteration to which they are subject lies in that loss of livingness, that death which they are suffering even in their birth as living 'nows'. Once dead and entered into history they suffer no further change except in respect of their proximity to the uniquely living surface (and the fresh relational properties implied in the specific character of the fresh matter which covers it).

Undoubtedly such a view has a certain naturalness, doing justice, as it does, to two vaguely felt demands of common sense. On the one hand it offers a 'real past' by correspondence to which historical beliefs can be true (and thus avoids the absurdity of the pragmatic view), on the other hand it preserves our sense of the open-ness of the future and of the real transitoriness of things in time (as the 'relational' view of past and future may fail to do). Yet it does not seem, in the last resort, coherent, a fact which adds strength to Santayana's theory, since this goes further towards meeting the same demands than any other alternative of which I know.

Certainly some of the objections liable to be pressed against it are without force. Its proponents are quite aware, for instance, that the change which events undergo from presentness to pastness, and in proximity to the present, is not the ordinary sort of change undergone by a thing as its character and relationships alter, but they would claim that the latter adequately conceived presupposes the former. Nor do they necessarily look foolish when asked the rate at which change of the first sort takes place, for they can answer that such a question only makes sense in the case of the latter sort (and that hence my use of 'for ever' and 'moment' in stating their position is not to be taken literally).[17] A more serious problem concerns the tenses of the verbs when, at time T, I say, truly according to the theory, that 'There are events before T to be referred to, but there is nothing thereafter whatever', since they are neither in the timeless present tense of mathematics nor in the ordinary present tense. Perhaps an interpretation can be found such that the proposition expressed is absolutely true, and not merely true as spoken on such and such an identified occasion (so that 'There are no events after this one' does not need the qualification 'as yet'), but is all the same 'fugitively' rather than eternally true. [18]

For the theory of Absolute Becoming, presumably, *events without successors* are all present in an absolute sense, and hence also simultaneous in an absolute sense, while past events are simultaneous with equal absoluteness if and only if they once belonged together in a set of events without successors. Whether the fact that the theory provides an absolute but operationally useless sense of simultaneity such as modern physics has no place for is a merit or a demerit is (genuinely) questionable. [19]

The incoherence of the view is probably brought out better in other ways. One might ask first, for instance, what stops an event which can change in one respect from changing in others. The death of Julius Caesar has exchanged presentness for pastness. May it not also have exchanged one degree of bloodiness for another? Yet if the past can change it is the past as it was when present which the historian is after, not the only past which is real according to this theory.

One may say that such exchange of other qualities is metaphysically impossible. But even to say this is to allow a contrast between an event in the state of pastness and the same event in the state of presentness and to say that they are otherwise alike. The reality of the event *become past* is insisted on so that historical statements have something to which they may correspond, yet such correspondence is only of value because the event as past corresponds to itself as it was when present. The latter correspondence is insisted on in the denial that events change in other respects besides degree of pastness, but it makes the event as past an altogether otiose metaphysical construction since if *it* can correspond to the event as present the historical statement may as well also do so (doubtless in a different sense of 'correspond') directly.

The truth is that events gone dead, bad, or past, as this theory must conceive then are really strange iconic relics (or perhaps memories in a cosmic mind as they seem to be for some followers of Whitehead) of the original events which had the quality of living realities. Had one somehow access to such realities they might be first class evidence of how things once were, though they could not be those events as they were in their presentness. As it is, they have no purpose whatever.

Theorists of Absolute Becoming sometimes seem to hold that to be past is simply to have successors, not to have lost any intrinsic quality of liveliness. 'Nothing has happened to the present to become past except that fresh slices of existence have been added to the total history of the world.' [20] This might seem to imply that it can *be* past while remaining just as much a living reality as in its presentness. This prompts a puzzling thought as I reflect on what I take to be my present sensations. How do I know that the fresh slices of existence have not been added 'already' so that really they are past, since this would make no difference to the state of mind which includes it? Once an event is past, its increasing degree of pastness may well be interpreted relationally by the Absolute Becoming theorist, as the increasing quantity of its real successors, but he can hardly avoid conceiving the exchange of presentness for pastness as an alteration internal to the event itself, otherwise it would make no difference to a state of mind from its own point of view whether it is present or past.

Santayana's view suggests, rather, that every state of mind, like every other fact, is present from its own point of view though past and future from other viewing points (though he can never say this quite explicitly in view of his belief that consciousness does not apprehend itself). It is hard, indeed, to know what a past state of mind is for the theorist of absolute becoming. Surely it must *feel* its own reality if it is indeed a state of mind, yet what could it feel like to be a past state of mind? Even to pose the question is to show how essentially right Santayana is in maintaining that to believe in a real past is to believe in a reality which is in itself as present as this moment and for which this present is just as truly a future as it is a past:

> Contradictory epithets of this sort are compatible when they are
> seen to be relative; but it must be understood that they are the
> relative aspects of something which has an absolute nature of its
> own, to be the foundation of those relations. And the absolute
> nature of moments is to be present: a moment which was not
> present in itself could not be truly past or future in relation to
> other moments. What I call the past and what I call the future
> are truly past or future *from here*; but if they were *only* past or
> *only* future, it would be an egregious error on my part to believe
> that they were past or future at all, for they would exist only in
> my present memory or expectation. In their pastness and futurity
> they would be merely specious, and they would be nothing but
> parts of a present image. If I pretended that they recalled or
> forecast anything, I should be deceived; for nothing of that kind,
> either in the past or in the future, would ever rejoice in
> presentness and exist on its own account. Thus only false memory
> and false expectation end in events intrinsically past or
> intrinsically future – that is to say, intrinsically sentimental.
> False legends and false hopes indeed have their being only in
> perspective; their only substance is the thought of them now,
> and it is only as absent that they are ever present. (RB, p. 265)

Though Santayana does not criticize the theory of absolute be-coming as such the criticisms of it I have advanced are implicit in his work, as in such remarks as the following: 'But words lead us to imagine that things can survive themselves. When Caesar has ceased to live, we half believe that he continues to exist dead. But nothing exists dead except dead bodies. Facts exist only as they occur, and the essence and truth of them, which indeed are eternal, are non-existent' (RB, p. 490).

We have already pointed out the limitations of Santayana's treatment of Time. Within those limitations it seems to me that his work has real value as an attempt to synthesize the view that time is merely one dimension of a spatio-temporal unity with that for which it is 'the jerky or whooshy quality of transience'.[21]

X

Santayana's Ethical Theory

1 The scope of Santayana's ethics

Santayana described himself as a moralist, meaning apparently that an essentially moral quest inspired his philosophy as a whole.[1] In spite of this, or perhaps as a consequence thereof, there is no single work – unless we so describe *The Life of Reason* as a whole, which in any case precedes the elaboration of many of his most characteristic doctrines – specifically devoted to the usual questions of the moral philosopher. If a unitary ethical theory is expressed in his works, we can arrive at it only through our own synthesis of what seems at first disparate. Nonetheless I believe that Santayana has a consistent system of moral philosophy, though it is never given any very organized statement, remaining largely the same from *The Life of Reason* onwards, except for certain clarifications regarding the status of good and evil made possible by the doctrine of essence.

Moral philosophers, at least since the publication of Moore's *Principia Ethica*, have often emphasized the importance of distinguishing between analytical and normative ethics (though the distinction has been made in a great variety of terminologies). Some have thought that the philosopher, as such, should be concerned only with the former but others have thought that the more general issues of the latter lie within his province. Although he has no regular terms for distinguishing the two, Santayana shows himself very conscious of this contrast, and would seem, upon the whole, to hold that a correct treatment of analytical ethics will show that normative ethics is too personal or subjective an affair to find place in a philosophical system; at any rate his own work belongs mostly to analytical ethics. We can only so classify it, however, if we take this in a broader sense than has been usual among analytical philosophers in the English speaking world,

188

who have conceived it usually as concerned with the analysis of term such as will occur in any, or almost any, system of normative ethics. Santayana certainly does deal with the questions of analytic ethics in this narrower sense (which I shall distinguish as meta-ethics), at least his comments upon the ontological status of *good* and *evil* can be reinterpreted as concerned with the meaning of 'good' and 'evil' (very much as Moore's statements about the object or notion *good* can be). Yet the greater part of his moral philosophy is concerned to analyse or clarify the content of certain specific normative ideals the concepts of which are by no means essential to every moral judgement. Since he is not concerned, *qua* philosopher, to argue for, or otherwise urge, the claims of these ideals his work here is not properly normative, yet because these ideals, in particular those of *the life of reason* and of *the spiritual life*, have a richness of content undiscoverable in the merely generic essences of good and evil, right and wrong, etc. and because Santayana is obviously inspired to clarify them through an at least partial commitment thereto, his writing on these topics is concerned with substantive moral issues in a way in which the purely analytic ethics we have distinguished as meta-ethics, to the increasing unease even of academic philosophers, is not.

2   *Value qualities*

Let us consider, first, the way in which Santayana deals with the more typically 'meta-ethical' questions. There are many scattered observations upon such matters in *Realms of Being* but their only at all systematic treatment is the chapter on 'Moral Truth' in *The Realm of Truth*. This gives an admirable statement of certain aspects of his viewpoint, but a better overall idea thereof is probably given by the much earlier 'Hypostatic Ethics' (*Winds of Doctrine*, Chapter IV § IV) and I shall proceed with an outline of this, supplemented by material drawn from elsewhere.[2] What we have here is a discussion of Bertrand Russell's essay 'The Elements of Ethics' (from *Philosophical Essays*; 1910) which was virtually a summary statement of the position of *Principia Ethica*, a position in which Russell lost faith not long after, partly as a result[3] of this criticism of Santayana's (which first appeared in 1911 in a review of Russell's book).[4] Santayana refers from time to time directly to Moore, and as the intuitionism he discusses, and in contrast to which he develops his own view, is so much more typical of Moore than Russell, I shall mostly refer to its target as *the Moorean*.

Santayana begins by noting how he, as an ethical naturalist (one whom he says the Moorean would call an ethical sceptic) agrees with the Moorean in two preliminary points, first that actions are good only in virtue of being means to other things which are good in themselves, and secondly that 'good' in this latter case names an indefinable quality and has meaning for us only because we encounter it in intuition. He seems to accept the Moorean's reasons for saying that good is indefinable, namely that all so-called definitions of good really only specify classes of facts which their proponent personally judges to possess 'the abstract quality "good"', but dismisses the point (we may think somewhat unreasonably) as too obvious to deserve the elaborate treatment it receives from Russell and Moore. He goes on, however, to take issue with the Moorean over the 'portentous dogma' which he derives from this somewhat 'trifling' truth, the dogma namely that (quoting Russell) 'Good and bad are qualities which belong to objects independently of our opinions, just as much as round and square do; and when two people differ as to whether a thing is good, only one of them can be right, though it may be very hard to know which is right.'

With a modest admission, which may not be entirely ironic, of the limitations of his own logical powers in comparison with Russell, Santayana argues that there is no valid inference from the indefinability of good to its being an absolute or primary quality of certain things. He points out that green is indefinable and yet things may truly be said to be green from one point of view and not from another; that right and left are indefinable and that the difference between them 'could not be explained without being invoked in the explanation', yet things are only right and left from a certain point of view, and that, for all that has been shown, the Moorean might as well say that 'if a man here and another man at the antipodes call opposite directions up "only one of them can be right, though it may be very hard to know which is right"' as maintain this in connection with good and bad.

Santayana can only find two reasons advanced in Russell's essay against the view that good, though an indefinable quality, is still 'a relative quality' which things may possess from one person's point of view and not another's. First there is the point that, as a matter of fact, and in general, when one man thinks something good and another man thinks it bad, we conclude that one must be mistaken, as we do not when one man likes oysters and another does not. Second, there is the point that if what makes a thing good from one man's point of view and not another's is supposed to be the fact that only the first man desires it, a man could not regard some of his own desires as desires for what is bad, as in fact he may do.

The first consideration Santayana dismisses as 'an idol of the debating chamber', describing it as a 'singular' reason for insisting on the absoluteness of values that only thus can we quarrel about them as men mostly do not about oysters. Concerning the second he makes the admission that a distinction can be drawn between what is 'really' good and bad from my point of view and what is only apparently so, but interprets this as the distinction between the goodness and badness found in things when one's momentary state is a fair reflection of one's abiding constitutional interests, and that found when one's conscious state reflects only some 'momentary and partial interest', and suggests that even in the latter case the things in question do truly possess 'a certain real and inalienable value' from the point of view of that sub-system of the personality.

The nature of Santayana's own positive view will have begun to be apparent, and may be stated more fully as follows (with the help of other sources). The desires or impulses of a man, conceived as psychic dispositions rather than as states of consciousness, consist in his physical tendency so to act as to produce certain results, but they manifest themselves in consciousness as an envisagement of things *sub speci boni* or *mali* according as they further (or belong to) those results or hinder them. From the outsider's point of view these acts of envisagement are emotions rather than cognitions, are in fact *desires* when this term is taken in a 'spiritual' sense, but what is presented to them is not a state of the present self, but the goodness or badness of some fact beyond (which may or may not concern one's own fate). (Santayana gives this sort of account of conscious emotion in general, and one may feel that he has made a general rule of what is only true of many cases.) This goodness or badness is a perfectly genuine quality or essence, but from the point of view of the reflective ontologist it may belong to things only in the sense that they do or would appear as possessing it to one or more specific psyches, and may be described as 'really' good or bad from the point of view of those psyches if such appearance expresses their more abiding impulses. (It is in this connection that Santayana often describes the purpose of normative ethics as a form of self-knowledge, since in determining what is truly good or bad one is in effect discovering what it is that one truly wants. He compares it in this respect with that dialectic – or conceptual analysis as we might call it – in which one tries to bring to light what one really means by certain terms; the two activities together constitute the Socratic method and serve to make the immediate contents of consciousness, and the finer modes of activity associated therewith, a more adequate reflection of one's deeper psychic intentions, behavioural or conceptual.)⁵

It cannot be said that Santayana offers much by way of positive argument for this position, either in the discussion of the Russell-Moore view or elsewhere, probably thinking its truth sufficiently obvious once the sophistry and emotional dogmatism of absolutism are assuaged. He certainly thinks it relevant to point out that the Moorean's expectation that certain value judgements will seem self-evident to his reader rests on the presumption of his reader being a certain sort of man and that there are always some to whom their contraries would seem equally so, but this cannot be the whole story, for he also urges that even if there were complete unanimity on value that would only show that everyone had the same arbitrary constitution. The main basis for his view would seem to be that a proper examination of the quality *good* shows that it, like the pleasant, is one of those aspects under which other essences are envisaged by spirit and like the others of this class is not formally exemplifiable, but can only belong to that to which spirit ascribes it speciously. (We have already considered what grounds there may be for saying this about these aspects in general.)[6] A subsidiary consideration (not without force, I think) is that if there were a good somehow present in the intrinsic essence of objects it would be of no possible interest to us, who can only be attracted by a good which we intuit.[7]

In his own rather different way Santayana thus makes the Humean point that unless value judgements are somehow intrinsically connected with the passions the special part they play in moving us to action is inexplicable. One might say that for Santayana value judgements express passion in a double sense, for, first, the envisagement of something as good, though it consists in the thing itself appearing to one in a certain way, is itself a passion, insofar as passions are conscious states, and, second, it 'expresses' a passion conceived as a disposition of the psyche. Although he hardly elaborates the point, it appears that Santayana thinks of the essence of good as an intrinsically suitable symbol of the fact that the psyche is in pursuit of what it appears to characterize, a view which, as I have said before, does not involve a synthetic *a priori* truth regarding what produces what but does involve a kind of affinity between distinct essences such as is not commonly recognized by empiricists.[8] Santayana's position shares some features with those attitudinist theories of ethics or values for which value judgements express attitudes rather than beliefs, but differs from them over the phenomenology of value (as one might put it) holding that it is not simply ethical words which have a magnetic quality, but that the situations to which we apply them are experienced by us, not as mere facts about which we have certain feelings, but as facts with a quality of beckoning magnetism as part of their very being. Santayana, one might say, thinks of Moore's theory as correctly describing how things appear to the valuing or moralizing subject,[9] while offering a more attitudinist theory from the point of view of ultimate ontology, though if Santayana thought of his theory in this way it would rather be as a synthesis between Platonism and Spinozism.

After noting the dogmatism (involving the exaltation of one's own personal values to the status of objective truths about the world) with which the Moorean disposes of hedonistic and egoistic ethics, Santayana concludes with the observation that ethical relativism, as he conceives it, the view that things are not really good or evil in themselves, but only from the point of view of one or more specific psyches, is a theory likely to breed greater tolerance and true sociability than an absolutism for which 'things have intrinsic and unchangeable values, no matter what the attitude of any one to them may be. If we said that goods, including the right distribution of goods, are relative to specific natures, moral warfare would continue, but not with poisoned arrows.'

Santayana's position regarding the relation between relativism and tolerance is, I believe, a somewhat subtle one. He does not forget that a moral judgement, as opposed to an observation about moral judgements, must express the speaker's own attitudes, and suppose that I am logically compelled to recognize something as good because another man does, thus putting all men's values on a par in an omni-tolerance.[10] On the other hand, he does think that the absolutist fails to take in that what he dismisses as an evil may really sparkle for another man's vision with that very same quality of goodness which belongs for him to his own ideals, and that one cannot grasp the truth that this is so without some lulling of one's antipathy. Each man or society must live by their own values, since there is no alternative, and this may sometimes even mean fighting for them as against the values of others, but at another level one may transcend this moralistic point of view and see that every envisaged good is equally genuine a good (though it may not be producible in the way supposed), an insight which may purge one's morality of its rancour without any weakening of its vigour.

There is, I believe, much wisdom in this ethical relativism of Santayana. The typically Santayanian urge to synthesize points of view usually advanced as contraries here reaches heroic proportions, yet it would seem to be coherent in its main upshot. Nonetheless the theory lacks completeness and gives at least an appearance of vagueness on quite a number of important points. It will be as well to consider some of these one by one.

1 The relation between good and bad (or *evil*, in the sense in which the word applies to evils in general, and not only to wicked agents)[11] on the one hand, and right, wrong, and duty on the other, have been the subject of much dispute, with the ideal utilitarianism of Moore and the theory of duty of W. D. Ross representing two extremes which have continued to find their echoes in later work. While Santayana is certainly disposed on the whole towards the former view, according to which a judgement that one ought to do something is equivalent to the judgement that by so acting one will produce results better on the whole than by any alternative which suggests itself, he can hardly

be said to have held it in any dogmatic way, and, in fact, he recognizes that for some moralities certain actions are *wicked* in themselves.[12] Clearly his main intention is not to analyse all moral concepts in terms of two basic essences *good* and *bad*, but to make the general point that things present themselves to us in 'moral colours' which 'express' our psychic impulses towards them, a point which can be applied to the thought of certain actions as such as *ought not to be done* as much as to the *good*. As to whether *good* (and *evil*) is a single essence, the points I made above about *beauty* would seem to apply.[13]

2 Santayana describes good and bad as relative qualities, and by this he seems to mean qualities which a thing wears for some, but not necessarily all, conscious beings, and which do not otherwise belong to the literal truth about it. (I assume that in some contexts we may understand 'wears' as also covering 'or would wear'.) A relative quality, in this sense, is, of course, something quite different from a relational property, that is from the property of being in a certain relation to something. It seems doubtful whether Santayana had any clear idea of this distinction. Certainly it would require some argument to show that up and down, right and left, are the former rather than the latter (though perhaps, in the end, this is true), yet Santayana compares the status of good and evil to these, as well as to green, which is in some ways a better example of what Santayana seems to mean by a relative quality.[14]

But though he over-simplifies in the presentation of his position, I still think he is essentially right in maintaining that good and evil may very well be indefinable qualities without belonging to things other than for human, or animal, consciousness.

3 I have suggested that Santayana, in effect, regards Moore's account as right about the phenomenology of valuation. This requires qualification. The complete contrast which held for Moore between natural 'objects', even indefinable ones such as pleasure, and the non-natural quality of *good* finds no echo in Santayana, for whom it would seem that pleasure essentially is the intuition which 'expresses' the attainment of something which unattained presents itself under the aspect of the good, so that pleasure, in a broad sense, and good are intimately related.

Moore gave various rather unsatisfactory accounts of what he meant by calling good non-natural. It seems likely that one point he really had in mind is that goodness pertains to individual situations not in a random way which could vary independently of other features, but in virtue of their total natures or essences, which essences are good, in the sense that they ought to exist, with a non-analytic necessity.

There are issues here concerned with 'universalizability' which Santayana does not discuss, but I think he tacitly allows an aspect of universalizability to evaluation by taking good as more essentially a predicate of essences than of facts. A certain ambivalence in his whole way of talking about good, so that at one time what anyone envisages as good is inalienably an eternal form of the good, while at another time it is only good so long as that person desires it, may be explained (I believe) precisely as we explained the similar ambivalence regarding beauty. [15]

Santayana was certainly vividly conscious of the fact that two people may envisage the same object without there being any difference in the way in which they conceive it other than the one vital fact that for one of them it may may glow with a goodness which seems quite inseparable therefrom while for the other it lacks all such lustre or is positively repellent. A striking example to which he points is the condemnation by Plato and the Moorean of a mindless unintellectual state of pleasure worthy rather of an oyster than of a man, and thereby constituting the *reductio ad absurdum* of hedonism, which is hardly distinguishable from the state of pure bliss to which the mystic aspires as his highest good:

> [The Moorean] repeats, in effect, Plato's argument about the life of the oyster, having pleasure with no knowledge. Imagine such mindless pleasure, as intense and prolonged as you please, and would you choose it? Is it your good? Here the British reader, like the blushing Greek youth, is expected to answer instinctively, No! . . . He is shocked at the idea of resembling an oyster. Yet changeless pleasure, without memory or reflection, without the wearisome intermixture of arbitrary images, is just what the mystic, the voluptuary, and perhaps the oyster, find to be good. (WD, p. 147)

Here, as elsewhere, Santayana supports his relativism, not by merely pointing, in a conventional way, to the variety of moral codes, but by making us sense how something which we condem may have a palpable goodness, beyond all argument, to others just such as our most cherished ideals do to us. That a recognition of this would lead to a greater tolerance seems to me quite true, and it is a recognition quite absent from many who would repudiate any theory of ethical absolutism. How few people possessed of a political ideal have any real sense of the way things glow or lower for their opponents.

Some doubt may still be felt as to the exact sense in which Santayana wishes to support *ethical relativism* and as to how he conceives its relation to a tolerance of diversity in morals. Certainly the term tends to be a vague one and has been given various meanings by philosophers and others. Sometimes it names the view that statements of such forms as 'X is good' are incomplete, and become significant only

195

when something like 'from the point of view of Y' is added or understood. Sometimes it names the view that all moral systems are equally good or bad, perhaps with the implication that one ought to abide by that of the community one is in at present and not criticize it by standards drawn from elsewhere. Relativism of both these and other forms has been the subject of a good deal of attack recently, especially from those whose theories have seemed to the vulgar to support them.

Emotivists, in particular, have seemed almost to vie with one another in claiming the right to a moral intolerance and dogmatism of which relativism is conceived as the denial.[16] The philosophical position of the former is that moral judgements express emotional or affective attitudes which cannot be classed as true or false, unless these words themselves function merely as terms of praise or dispraise, and that if one person says that X is good and another that X is bad, there is no sense in which one can be the objectively correct opinion. Granted important differences, there is a good deal in common here with Santayana. Quite rightly, however, they go on to insist that it would be sheer confusion to think that they are committed thereby to saying that X is both good and bad, pointing out that this would be to express a moral attitude of tolerance no more implied in the realization that moral judgements express attitudes than is any other attitude. Is Santayana victim to a confusion similar to that the emotivists condemn?

Actually Santayana criticizes this sort of *non sequitur* himself, but since he does also at times suggest that relativism has some sort of connection with tolerance, there is a certain appearance of confusion. This, together with the precise nature of his relativism can be cleared up, I think, if we recognize that for Santayana there are various different levels at which we may consider values.

A man who is looking at things from the moral point of view will regard some of them as good and some as bad, that is, he takes them as possessing those moral colours, in which they appear to him, as a part of their very nature. Although this belief of his will not be literally true, it will possess a kind of symbolic truth if the impulses it expresses are stable, registering the literal truth that things of a certain sort will satisfy the psyche. One might urge that the belief is literally *false*, but I suspect that Santayana would think this failure-implying description apt only if the belief deliberately claims literal truth for itself, and not if it is merely a way of looking at the world which is not self-conscious about its own status.

Judgements or beliefs of this sort ascribe moral qualities to things in an absolute way, that is, their form is simply 'X is good', not 'X is good from point of view Y'. If, however, one reflects philosophically and rises to what might be called the ontological point of view, one will recognize that these qualities of good (and evil) have no place in

196

the world except as ways in which the spirit envisages actual or possible things, and the moral judgement 'X is good' will be replaced by the more literal ontological judgement 'X is good from the point of view of Y'. It is at this level that Santayana is speaking when he talks of anything possessing its inalienable goodness which has been felt as a good.

Our explication of Santayana's position is incomplete, however, until we add a third stage in which the ontological insight reacts upon the moral judgement, for, according to Santayana, once we fully realize the literal truth that that what other men pursue possesses for their vision the same goodness that our goals possess in our eyes we are bound somehow to incorporate this vision in our own moral outlook. Certainly there is a difference between the factual truth that A finds G good, and the moral judgement that G is good, but one cannot really grasp the former fact, which involves imagining how things are from A's point of view, without this participation in A's vision setting up an aspect of goodness in G as one of the values of which one finds one must take account in one's own moralizing, though it cannot determine the precise weight one attaches to this good as against others, a matter which must be continually decided afresh in every individual mind. This will become clearer when we discuss *reason*.

Although Santayana does not make these distinctions as boldly as I have done, there seems no real doubt that this account correctly represents, in outline, what he has communicated in his richer, if less analytic, vein.

3 *Reason*

A view for which value qualities are merely the way in which the goals of our impulses and the obstacles in their way appear to us might seem to leave little room for any conception of the role of reason in morals other than that ascribed to it by Hume of pointing out the means to ends determined by the passions. True, Santayana differs from Hume and his modern followers somewhat on the phenomenology of the relation between facts and values, for these latter rather give the impression that the emotions on which morality is based are directed on to a world which presents itself in the first place as free of value, while for Santayana facts present themselves as essentially value charged. Nonetheless one might expect the upshot, from the point of view of ethical methodology, to be much the same, since in neither case does there seem to be any sense in which one 'ultimate preference' can be more reasonable than another. In fact, however, Santayana understands by 'reason' something which can play a much more commanding role than is usually allotted to its referent by ethical naturalists. His main account thereof is to be found *passim* in *The Life of Reason*, but when he took up the theme again thirty-five years later in the 'Apologia' (in PGS) he still describes reason in essentially the same fashion. Empiricists have usually agreed with Hume that, so far as practice goes, 'Reason is, and ought only to be the slave of the passions, and can never pretend to any other office than to serve and obey them'. Conceiving reason as the power of deductive or inductive reasoning they have thought it incapable of selecting a goal, and have limited its practical task to that of discovering the means to ends set by nonrational impulse. More rationalistic philosophers have usually sought a more masterful role for reason, but they have agreed in setting it in contrast to passion or impulse. Santayana, like the rationalist and unlike Hume, ascribes an active controlling function to reason, but unlike both rationalists and empiricists, he conceives reason as essentially an impulse among impulses, almost, one might say, a passion among passions. It is the impulse to organize other impulses, or the interest in organizing other interests (for Santayana tends to identify these two) into a harmonious system. A man is rational to the extent that he is not so given over to the impulse accidentally dominant at any one moment as to forget the claims of those values which beckon him at other times. We will see subsequently that these values comprise the objectives of all impulses, whether originally located in himself or others, of which he ever has cognizance. The rational man is one who feels the *prima facie* right of every impulse to satisfaction, of every envisaged good to actualization, and who has as his controlling ideal a form of life in which a maximum of impulses find a harmonious satisfaction. 'Reason as such represents or rather constitutes a single formal interest, the interest in harmony' (LRI, p. 267). The ultimate controlling factor in the rational man's behaviour is always the total system of impulses ever active in him, not merely some impulse which happens to be pressing at the time. This is not, of course, a matter of never aiming at anything in particular, but of being guided by a sense of the relationship in which one's present objective stands to a system of objectives which one's life realizes as a whole, and which brings about as much as possible of what one looks upon from time to time as good.

Rationality is essentially an impulse, an impulse to harmonize other impulses, but like any other impulse it enters consciousness as the envisagement of a certain ideal, of certain contingencies *sub specie boni*. Santayana seems somewhat vague as to whether what the rational man envisages as good is a state of affairs which comprises as many as possible of the contingencies which are good from the point of view of other impulses, or whether what he envisages as good is the satisfaction of these other impulses. The distinction may seem trifling, yet it is not altogether without significance. Perhaps Santayana's position is that the rational ideal is a harmony of goods deliberately recognized as such only because they are the objectives of impulses.

Reason itself, and the harmony of other values which it pursues (here again Santayana does not distinguish between the value of the impulse and the value of its objective very clearly), is a relative good in just the same sense as any other good. Reason, and its goal, is good from its own point of view (though Santayana suggests that reason may sometimes have to inhibit even itself in the interest of its own ideal of harmony) but it may be as truly an evil from the point of view of some other impulse, which seeks a more dominant role than reason can allow it. 'Reason alone can be rational, but it does not follow that reason alone is good. The criterion of worth remains always the voice of nature, truly consulted, in the person that speaks' (PGS, p. 563). Moreover, there is no one single solution to a practical problem which is *the* rational solution, and the value of alternative rational solutions is relative to the particular balance or synthesis of forces within a judging psyche. Every harmonization of conflicting impulses demands that some of them be modified or even suppressed (though always with the sense that ideally all of them ought to have been satisfied) and there will always be alternative solutions equally rational but unequally good from any given point of view.[17]

Clearly a man is not rational for Santayana merely because he has a vaguely passionate desire for harmony such as might belong to a drunken sot even while he is sacrificing all his interests to one. Reason is a hidden psychic mechanism which modifies the satisfaction of immediate impulses in the interests of remoter ones, a process whose conscious expression is the reproduction of these latter in imagination.

On the face of it, someone might remember that he often had a certain impulse as the drunkard might remember his impulse at other times to earn a living, and be quite uninfluenced thereby. It would seem, then, that it is not mere recollection of such impulses, but a recollection which restores their potency, which expresses reason. According to Santayana, however, the conceiving of an impulse involves its partial re-enactment, a re-enactment the more complete the more vivid the conceiving,[18] so that one cannot really take in the fact that at other times one feels a certain want without the object of that want appearing as a good to one now. To think of a variety of impulses is, therefore, *ipso facto* to have a variety of present aims, and thereby to be in a state of distraction until one can somehow harmonize them; indeed Santayana seems to hold that to be thus aware of two interests at once is necessarily to desire their harmonious satisfaction:

When two interests are simultaneous and fall within one act of apprehension the desirability of harmonizing them is involved in the very effort to realise them together. If attention and imagination are steady enough to face this implication and not to allow impulse to oscillate between irreconcilable tendencies, reason comes into being. Henceforth things actual and things desired are confronted by an ideal which has both pertinence and authority. (LRI, pp. 267–8)

This suggests a kind of inevitability for the ideal of rationality hardly congruent with the emphasis laid elsewhere upon its relativity. The most that he should have said is that the search for a course of action which will resolve the conflict of all presently conceived impulses is inevitable, while allowing that the resultant may not correspond to any ideal which could be called rational. It might fail to do so either because so few relevant interests are conceived, or because their conflict is resolved by the sacrifice of the remainder to the goal of one which is treated as supreme.

But although one may decide to sacrifice a conceived impulse, one cannot, on Santayana's view, be entirely indifferent to it, so that mere awareness of a wide range of interests which might be affected by one's action takes one more than half way to rationality. In the light of this Santayana presents rationality as bridging the alleged gulf between egoism and altruism, an important point since otherwise reason, as he describes it, might seem virtually the same as the principle Bishop Butler called self-love:

The conflict between selfishness and altruism is like that between any two ideal passions that in some particular may chance to be opposed; but such a conflict has no obstinate existence for reason. For reason the person itself has no obstinate existence. . . . The limits assigned to the mass of sentience attributed to each man are assigned conventionally; his prenatal feelings, his forgotten dreams, and his unappropriated sensations belong to his body and for that reason only are said to belong to him. Each impulse included within these limits may be as directly compared with the represented impulses of other people as with there presented impulses expected to arise later in the same body. Reason lives among these represented values, all of which have their cerebral seat and present efficacy over the passing thought; and reason teaches this passing thought to believe in and to respect them equally. Their right is not less clear, nor their influence less natural, because they may range over the whole universe and may await their realization at the farthest boundaries of time. All that is physically requisite to their operation is that they should be vividly represented; while all that is requisite rationally, to justify them in qualifying actual life by their influence, is that the present act should have some tendency to bring the represented values about. In other words, a rational mind would consider, in its judgement and action, every interest which that judgement or action at all affected; and it would conspire with each represented good in proportion, not to that good's intrinsic importance, but to the power which the present act might have of helping to realise that good. (LRV, pp. 250-1)

We may see here an analogy with Santayana's treatment of 'romantic' solipsism. There is nothing particularly rational in merely believing in the existence of one's own stream of consciousness, since in believing in that the passing thought is already acknowledging the existence of outlying facts, and there is no natural boundary which encloses merely the facts of one's own sentience. There is likewise no natural boundary enclosing the impulses of the single person, and the process whereby the passing thought represents impulses of the individual whose primitive dominance belongs to other moments is essentially the same as that whereby it represents impulses whose original basis is in another individual. It is the comprehensiveness of what is represented in thought, or in thought's basis, at any one moment, which determines both the extent of concern for one's own needs in later life and of concern for others. Thus Santayana again exhibits a tendency to follow James and Bradley in regarding the passing thought as the true subject and to assimilate (as Bradley does) its sense of the self which owns it to that which it has of conscious life as a whole, a tendency somewhat antithetical to his otherwise rather excessive individualism.[19]

On the moral question whether one should be an egoist or a universalist Santayana is as relativistic as on all moral questions. In 'Hypostatic Ethics' he maintains that the real egoist has a certain ideal, not the preservation of a certain bare particular, but the continued exemplification of a certain essence, his own personality, to which he attaches supreme value, and that, whatever others may think of this evaluation, it is not 'the thin and refutable thing' attacked by the Moorean. In effect, though the point is formulated somewhat differently, he is saying that the judgements of the egoist are as logically universalizable as any other value claim, since they concern the value of a certain specific *sort* of thing. There is a good deal of force, I think, in this claim that the beloved self is conceived as what has certain qualities and exists in a certain sort of context, but it may not do complete justice to what each person means by himself.

What is not so clear is whether Santayana thinks that reason (whose ideal, we must remember, is only one among many) is essentially altruistic (or rather universalistic, i.e. equally concerned with the interests of all, oneself included) or only that it is susceptible of such a development.

His position, I take it, is upon the whole as follows. The rational man is one who preserves at each moment a sense of the value of all that he ever values, and lives by an ideal which, so far as is possible, synthesizes them all, making none the sole arbiter of the remainder's right, as does the ideal of the fanatic. His behaviour advances an organized system of impulses, neither controlled (like that of the 'pre-rational' man) by a mere succession of different impulses which prevent their successors' satisfaction, nor (like that of the 'post-rational' man)[20] by some dominating impulse such as maims all other aspects of the personality. Since the impulses thus organized and the values thus synthesized include not only his personal impulses, but all those represented or conceived ones which have become to some extent his own, such rationality is by no means limited to personal prudence, and has even a certain intrinsic tendency to universalism, for one cannot organize one's own impulses without the representation of outlying facts, and when these outlying facts are the impulses of others their very representation serves to recreate them in oneself.

But if some concern for the needs of others is thus virtually inevitable in the rational man, Santayana is still insistent that the weight to be attached to different rival claims is not determinable by any method common to every rational ideal. He repudiates the utilitarian calculus and denies that different values are commensurable in any straightforward way. The choice of synthesis, especially if every possibility requires that some value be sacrificed, must in the end express a higher order impulse in the judging psyche logically undetermined by the lower order impulses whose equal initial legitimacy it acknowledges:[21]

> The standard of value, like every standard, must be one. Pleasures and pains are not only infinitely diverse but, even if reduced to their total bulk and abstract opposition, they remain two. Their values must be compared, and obviously neither one can be the standard by which to judge the other. This standard is an ideal involved in the judgement passed, whatever that judgement may be. Thus when Petrarch says that a thousand pleasures are not worth one pain, he establishes an ideal of value deeper than either pleasure or pain, an ideal which makes a life of satisfaction marred by a single pang an offence and a horror to his soul. If our demand for rationality is less acute and the miscellaneous affirmations of the will carry us along with a well-fed indifference to some single tragedy within us, we may aver that a single pang is only the

thousandth part of a thousand pleasures and that a life so balanced is nine hundred and ninety-nine times better than nothing. This judgement, for all its air of mathematical calculation, in truth expresses a choice as irrational as Petrarch's. It merely means that, as a matter of fact, the mixed prospect presented to us attracts our wills and attracts them vehemently. So that the only possible criterion for the relative values of pains and pleasures is the will that chooses among them or among combinations of them; nor can the intensity of pleasures and pains, apart from the physical violence of their expression, be judged by any other standard than by the power they have, when represented, to control the will's movement. (LRI, pp. 238–9)

How satisfactory, taken as a whole, is this account of reason?
1 One might object, first, that Santayana's apparent supposition that a conceived impulse is necessarily to some degree participated in, so that 'to understand is more than to forgive, it is to adopt' (LRI, p. 259) is either erroneous or quite unproven. Certainly, on the face of it, I can be clearly conscious of your aims and remain wholly unsympathetic therewith.

Santayana might reply that I can certainly be conscious of your aims as behavioural tendencies without such sympathy, but that I can only really bring home to myself their expression in consciousness by seeing things for the moment in the same moral colours as you do, and that if this has its usual physical basis it must include a factor tending, however feebly, to forward the same objectives. This does not apply, he would need to add, if my acknowledgement of the facts about your consciousness is merely verbal, but only when I really bring home to myself the nature of the facts.

It must be allowed that Santayana does not deal with this important matter at all adequately, though he may well be right in the main point, perhaps for reasons which do not fit in too well with his later views. It may be, for instance, that the very notion of believing in the existence of something implies the treatment of its representation as one would the corresponding reality, and that in the case of a desire this means treating it as I would a desire which I *feel* and do not merely imagine.[22] Santayana could not accept this, however, since the contrast it implies between acquaintance with representations and with the represented is inconsistent with his analysis of consciousness. Perhaps we may add the following reflection. If it can be established, in whatever way, that I cannot really take in the fact that another man has certain desires without seeing their satisfaction as a *prima facie* good, it is not only the opposition between egoism and altruism, but that between the *is* and the *ought*, which will take on a new aspect. One could still rightly insist that no factual statement entails an ethical one, but one would have to admit that one could not genuinely acknowledge the existence of certain facts without adopting certain values. (This should not be confused with the bizarre doctrine that the judgement that an individual is conscious or sentient does not express a factual belief but a moral decision to treat it in a certain way.)

2 If reason strives to harmonize all represented impulses, it might seem that the impulses of the dead, as also recollected impulses of my own which would never naturally arise again, would be on a par for it with those of the living, and of my living self. Yet one must doubt whether Santayana would really describe as reasonable the attempt to achieve a goal which would satisfy no living person. [23] Even if he argued that they have become living interests once more by their re-enactment in my mind one may still ask whether the complex goal of reason could include objectives which would exist only after interest in them had ceased, as say in a social order more adorable in prospect than in achievement.

This is a case where the ambiguity we noted previously as to reason's ideal becomes important. Is the harmony it seeks a harmony of satisfied impulse or a harmony of the goods envisaged by those who feel those impulses? As ethical relativist Santayana could acknowledge the possibility of taking either as an end, but it remains unclear which he regards as the end of reason. I find it hard not to believe that the first represents his deeper intention, but he certainly often thinks rather in terms of the second.

3 It is often thought that any theory for which moral judgement belongs to the volitional or affective side of our nature must accept Hume's view that only means, as opposed to ends, can be rational or irrational (in a pejorative sense). Santayana avoids this by describing ends as rational which belong to, or constitute, a harmony between the individual's various ends in the manner described. Although he does not do so explicitly, he might have recommended his theory as a means of avoiding Hume's rather shocking claim that ' 'Tis not contrary to reason to prefer the destruction of the whole world to the scratching of my finger'.

This, it may appear on reflection, is a mere verbal trick depending on a special definition of *reason* which leaves Hume's essential point standing.

In fact I think this objection unfounded. If the usual use of 'reason' in relation to practice is as Santayana describes it, then it is Hume who is misleading in suggesting that there is no sense in describing ends as rational or otherwise.

But is this the usual use of reason, and is Santayana concerned to claim that this is so? Surely the truth is that reason is a somewhat vague word, sometimes bearing or at least including much the sense Santayana gives it (as when we call a thoroughly disorganized life an irrational one, however well judged the means adopted for each momentary purpose may be) but often confined to a sense more like Hume's. What then is the real nature of Santayana's claim?

It rather looks as though Santayana, however he saw it himself, is giving what C. L. Stevenson has called a 'persuasive definition', that by giving his own definition of a word normally vague and fluctuating in descriptive content, but constant in favourable emotive force, he is inducing us to share his own favourable attitude to what he has made it label.

This is a tempting interpretation of Santayana's strategy, but I think it is only an approximation to the truth. Santayana, after all, is at pains not to coax us into treating a high valuation of reason as inevitable. We would do better, I think, to say that he has selected one among the various possible ways of giving precision to a somewhat vague word, because it then specifies, especially in the phrase 'the life of reason', one of the great guiding ideals which men have from time to time set before them, and which, because it is dear to Santayana himself, he seeks to become clearer about, but that he is not using his definition as a device for recommending reason to those not already attracted by it. This usage (he should have pointed out) is not compulsory, yet it is important to be aware of it, since otherwise one will be mistaken as to what it is that those who recommend a life of reason are recommending, and may wrongly suppose that those who talk of ends as being rational or otherwise are talking nonsense. Taken in this way, I find Santayana's position largely acceptable and of some importance as showing that we need not mean by a rational man merely one who knows how to bring things about.

4 Santayana's account of reason seems, at most, an account of practical reason, and it may seem odd that he does not make this clear. Would not Santayana himself want to say, in contrast to Hume, that a man could be intellectually rational, and even be guided in practice by this intellectual sort of reason, while living according to pre-rational or post-rational ideals such as do not bring all sides of his life into a co-operative harmony?

Santayana's failure to distinguish between practical and cognitive reason (a better term, I think, for the set of skills requisite for the enlargement of knowledge than theoretical or speculative reason) is quite easily explained by his tendency, especially in *The Life of Reason*, to treat knowledge and the skills which enlarge it as too intimately bound up with reason, as he describes it, to require a separate mention. An impulse, after all, which does not bring some conception of its goal and of the means thereto is either impossible, or below the level of those which reason seeks to organize, while this organizing power is itself conceived as operating upon and by means of representations of impulses and of the world in which they will or will not gain satisfaction, and thus as containing the quest for knowledge within its very essence (a point on which I have not dwelt before as I thought it required independent treatment). Even in his later writings, Santayana treats science as mainly a form of useful know-how, and though he honours the pure visions of truth, possibility, and dialectical relationships, he is inclined only to call them knowledge insofar as they enlighten practice. Practice, indeed, is not always very rational in Santayana's sense, but he would seem to think of the organization of cognition as being susceptible only of minimal development when impulse itself is disorganized. From Santayana's point of view, then, it would be very artificial to divide reason into two branches, the practical and the cognitive, since he thinks of the reason I call cognitive as essentially an aspect of the organization of impulse.

There is certainly something in this, but I cannot think it satisfactory altogether to by-pass the notion of a pure cognitive reason. There are, in any case, hints of a rather different and more satisfactory way of regarding the relations between reason as applied to facts and reason as applied to values, for which the first is the effective urge to attain a coherent and abiding system of beliefs, and the second the urge to attain a coherent and abiding system of values, so that while its raw material is different in either case, its treatment thereof is similar.[24]

This fits in with the epistemology of *Scepticism and Animal Faith* better than may at first appear. Santayana would have no truck, of course, with a coherence theory of *truth*, nor would he locate the genesis of knowledge in some ethereal striving towards some conceptual structure immanent within it. One believes because one cannot help believing, and one's beliefs concern a world of independent substances, including oneself as that substance in whose buffets from the rest they recognize their cause. Yet if one asks what, on his theory, constitutes the rationality or irrationality of a sincerely held belief as opposed to its truth or genesis, it would seem to be its coherence or otherwise with the body of beliefs to which I am non-rationally prompted, just as the rationality of an ideal turns on its harmonizability with other initially non-rational ideals. In the latter case, however, the raw material is arrived at in a more *a priori* manner since the moralist arrives at his initial ideals (just as he does at the abstract ideal of reason itself) by consulting his own heart, that is by a process whereby he brings to consciousness the ideals implied by his own perhaps deeply buried impulses, impulses which Santayana has a strong tendency to think of as innate. It is in this connection that he talks of self-knowledge as the end of moral thought.[25]

It is natural to conclude that reason in general is the effective urge for a coherent and abiding system of beliefs and ideals together, and this would largely fit in with Santayana's position. Yet we must be careful how we understand this suggestion. The rational man modifies his beliefs in the light of other beliefs, and his ideals in the light of other ideals. Does he modify his beliefs in the light of his ideals? Santayana certainly condemns any such disrespect for truth and would never call it rational. Does he modify his ideals in the light of his beliefs? This is a more difficult question. Santayana often condemns this as a betrayal of the ideal, yet clearly he would think it irrational to continue an impossible ideal's pursuit. The idealizing reason, so one might put his thought, will retain a spiritual allegiance to the ideal impossibility, but the practical reason will work for humbler ends.

In any case, something along these lines seems the essentially right account of the matter and incorporates what is of value in Santayana's more 'official' definition of reason. The rational is essentially the coherent – at least no alternative definition seems to specify any concept of much significance. Many questions remain concerning the various factors involved in coherence (for coherence is something more than mere logical compatibility) about which Santayana has little to say, but one may still agree that he is pointing in the right direction.

Such must suffice as an account of Santayana's ethical theory, though it is impossible within one chapter to do justice to its various strengths and weaknesses. Its weakest point, I think, lies in the minimal attention given to the more peculiarly moral concepts, such as duty, and what goes with this, its excessive individualism. Though he sometimes discusses such things, he hardly does justice to the social nature of moral concepts, and sometimes gives the impression of holding that a man's values are determined almost entirely by the innate needs of his psyche.

As Santayana uses 'moral', tigers may be presumed to see things in a moral light as much as men do, for any situation is conceived morally in his sense if it presents itself as intrinsically desirable or undesirable. Such language blurs distinctions of importance which are not re-established by the admission that tigers do not aspire to live the life of reason. Tigers lack morality because they do not assess their behaviour by rules which represent the pressure of a social group upon the individual, and the same might be true of one whose life was rational in Santayana's sense. It is arguable that behaviour directed by rational foresight of goods to be achieved and evils to be avoided is an advance upon that determined by socially inculcated principles, but one hardly has a morality in the usual sense without the latter, [26] and even the notion of goods and evils tends to lose its usual sense when their felt values owe nothing to, or at least when they stand in opposition to, socially inculcated mores.

Yet Santayana's insistence that one envisages things *sub specie boni* or *mali* whenever one is attracted or disattracted by them serves to remind us of something too often forgotten by moralists, namely that when moral terms are used sincerely they point to an immediately felt value in envisaged situations which is equally present when these are such as the social nature of language makes it hard for us to describe as good or evil, as (for example) when they are such as satisfy or frustrate impulses which are frankly vindictive. Though I do not normally describe something as a good or evil unless its magnetic or repellent quality is such as social norms countenance, yet social norms themselves are only effective insofar as their prescriptions forward and prevent things whose positive or negative value is just such a real felt presence as Santayana means by the given essences of *good* and *evil*. As such they must compete with other immediate attractions and re-pellencies which we refrain from calling goods or evils only in virtue of a social pressure productive of an unhealthy split in consciousness. Perhaps it is more honest, and in the end more favourable to all commonly acknowledged values, frankly to call good whatever has this special brightness for our consciousness, sacrificing its attainment, if we can be brought to see its consequences as in the end more dark than bright, without the attempt to exorcise its magnetism by denying it the title 'good'. Such is at least one important lesson we can learn from Santayana.

XI

Spiritual Life

A life of reason, we have seen, would be a life in which the satisfaction of every impulse in our being is treated as a good to be cherished if possible, and in which life is organized so as to satisfy as many of these impulses as possible, in a harmonious manner such as allows them to promote each other's values rather than be in competition. Such a life may impose sacrifices but no pursuit is sacrificed as being for something bad in itself; only as being for something incompatible with a greater body of good.

Attempts to chart the character of a life of reason constitute contributions to rational ethics, and Santayana regards Plato and Aristotle as still the masters here. His own *Life of Reason* approximates to an essay on rational ethics, but cannot really be described as such, even in intention, since it is too lacking in concrete recommendation. Its function is rather to chart the progress which has so far at times been made to a rational morality, that is to a form of life such as might be recommended in a rational ethics. This is a subject we are not pursuing here, but we may note once more that for Santayana there is no one type of rational morality. Alternative and incompatible modes of life might each obtain a high degree of rationality.

In later years Santayana seems to have taken a dimmer view of the possibility of a rational morality ever arising, the two world wars greatly contributing to his pessimism in this regard.[1] His attention thus turned more and more to the solace to be provided for the individual in an irrational world by the development of an inward spiritual life.

This was indeed a kind of development which had to some extent been deprecated in advance in *The Life of Reason*. He there distinguished three types of morality (the second, however, only existing as an ethics, that is, in idea); pre-rational, rational and post-rational.[2] Pre-rational morality is a moral system based on various distinct principles, each presenting a response to some recurrent type of situation, but without forming a well-integrated whole; rational ethics we have already characterized; and post-rational morality is any way of life based on the sacrifice of all other impulses to some single aspiration towards a distinct form of good. Whether any society, except one in distintegration, has had a morality which answers to what Santayana calls the pre-rational type may be doubtful, but perhaps the system of ethics established in the work of such a philosopher as W. D. Ross with its loosely knit group of *prima facie* duties is somewhat of this type. As regards post-rational ethics Epicureanism, Stoicism and some forms of Christianity – the systems which exhibit what Gilbert Murray described as the great failure of nerve[3] – are examples given by Santayana himself. Clearly a complete commitment to what Santayana calls the spiritual life would be the adoption of a post-rational morality. On the whole it would seem that a spiritual, as opposed to a rational, life is regarded by Santayana as more within the power of the individual to realize even in an unfavourable society, but the actual definition of these concepts does not seem of itself to imply that a rational morality is something present in a society and a spiritual life something resident in the individual.

Some commentators on Santayana have seen his own turning from the rational to the spiritual life as a personal 'failure of nerve'.[4] Regarding this we may point out first that it was a return, perhaps at a higher level, to the more meditative outlook of his early poetry and philosophy from which, as I am inclined to think, *The Life of Reason* was a somewhat forced departure, and second that a certain failure of nerve may be a quite proper response on the part of a man with a rich vision of the good to the world in its actual constitution. In any case, there will always be those who, like Santayana, find the existent world largely uncongenial and for whom life can be a good only to the extent that they cultivate a contemplative spirit.

It must be borne in mind, in any case, that Santayana entirely foreswore all moral dogmatism, and was simply exploring that form of the good for which his own personality and opportunities suited him and setting it before those similarly placed.[5]

Actually, contrast between the life of reason and the spiritual life, as Santayana describes them, is far from clear cut, partly through a genuine complexity in his viewpoint, partly from a tendency to vary the meanings attached to these expressions.

The spiritual life, as conceived by Santayana, is one dedicated to pure intuition, but a certain ambiguity in this phrase infects the former.[6] Pure intuition can mean the trance-like state of the sceptic who merely lets ideas and impressions float through his mind without their symbolizing for him any beyond at all. On the whole it does not seem that the man whom Santayana calls spiritual is really supposed to be in this state, though his language sometimes suggests this. This use of 'pure intuition' is the one which figures in Santayana's epistemological discussions, where pure intuition is depicted as the state to which one who would believe nothing he could conceivably doubt would eventually be reduced. When he discusses questions of value it would seem that by 'pure intuition' he means rather a state of mind in which, though a perfectly adequate sense of surrounding existences is retained, these existences are valued for the essences they present or suggest to the distinterested imagination, which delights in the forms of things actual or possible, and not for the satisfactions or hindrances they promise to the restless willing of personal advantage and animal satisfaction.

But even granted that the spiritual life is one in which pure intuition, in this latter sense, provides the dominating interest, a certain ambiguity remains. For sometimes Santayana seems to think that a man is spiritual, lives the life of spirit, to the extent that he has any real sense of values at all, but at other times that the spiritual life is a special vocation alternative to other lives which may be as good in their own way as it is. In the former sense the spiritual life is implicated in the life of reason, in the latter it is an alternative to it.

I think we may explain the source of this ambivalence thus. Any state in which spirit finds itself is, for Santayana, describable as the intuition of a certain essence. Thus anyone who has a clearly envisaged goal, or who has any conscious sense of his achievement, intuits an essence such as constitutes a form of the good. Now there are irrational people who are so dominated by mere will that they never bring to any vivid realization either what they seek or what they have attained. Lives such as this are poor by any standard with which we can expect Santayana (or ourselves) to sympathize. Everything is pursued by them for the sake of notional goods beyond, which never come to any genuine conscious life. No life of reason could take this form, for in such life no impulse would ever receive real satisfaction, for it is evident that the impulses organized by reason are those which have some manifestation in the realm of spirit (i.e. in consciousness). When reason operates it does so because it, or its equivalent in the realm of spirit, conceives the goods for which the various impulses of our being are striving, and it rejoices with their fulfilment. The spiritual life in this sense is any life lived with any vividness, and the life of reason, unless it itself takes on a rather debased meaning (as perhaps it occasionally tends to do in Santayana's later writing) is bound to be at least one form of the spiritual life in this sense.

But a life of reason is essentially an 'engaged' and active life, and it is one which risks real setbacks and disappointments, one which does what it can to realize the good, but risks sufferings which it can do little within its own terms to assuage. The spiritual life, as Santayana at other times conceives it, is one which offers a release from a world full of risk and failure. Its eyes are turned on the forms of things actual and possible for their own sake, forms which could not be other than they are. It should be noted that Santayana sometimes indicates that it is not all forms which receive the indiscriminate attention of the spiritual mind, but those forms which appeal to it as good or beautiful. The other forms, of evil and disaster, have being as much as these, but the spirit has no call to turn to them. At other times, however, it is implied that all forms offer an equally suitable theme for a meditation which delights to take in form for its own sake, and to study their intrinsic relations to each other so far as it has power. (Presumably we must resolve certain difficulties here by saying that the essences *under the aspect of which* the forms are then intuited do not include the forms of good or evil, but rather the aspect of 'something of interest for its own sake'.) The spiritual life, in this sense, is the life of 'pure intelligence' in a certain sense of the expression (covering not only the insight into logical connections but also the 'taking in' of forms aesthetically, whether the forms of historical events, of visible phenomena, or whatever), the life of Aristotle's God, to whom Santayana refers in this connection.[7] The spiritual man will probably be especially interested in those aspects of the *existent* world which he understands because their character provides a steadier and richer object for contemplation than the vagaries of fantasy, but where the facts suggest, without exemplifying, a form especially rewarding for exploration, his attention may well centre on that.

I have used the word 'exploration' to suggest again that I do not think Santayana really means by 'pure intuition' in this connection, a blank and helpless attention to whatever thrusts itself forward. On the other hand he certainly does imply by the term that the state of mind in question is one in which one brings to vivid attention at each moment some aspect of one's subject matter, and consciousness is more than that vague buzz accompanying preparations for action, speech, etc. such as is even a fair amount of so-called intellectual activity.

We have seen that the spiritual life is sometimes so understood as to be an essential aspect of the life of reason but sometimes rather as an alternative to it. But even in the latter more restricted sense Santayana does not really intend to exhibit them as rivals, for, when he is taking the spiritual life thus he describes it as satisfying a particular human impulse which, for reason, has its claim as much as, if not more than, other impulses. The rational statesman for example, who wishes to promote the life of reason in society at large will have no wish to hinder contemplative activity as such, but he will regard it as only one human need which should not be allowed satisfaction at the expense of others.[8] But here again the flexibility of these key terms tends to produce at least an appearance of inconsistency, for looking at spiritual life as present in any real satisfaction, or even conscious sense of value, Santayana is inclined at times to speak as though the encouragement of spirituality were the sole ultimate justification of society.

Santayana's overall position, however, is fairly clear. The satisfaction of any vision of the good, and even perhaps the conscious discrimination of something as good, should, ideally, have its place within the ideal pursued by reason, whose good is precisely a harmony of all such satisfactions and aspirations. All such satisfactions and aspirations are in one sense spiritual, but a certain class of them, the more contemplative ones, are marked off as spiritual in a more limited sense, and these have no essential rights, from reason's point of view, beyond those of the others, except what springs from their especial readiness to be harmonized with other impulses. For the contemplative man, on the other hand, the good of contemplation may seem better than a harmony in which it is only one element. The question whether he is right or not has no real answer, unless taken as a question as to whether some individual has worked out a system of values with which he himself will really be able to rest content.

I may seem to have implied just now that the spiritual man (in the restricted sense) sees contemplation as the highest good, and one may ask 'His contemplation or that of others?' But Santayana would say that the good for the spiritual man is not his or anyone else's meditation but that upon which he meditates. He is drawn to meditate upon these essences not because he sets his meditation before him as a goal but because they continually solicit his delighted attention. Thus his valuation does not really represent a view as to how life should be lived or organized at all, but a state of delight in the forms of things which sustains itself, possibly at the expense of other proclivities. Once he asks himself how the value of his or another's meditation upon this theme compare with each other and with other states of existence as proper goals of endeavour, he has ceased to be spiritual and must adopt the point of view of the life of reason or of some pre-rational or post-rational ethic. If this is Santayana's view, and though he does not make it very explicit it seems to be what he intends, he should not have described, as he sometimes does, the spiritual life as a form of post-rational morality. It is not really an ethical view at all, but a state of mind which may be valued ethically. In general, I think Santayana is rather unclear as to the relation between the good found in objects of contemplation and goodness as a characteristic of certain states of existence including the contemplation of the good in the former sense. Both goods solicit, but the one as a magnet for attention, the other as a goal for action.

Just as we sketched the abstract form of a life of reason as Santayana sees it, without going into his detailed application of the concept as an instrument for evaluating various forms of life, so we must remain content with this abstract sketch of the life of spirit, without pursuing Santayana in that description of its more concrete character, and of the difficulties which especially beset its emergence, which forms the bulk of *The Realm of Spirit* as of the earlier *Platonism and the Spiritual Life*. But the distinction at which we have arrived between spirituality and the pursuit of spirituality seems to cast some light upon one question which troubles those pages from time to time, the question namely whether the spiritual life is 'selfish'. Certainly the pursuit of one's own spirituality is a selfish pursuit so far as it goes, though not necessarily therefore reprehensible, while a wish to promote spirituality generally is so far unselfish, though not necessarily therefore good. On the other hand the delight in forms of the good and the spontaneous turning of attention in the direction of whatever appeals to such delight, is not selfish, for it is not an action with a goal at all.

Santayana virtually offers this answer himself at times,[9] but he also gives another answer of rather doubtful value. In giving this answer he thinks of the spiritual life as that lived by one who deliberately adopts a spiritual attitude, thus treating existence as a means to satisfying his own delight in form. Clearly Santayana has sympathy with such a stance, and he is inclined to justify it by an appeal to his version of epiphenomenalism, the doctrine that spirit is not a cause but only an effect, the flower but not the root of existence. Thus he says that since spirit is impotent, can make no alteration in the flux of events, it can absolve itself from guilt and perhaps from active concern about them, and give itself to the one thing it can do, which is contemplate both what is and what is not.[10]

There is something rather specious about this argument, for on his own doctrine it is not really spirit which chooses but the pysche (an entity – it may be recalled – which Santayana explains along lines which we can briefly sum up by saying that it is a logical construction from the behavioural tendencies of the organism) and this not in certain cases but in all. The question, therefore, how far to be active and how far to be contemplative, is a question directed at the psyche, and the psyche certainly is not impotent. Perhaps there was a tendency as years went on for Santayana to pass from an epiphenomenalism which has no implications regarding the impotence of man in face of his fate, to a certain fatalism about the course of events and the relative impotence of *decisions* to affect what is determined far more deeply. The later opinion may or may not be correct (it is anyway a matter of degree) and if it is, it may even suggest, as Santayana sometimes likes it to do, that it is the better part to accept what comes and to enjoy the conceiving of it, than to kick against the pricks – but it is certainly not implied by epiphenomenalism, which has no implication as to the degree to which deliberate decision making is a factor in modifying the world (since on Santayana's view decision making has both its psychic and its spiritual aspect and in its former is certainly not impotent). Thus, we must dismiss the appeal to the impotence of spirit as a case of special pleading on behalf of the pursuit of spirituality.

Yet there is a residual point which perhaps has a certain force. The recognition that spirit is impotent, if it is, may at first dismay us and we may be inclined to dismiss spirit as a useless excrescence or secretion which the organism might as well be without.[11] Yet on further thought we may agree with Santayana that in point of fact we cannot seriously attach value to the existence of the organism except insofar as its fate either produces certain forms of spirit or provides spirit with an object of contemplation. Having got so far, we will see that all that matters in existence in the end is the form of spirit which it evokes, and this is to agree that spirituality in the broader sense is the only ultimate end we should really set ourselves, and that in the narrower sense it represents a main component of such an end. This is not a deductive argument in favour of an ethical conclusion, but it is a manner in which the ontological doctrine of epiphenomenalism may serve to prompt a clarification of our sense of values. This is the better part of Santayana's obvious affection for epiphenomenalism and dislike of the pragmatist view which so insists on the instrumental value of consciousness, that we are perhaps led to think that this is its only value. Obviously this lends no support to the truth of epiphenomenalism. Properly thought through it establishes the ethical irrelevance of the question whether consciousness or only its physical basis has effects.

The issue whether the pursuit of one's own spirituality is selfish in a bad sense is a real one, and clearly one which was personally important for Santayana. It is not my task to pass judgement on his life, though, without calling him 'a saint of the imagination',[12] I do not think his shade need fear judgement whether this is based on its fruits or its intrinsic charm. Nor should we take his philosophy as intended to vindicate his own sort of retired life, for while he doubtless defended this he was far from claiming it to be a model either of rationality or spirituality.

It is evident, I think, that spirituality does not function for Santayana as the expression of any single abstract conception definable by sufficient and necessary conditions. It is in the end a term which as much acquires its meaning (as some have said that all terms do) by the things to which it is applied as it has a prior meaning determining its application. Thus we cannot pretend to have offered any complete elucidation of it here. But there is one more point we shall make upon the subject.

If we look once more at the notion of spirituality, clearly distinguishing this from any selfish wish to feed one's own spirit with delight, we may note that the main characteristic of it as a type of life is its spontaneity, for its basic character is the spontaneous delight in whatever hints at some form of the good or the beautiful. This is, in fact, a feature of spirituality much emphasized by Santayana, as when he talks of the spirituality typical of childhood in its better moments, and of the greater spirituality found in many a sinner than in the puritan. If one does not realize the importance of this in Santayana's notion of spirituality, and thinks of it rather as the aesthete's quest for self-delight, one will be more perplexed than one need be as to how he can see Christ as the great example of, and delighter in, spirituality. Santayana sees him as (among other things) the highest type of the spontaneous lover of the good in all its various forms.

> It is indeed one of the beauties in the idea of Christ that in spite of his absolute holiness, or because of it, he shows a spontaneous sympathy, shocking to the Pharisee, with many non-religious sides of life, with little children, with birds and flowers, with common people, with beggars, with sinners, with sufferers of all sorts, even with devils. This is one of the proofs that natural spirit, not indoctrinated or canalised, was speaking in him. Wherever it peeped, however rudimentary or hidden or contorted it might be, he recognised it, and wished to liberate and draw it out, as far as it would come. Was it not the fate hanging over these poor beginnings or sad frustrations of life that saddened him and carried him first to the desert and at last to the cross? Spirit was everywhere so smothered and tormented that nothing short of death to this world could save it. It could be saved if it saw that in Christ, with his voluntary Incarnation and Passion, it had its saviour and exemplar. However brief or troubled its career might be, it would be justified if ever the same light touched it that shone in Christ. This was the light of ideal union with God, and all else was vanity. (ICG, pp. 251-2)

Death to this world is understood by Santayana as symbolizing a submissive acceptance of the frustrations that must always in the end meet one's animal will to live, and a readiness to adore as eternal ideas whatever forms of the good come to mind when, checking mere animal urgency, one asks oneself what would really satisfy the heart's yearning. If one's hopes are all based upon the lasting *exemplification* of some form one will never have peace, but if one loves the form one envisages simply as form then one's affections are set on something eternal. Although traditional other worldly religions do not explicitly set themselves such an aim, their effect is, where they really enrich life, to set forms of the good before the imagination which are loved for their own sake, and not as mere forces at work in the world.

Christian charity Santayana sees as essentially one with Christian spirituality, for the spiritual mind sees in each inadequate human person a suggestion of some form of the good such as he would reach if not hindered by a cruel world, and this inspires love and pity. It is evident that such spirituality is taken as including the love of spirituality as it appears in any person. Santayana also evokes in this connection the more Indian notion of spirit recognizing essentially the same essence of spirit as present in all its instances, and as therefore moving beyond the ordinary selfishness of the psyche.

The further pursuit of these themes would demand a thorough study of Santayana's philosophy of religion such as we are deliberately not undertaking here. So much must therefore suffice as a hint of the way in which Santayana's ontology branches out into a general vision of human life and good. Our business has been with the more abstract features of Santayana's viewpoint, and that business is now almost at a close.

XII

Concluding Remarks

Our survey of Santayana's philosophy is at an end. We have studied in some detail the main features of his mature epistemology and ontology, and of his moral philosophy in its more abstract aspects. Others, of course, will find many riches in Santayana's treatment of these topics such as are unexploited here, especially as Santayana's prose, in spite of its apparent lushness, is mostly a highly concentrated means of communication. There are, in any case, aspects of Santayana's philosophy which we have largely or entirely ignored: his treatment of religion; his aesthetics; his political philosophy.

If the reader doubted it before, it is to be hoped that he will now agree that Santayana is an important philosopher whose work is of continuing significance. Its range is wide but six themes may be mentioned again as of especial interest.

1 Santayana's treatment of scepticism, and of what would now be called reductionism, carries a message which philosophers have still not learnt. The urge persists to explain certain classes of common sense objects away on the grounds that only as thus explained can they be objects of knowledge. Certainly the victims and the style of murder alter but the homicidal motivation remains, directing itself now mainly at so-called private experiences. If the view that knowledge must have foundations of some ultimate sort is a largely abandoned dogma, it is more because ultimate epistemological issues are shirked than because any radical alternative such as Santayana offers has been found. Some see an alternative in a generalization of the hypothetico-deductive method, but this will hardly do, for the most basic beliefs of common sense can only be tested by those who assume their truth. Santayana's demonstration that there is no satisfactory half-way house between a trusting animal faith and a solipsism of the present moment may still serve wonderfully to clear the air in these sophisticated days.

2 With his strong sense for the wonder of the immediate, Santayana, in his doctrine of essence, draws our attention to an aspect of reality of great spiritual significance. Naturally he is not alone among philosophers in this, but he is particularly successful in disengaging this recognition of the immediately given from the notion of raw uninterpreted data which provide the foundations of knowledge. The given is significant for providing existence at its richest with a worthy end, not for providing knowledge at its poorest with a possible beginning.

3 More generally Santayana's attempt to chart the relations between his four realms of being, and his characterization of each realm, is a major contribution to the seemingly abstruse, but in truth widely relevant, discipline of ontology. The relations of particular to universal, the contrast between internal and external relations, the status of past and future, the relation of things in themselves to phenomena, and the 'inner' nature of the former, are matters of abiding interest arising in ever fresh connections as human knowledge advances. Taken all in all, Santayana's attack upon these problems (though he would hardly have expressed it thus) is one of the most sustained and serious undertaken in this century and, in English, Whitehead's is the only comparable contribution. Santayana suffers by comparison as regards his comparative ignorance of modern science and in his reluctance to become involved in logical technicalities, but in general level-headedness he has no mean advantage.

4 Santayana's type of materialism and, in particular, his epiphenomenalism, are of special interest at the present day, when the progress of psychology, neuro-physiology, and artificial intelligence research seems to point ever more steadily to a mechanistic view of man. In his treatment of mind and body he is certainly grappling with issues to which he finds no complete solution, for the manner in which spirit emerges from and expresses the activities of the psyche remains in great part mysterious on his account; nonetheless it seems to me that if man is at one level explicable mechanistically then some sort of epiphenomenalism must be true, and that Santayana's attempts to make sense of the theory are peculiarly instructive. Certainly his position is worthy of greater respect than that of a so-called identity theory which simply seeks to purge us of any conception of what it is which really matters about human beings.

5 Santayana's elaborate examination of spirituality as a human ideal is perhaps unique in being that of a convinced materialist. As such, it may repel both materialists and spiritualists (to use that word in its better sense) of the more bigoted kind but it is, surely, an enterprise of some significance. Almost all who have celebrated what Santayana calls spirituality have associated it with a conception of reality increasingly difficult to sustain in a scientific age, while materialists tend to

be dead to its values. Here again Santayana seems to me a significant thinker for the present time.

6   Finally I would note Santayana's particular type of ethical relativism as being especially worthy of attention. That his ethical theory is inadequate in some important respects I have endeavoured to show; nonetheless his central relativistic insight is peculiarly compelling. There is, of course, nothing original in the mere assertion that values are relative. Where Santayana's treatment of this topic is so pregnant is in his sense of the almost palpable reality for different people of opposing value qualities, and of the way in which our grasp of this may be expected to affect our attitude to one another's projects.

Santayana certainly has his defects as a thinker. There is a failure to enter into detail on many matters which one would think essential to the establishment or clarification of his position, he is content with arriving at a general idea as to where the truth lies without trying to pin things down more precisely, and there is a tendency to make general statements about a class of objects which only apply to the subclass which mainly engages his interest (as often with essences). We may note also that he is usually at his weakest on such occasions as he makes comments about the nature of language, and his theory of thought, though he has insights which should find a place in any adequate treatment, is somewhat crude.

There is little point, however, in dwelling on the weaker aspects of a philosopher's thought unless either he has become influential in precisely these respects or they invalidate his work as a whole. Neither is true of Santayana's defects, which are indeed the reverse side of excellencies peculiarly lacking in the present philosophical scene, namely a breadth of vision, a directness in coming to the heart of the matter under discussion, and a style of philosophizing which is a unique blend of analytic pithiness and poetic vision. Above all, Santayana's philosophy is to be recommended for the manner in which it combines into a working and coherent whole the contrasting insights of so many schools of thought usually conceived as standing in blank opposition one to another.

Notes

I Introduction

1 Santayana commented on his own style that it hid the fact that at heart he was 'a Scholastic' in his principles, though not in his ways, but he adds that if he had written more austerely his books 'would have been much more solid, and nobody would have read them' (PGS, p. 604). However, when one considers the contribution which the barbarity of their style seems to have made to the growth of commentaries on some philosophers, one wonders whether a more forbidding and less attractive presentation of his thoughts might not have stood Santayana in good stead, had he wanted to be a subject of academic study. Perhaps one role of the present book is to show that Santayana's ideas do not have to be presented beautifully.

2 The only aspect of his philosophy almost totally ignored in this book will be his political philosophy. My main concern is with his epistemology and ontology.

3 *Physical Order and Moral Liberty* (POML), ed. J. and S. Lachs (Vanderbilt University Press, 1969).

4 As is suggested by J. Passmore in *A Hundred Years of British Philosophy* (Duckworth, London, 1957). It seems a pity that Santayana represents one of the few cases where the author of that peculiarly unpartisan history appears to denigrate one of the authors whose positions he summarizes.

5 I am thinking particularly of the work of W. V. O. Quine.

6 As witnessed by the following publications:
George Santayana's America. Essays on Literature and Culture, ed. J. Ballowe (University of Illinois Press, 1967); *The Genteel Tradition. Nine Essays by George Santayana*, ed. Douglas L. Wilson (Harvard University Press, Cambridge, Mass., 1967); *Santayana on America*, ed. R. C. Lyon (Brace & World, New York, 1968).

7 In PGS, Russell exhibits an admiration for Santayana's philosophy which seems sincere, but he virtually omitted reference to his work in his *History*

of Western Philosophy (Allen & Unwin, London, 1945) and is said to have justified this in conversation by saying that Santayana's philosophy was too largely derivative from Leibniz, a curious opinion.

8 Cf. Russell – *Our Knowledge of the External World* (first published 1914. Allen & Unwin, 1922); *Mysticism and Logic* (Allen & Unwin, 1917).

9 I have seen it stated that Whitehead remarked that Santayana was the philosopher of his time most likely to be read in the future. Whitehead's *Process and Reality* (Cambridge University Press, 1929) refers quite often to *Scepticism and Animal Faith*. There is really quite a lot in common between their two philosophies, and where the difference might sometimes seem greatest they sometimes turn on different uses of words, as, for instance, of 'substance'. However, Whitehead's world is far too animistic and uplifting for Santayana. Comparisons between them are made at several points in the present book.

10 'My own philosophy, I venture to think, is well-knit in the same sense, in spite of perhaps seeming eclectic and of leaving so many doors open both in physics and in morals. My eclecticism is not helplessness before sundry influences; it is detachment and firmness in taking each thing simply for what it is. Openness, too, is a form of architecture' (RB, p. xviii).

11 Cf. note 7.

12 For an excellent discussion of Santayana's relation to various historical philosophers see 'Santayana's Philosophical Inheritance' by Celestine J. Sullivan Jnr in PGS.

13 All the books in the above list, and in that which immediately follows, were first published in the USA by Charles Scribner's Sons, New York, with the following exceptions:
Lotze's System of Philosophy, George Santayana ed. P. G. Kuntz, Indiana University Press, 1971 (as the editor says in his valuable introduction this doctoral dissertation shows Santayana dwelling on themes which otherwise only became conspicuous in the mature ontology and which are left in the background in the period of *The Life of Reason*); *Sonnets and Other Verses*, George Santayana, G. S. Stone and Kimball, Cambridge and Chicago 1894; *Lucifer; A Theological Tragedy*, George Santayana, Herbert S. Stone, Chicago and New York, 1899; *Three Philosophical Poets: Lucretius, Dante and Goethe*, George Santayana, Harvard University Press, Cambridge, Mass., 1910; *The Philosophy of George Santayana*, P. A. Schilpp (ed.), Tudor Publishing Company, New York, 1940 and 1951 (this work contains a thorough bibliography of Santayana's writings); *The Idler and His Works*, George Santayana, ed. Daniel Cory, Braziller, New York, 1957; *Animal Faith and Spiritual Life (Essays by and on George Santayana)*, John Lachs (ed.), Appleton-Century-Crofts, New York, 1967; *George Santayana: The Birth of Reason and Other Essays*, Daniel Cory (ed.), Columbia University Press, New York, 1968; *George Santayana–Physical Order and Moral Liberty*, John and Shirley Lachs (eds), Vanderbilt University Press, New York, 1969.

14 Cf. MS., pp. 156–7.

15 See Chapter IV, no. 8, of the present book.

16 Cf. note 38 below.

17 The mutual reactions of the Harvard intellectuals and Santayana are described very well by Jacques Duron in *La Pensée de George Santayana: Santayana en Amérique* (Nizet, Paris, 1950). See also R. C. Lyon's introduction to his collection *Santayana on America*, especially pp. xxiii–xxiv and Chapter I of *George Santayana* by George Howgate (University of Pennsylvania Press, Philadelphia, 1938, reprinted 1961).

18 Dewey described it as 'The most adequate contribution America has yet made, always excepting Emerson, to moral philosophy'.

19 For a useful account of American naturalism see the essay by H. A. Larrabee in *Naturalism and the Human Spirit*, ed. Y. H. Krikorian (Columbia University Press, New York, 1944).

20 On checking the reference I find that the actual phrase was: 'The nacre of his prose, precious with a sanity so polished as to seem more morbid than another man's madness . . .' ('Of Essence and Existence and Santayana' *Journal of Philosophy*, 51, (1954), pp. 31–4, reprinted AFSL).

21 'He [a critic who had contrasted his earlier and later philosophy to the disadvantage of the latter] almost persuades me that, without feeling it, I may have become a different person, intensely and clearly as I seem to myself to have remained the same. I should say that, during a long life, I have expressed in turn different sides of my nature, and developed different parts of my innate philosophy' (PGS, p. 538).

22 This hostility is evident in some of the contributions to PGS (in particular, the papers by Edman, Vivas, and Munitz) and also in *The Moral Philosophy of George Santayana* by M. K. Munitz (Columbia University Press, New York, 1939).

23 See, for instance, PGS, p. 503.

24 This is not entirely fair to Dewey who laid great emphasis on the fundamental place of ends or consummations in life. What, however, distinguishes Dewey from Santayana here is that by Dewey intellectual operations seem to have been conceived as purely instrumental, and the ends seem to have consisted in somewhat dumb and unintelligent satisfactions, while for Santayana an intellectual vision of an ordered whole, true or imaginary, was the highest satisfaction, and was that in which thought in the highest sense consisted.

25 Santayana does, however, point out that his claim that spirit has no efficacy does not mean that rational planning, understood as an activity of the psyche, has no efficacy. (See, for example, PGS, p. 541.) As to the degree of its efficacy his hopes seem to have declined from the period of *The Life of Reason* onwards. The issue is discussed in Chapter XI of this work.

26 In short, great emphasis is laid on what Bentham called the dimension of fecundity. In the later works where he is discussing rather the life of spirit the emphasis is primarily on intensity.

27 Cf. LRI, Introduction, pp. 3–5.

28 Richards's doctrine of the two uses of language is presented in his *Principles of Literary Criticism* (Routledge, London, 1924).

29 Quoted by R. C. Lyon in his introduction to his collection *Santayana on America*. I forget, or have never known, the 'draft' in which it occurs.

30 From an essay on Berkeley written for *From Anne to Victoria, Essays by Various Hands*, ed. Bonamy Dobrée (Cassell, London, 1937). Reprinted in AFSL. The quoted passage is on pp. 103–4 of this last.

31 COUS, pp. 108–9, in the essay on Royce. It is a nice case of Santayana enjoying James's style and developing a thought of his along his own lines.

32 Cf. the following passage from his novel:

His education, in spite of such excellent diligent masters, was carried on exclusively by himself. It consisted in learning the places of goods and evils, and the way they followed one another. That wagging of arms and legs, together with the habit of staring and following the light with his eyes, proved to be very useful for this ethical purpose. Goods and evils turned out to be arranged in a circle or sphere, in what nurse called his skin, or a little under this, in what she called his tummy; but there were some goods and evils that escaped beyond or came from beyond, such as the bottle when it was not yet or no longer in his mouth; and these potential goods and evils, which nurse called things, extended very far and had a tremendously complicated life of their own, which Oliver himself afterwards called the world. Even that was not all: for deeper down and higher up than his tummy, there were a lot of other goods and evils, not traceable by the eye, nor possible to run after and take hold of with the hand, when they showed a tendency to run away: and these were himself, his mind, or soul. The mind was the most entertaining and satisfactory region of all in which to keep your goods and evils: nobody else could get at them: and provided the evils were not too violent, like being carried away from what you wanted to do to what you didn't want to do, it was most amusing to have that private world of your own, and talk to yourself about it. (*The Last Puritan*, pp. 97–8)

33 In the essay on Shelley in WD the poet is praised for his possession of the kind of intelligence which transforms into an articulate and coherent ideal the usually dumb and unorganized yearnings of the heart, in spite of the fact that he lacked that more familiar kind of intelligence which consists in a grasp of how things are and of what is practicable. In the treatment of ethical intuitionism in that same book (pp. 138–54) Santayana also shows sympathy with the determination of G. E. Moore and the early Russell to make a sharp separation of judgements of what ought to be from judgements of what is. (See also Chapter X of the present book.)

34 See 'Preface to the Second Edition' (1922) in LRI (in editions after 1922, including the Collier paperback, but not in the 1952 one volume version of *The Life of Reason*).

35 See LRI, Chapter VIII.

36 This brief outline of Santayana's life is based largely on the three volumes of his autobiography, *Persons and Places*. Use has also been made of *The Letters of George Santayana*, ed. D. Cory and *Santayana: The Later Years* by D. M. Cory (Braziller, New York, 1963). Santayana's autobiography was written when he was an old man and may sometimes have been inaccurate, but it has scarcely seemed appropriate for the present limited purpose to check his statements in any systematic way.

37 Cf. PP, pp. 134–5.
38 James's description of *Interpretations of Poetry and Religion* as 'the perfection
   of rottenness' (cf. *Letters of William James*, ed. by his son Henry James,
   Longmans, London, 1926 (2nd edn), pp. 122–3) is often quoted, but,
   apart from the fact that even this is in part complimentary when
   taken in context (for James also says: 'I have literally squealed with
   delight at the imperturbable perfection with which the position is laid
   down on page after page') for the meaning is that it represents the perfect
   development of a point of view which James thought morbid (because of
   its emphasis on the value of imaginative contemplation) the record
   contains many more appreciative comments by James on Santayana, as
   when he wrote to President Eliot concerning Santayana's 'style, his
   subtlety of perception, and his cool-blooded truthfulness'. (*The Thought
   and Character of William James*, ed. R. B. Perry, 2 vols, Little, Boston, 1935,
   Vol. II, p. 270) and in his praise of *The Life of Reason* (op. cit. Vol. II,
   p. 399). (See also correspondence with Shadworth Hodgson of 1887
   in op. cit. Vol. I, pp. 640–3 and other references to Santayana in these
   volumes). As for Santayana's attitude to James, he had the greatest
   admiration for *The Principles of Psychology* (first published by Henry Holt,
   New York, 1890. 2 vols, Dover Publications, New York, 1950) but took
   a fairly dim view of *Pragmatism* (1907) and kindred works. For James as a
   man and teacher he certainly seems to have had a considerable respect,
   and relations between them were much more cordial than they are sometimes represented as having been. (As is clear from Perry's two volumes
   on James, from the letters both of James and of Santayana, and from
   Santayana's comments on James throughout his writings.)
39 For an evocation of the Santayana of these days see *George Santayana* by
   George Howgate, Chapter 2.
40 'Of course the academic world was astonished. To leave Harvard in
   order to contemplate in Spain, in Paris, in Oxford and on the banks of the
   Cam was to cut off an enviable career for idle musing. . . . Besides, after
   so much admiration had been lavished upon him, it seemed ungrateful to
   scatter the incense to the breeze. And, really, how could one leave
   Harvard and Boston by choice?' From 'Santayana at Cambridge' by
   Margaret Munsterburg (daughter of the Harvard psychologist, Hugo
   Munsterburg, a contemporary of Santayana) in *American Mercury*, vol. I
   (1924) quoted in George Howgate, op. cit., p. 1.
41 Cf. *Letters*, p. 405.

II Scepticism

1 The first two sections of this chapter are based mainly on SAF, I–III, and
   Preface, but here, as throughout, my understanding of Santayana
   represents a response to his total published output, but especially RB.
2 Cf. Josiah Royce – *The Spirit of Modern Philosophy* (first published 1892.
   W. W. Norton, New York, 1967), pp. 378–9. There are many such oblique
   references to Hegelian positions in Santayana's writings, and indeed with
   regard to Royce it is arguable that there was more positive influence than
   Santayana recognized.

3 Cf. SAF, pp. 40–1.
4 SAF, Chapters IV and V.
5 SAF, pp. 290ff. See also SAF, pp. 17 and 35 and Chapter IV.
6 This section is based mainly on Chapters VI–VIII of SAF.
7 Essences are introduced in Chapters IX and X of SAF.

III   Animal Faith

1 SAF, pp. 100; 186; and *passim*.
2 PGS, pp. 586ff.
3 SAF, Chapter XII.
4 SAF, Chapter XIII.
5 SAF, Chapters XIV–XVI.
6 SAF, Chapter XVI.
7 Cf. SAF, pp. 184–5.
8 Cf. SAF, pp. 294ff.
9 See 'Inference from the Known to the Unknown' by J. Watling in *Proceedings of the Aristotelian Society (1954–5)* and *A Materialist Theory of the Mind* by D. M. Armstrong (Routledge & Kegan Paul, London, 1968), Chapter IX. The main statement of Santayana's position is SAF, Chapter XVIII.
10 SAF, Chapters XIX and XX.
11 SAF, Chapter VII.
12 Cf. J. Bennett – *Kant's Analytic* (Cambridge University Press, 1966), pp. 184–7
13 Santayana's views on space and time, which belong here, are discussed in Chapter VI.
14 SAF, Chapter XXII.
15 SAF, Chapter XXIII. See also LRI, Chapter V and VI, and RS, Chapter III.
16 Cf. SAF, Chapter XXIV.
17 SAF, Chapter XXVI.
18 Cf. J. Wisdom, *Other Minds* (Blackwell, Oxford, 1952); N. Malcolm, 'Wittgenstein's "Philosophical Investigations"' in *The Philosophy of Mind,* ed. V. C. Chappell (Prentice-Hall, Englewood Cliffs, 1962); J. T. Saunders and D. F. Henze, *The Private Language Problem* (Random House, New York, 1967), and other writings too numerous to mention.
19 There is some such exploration in DP.
20 Cf. especially Moore's *Some Main Problems of Philosophy* (Allen & Unwin, London, 1953); also 'A Defence of Common Sense' in *Philosophical Papers* (Allen & Unwin, London, 1959).
21 Cf. especially Karl Popper – *The Logic of Scientific Discovery* (Hutchinson, London, 1959).

IV   The Doctrine of Essence

1 Cf. RE, Chapters I–III, X and *passim*; SAF, VII–X; and 'Three Proofs of Realism'.

NOTES TO PAGES 65-78

2 For an elaborate critique by Santayana of Russell's notion of sense-data see 'What are data?' and 'Essences not abstractions' in POML.

3 The most influential attack upon such arguments in recent times has been that of J. L. Austin in *Sense and Sensibilia* (Oxford University Press, London, 1962). In my *Facts, Words and Beliefs* (Routledge & Kegan Paul, London, 1970), Chapter 1 sections 1 and 2, I have tried to show that Austin's critique of sense-data does not affect the main grounds which there are for speaking of them. Of course, Santayana's ontology does not include sense-data (conceived as particular existences) but I think some of the arguments I put in place of the so-called argument from illusion have relevance to the introduction of sensory essences. The term 'sense-datum' is an unfortunate one, in any case, as it tends to suggest the ill-conceived notion of the 'sensory core', whereas what is meant is the actual appearance of a thing, which is certainly largely the product of interpretative processes at the level of the 'psyche', so that, for instance, the sense-datum or appearance is different in character according as to how one sees an ambiguous drawing. There is a good deal to commend Santayana's insistence that this actual appearance is best thought of as a universal, not a particular. For Santayana on the absurdity of wishing for 'intuitions of things' see, for instance, SAF, Chapter X.

4 For a survey of some main notions which have gone under the title of 'the given' one may usefully consult *The Appeal to the Given* by J. J. Ross (Allen & Unwin, London, 1970). None of those discussed there correspond to Santayana's.

5 Cf. PGS, pp. 580–1; RB, p. 664.

6 Cf. 'On Synthesis and Memory' posthumously published in *Journal of Philosophy*, Vol. LXVIII, No. 1 (15 January, 1970). See also RB, pp. 203 and 651ff.

7 Cf. 'Penitent Art' in OS.

8 For the distinct types of exemplification discussed in this section see, especially, RE, Chapter IX.

9 Cf. RB, pp. 19, 23–4, 36, 66, 109, 224–5.

10 RB, pp. 32, 45, 72, 135.

11 Cf. RB, p. 131. Also perhaps 'comic' essences, like the round square, intuited when one confuses the distinct (SAF, pp. 120–3. RB. pp. 26–7, 56–7).

12 See *Santayana: The Later Years* by D. M. Cory, p. 45; also HW, Chapter II.

13 Cf. RB, pp. 93, 124.

14 Cf. RB, pp. 97ff.; also RB, p. 91. For an early treatment of the generic, by which he would probably have stood, see SB, pp. 118–19.

15 Especially in RE, Chapter II.

16 Cf. AFSL, p. 109; POML, pp. 96–101; PGS, p. 536; SAF, Chapter X.

17 Cf. RE, Chapters V, VI and X.

18 Cf. RB, pp. 33ff.

19 For an explicit and quite recent statement of this view see *Logic and Reality* by Gustav Bergmann (University of Wisconsin Press, Madison, 1964), p. 57.

20 See *Santayana: The Later Years* by Daniel Cory, p. 17. For Santayana's account of pure Being see RE, Chapter IV, and also 'On Metaphysical

Projection' in *The Idler and His Works*; AFSL, pp. 139–41; SAF, pp. 272–4; 'Some Meanings of the Word "Is"' in OS, etc. Santayana's somewhat Bergsonian discussion of nothing is interesting, especially as marking the contrast between his account of pure Being and the Hegelian one. (Cf. RB, pp. 45 and 53–4.)

21 Cf. POML, pp. 90–1; RB, pp. 46–9.

22 See, for example, RB, pp. 5–6, 18 and 56.

23 Cf. RB, pp. 67ff., and pp. 113–18.

24 Cf. RE, Chapters VI, VII, and IX, and RM, Chapter II. Also RB, pp. 3, 5, 35–6, 49, etc.

25 Compare 'the intrinsic qualities of a thing compose its essence, and its essence, when caught in external relations, is the thing itself' (RB, p. 44) with 'things . . . far from being identical with their essence at any moment, exist by eluding it, encrusting it in changing relations and continually adopting a different essence' (RB, p. 110). See also RB, pp. 21ff.; p. 39; pp. 120ff.; pp. 202–12; pp. 218–19.

26 RB, p. 76.

27 For Santayana's later views on beauty and related topics see; 'An Aesthetic Soviet' (especially footnote on pp. 190–1) and 'Penitent Art', both in OS; RE, Chapter I, especially pp. 6–11; Chapter VIII, especially pp. 110–14 (on prose and poetry); Chapter X, especially pp. 152–4; RT, Chapter XII (on Beauty and Truth); PSL, Section IV; AFSL, Part VIII, especially 'The Mutability of Aesthetic Categories'. Santayana himself denied that there was any definite subject describable as Aesthetics. In fact, in the last article listed, he describes it, without using the term, as what we might now call a 'family resemblance' word. Be that as it may, the passages listed modify the opinions expressed in such earlier works as SB; IPR, and LRIV. His literary criticism is collected in *Critical Writings of George Santayana*, ed. N. Henfrey (2 vols, Cambridge University Press, 1968).

28 Cf. RB, pp. 418–19.

V Spirit and Psyche

1 RM, Chapter VI.

2 For the psyche see RM, Chapters VII and VIII; RS, Chapters I and III; SE, Chapter 49; DP, pp. 14–17; and POML *passim*. RS, Chapter IV should also be consulted.

3 Cf. OS, p. 107; RB, pp. xxxi; 608, 609, 617, 659; POML, pp. 187–92; SAF, pp. 207–8.

4 Cf. SAF, Chapters XV–XVI, and pp. 293–7, etc.; RS, Chapter I; SE, Chapters 44–9.

5 Doubtless it also owes something to Spinoza's concept of *conatus*. For relevant references to Aristotle see RB, pp. 333, 571, 591. See also 'The Secret of Aristotle' in DL.

6 See Chapter IV, note 9.

7 George Santayana, 'Living without thinking', *Forum*, no. 68, 1922, pp. 731–5; reprinted in AFSL, pp. 275–8, a review of *Psychology from the*

Standpoint of a Behaviorist, John B. Watson, Lippincott, Philadelphia and London, 1919.

8 See especially SAF, Chapter XXIV; also RM, Chapter VIII; RT, Chapters VI and VII; AFSL, p. 277.

9 Cf. RB, pp. XXXI and 345; AFSL, pp. 80–1.

10 *The Explanation of Behaviour* by Charles Taylor (Routledge & Kegan Paul, London, 1964), Chapter I and *passim*.

11 Cf. PGS, 509–10; RM, Chapter VII; RS, Chapter IV.

12 Chapters I–III, and VI of RS provide the most unified statement of Santayana's general view of *spirit*, but my account is based on passages too numerous to cite from SAF, RB, POML, AFSL, PSL, PGS, and elsewhere.

13 See, for example, RB, pp. 603ff. It may be noted that when Santayana talks of 'moments of spirit' as not being 'situated by their external relations' (RB, p. 604) he presumably means their external relations *to each other*, and is not denying what on the whole seems to be his view that they are situated by their external relations to their physical basis. (Cf. RB, pp. 204–5.) However, as I try to bring out in what follows, Santayana's view as to how moments of spirit belong to particular spatio-temporal contexts is far from easy to grasp. There is a good deal in POML which shows the difficulty he had with this question.

14 See, for example, SAF, pp. 214–15; RB, pp. 129–30, 619, 677 and in RS *passim*.

15 Cf. DP, p. 55.

16 Santayana's epiphenomenalism (a term he disliked, however, on the grounds that only given essences, and not either matter or spirit, are properly 'phenomena') has very much the same character in LR as in RB and some of the finest statements of it belong to his earlier work; see, especially, 'How Thought is Practical' in LRI and 'The Efficacy of Thought' in AFSL. The doctrine plays an important part in RS; see especially Chapter V.

17 Sometimes he seems to want to dispense, even, with the demand of universality. (See letter to C. J. Ducasse in *Letters*, p. 213.) POML contains various attempts to wrestle with the problem; the paper on pp. 23–34 is of especial interest. For the line of thought developed below see, besides this paper, POML and RB *passim*, especially RS, Chapter V.

18 Cf. POML, p. 27; SAF, p. 219; RB, pp. 315, 564, 632–6, etc.

19 A useful account of their views may be found in W. James's *Principles of Psychology* (first published by Henry Holt, New York, 1890. 2 vols, Dover Publications, New York, 1950), Chapter V.

20 Cf. the review of James's *Principles of Psychology* reprinted in *The Idler and His Works*. See also AFSL, pp. 79ff.

21 AFSL, p. 80.

22 Cf. SAF, p. 221; RB, pp. 198, 344, 354, 597; PGS, p. 579.

23 Cf. RB, pp. 315 and 564.

24 Cf. STTMP, pp. 67–8; RB, pp. 807–8.

25 In fact something like this argument is found even so early as in his doctoral dissertation on Lotze. (See *Lotze's System of Philosophy* by George Santayana ed. P. G. Kuntz, pp. 149ff.) Cf. RB, p. 247.

26 Cf. SAF, p. 16; OS, p. 87.

27 Cf. SAF, pp. 276–7; RB, pp. 438 and 663ff.

28 Cf. SAF, pp. 168–9; RB, pp. 37, 67ff., 91, 97, 113–18. Santayana also sometimes describes the concentration on some one element in the given as a case of intent, but this is an extension of the term inconsistent with his usual usage.

29 Cf. RB, p. 146 and PGS, p. 579.

30 See, for example, SAF, Chapter XXXVI, also pp. 130 and 189–91; RS, Chapter VI; and the various references to 'moral essences' in RB.

31 His own use of 'feeling' is certainly thus ambivalent. I cannot trace a passage in which I seem to recall his explaining this. Elsewhere he makes the different but related point that 'we hardly have words for essences so generic and inarticulate as are given in sheer alarm, lust, impatience, or effort; these terms, which we say denote "feelings" really denote, for our adult minds, the occasions and actions that are visible when we use them. We never name our own passions, until we catch them in the mirror of the world' (RB, p. 664). All the same, he clearly does not want to hold, in Wittgensteinian fashion, that there *cannot* be names for such essences, still less that in lacking names they fail to be definite somethings. For an attempt to define 'feeling' see PGS, p. 578.

32 Santayana's fullest discussion of this topic is in SAF, Chapter XVIII.

33 Cf. 'Three Proofs of Realism' Section 1, last paragraph (in *Essays in Critical Realism* by Durant Drake *et al.* (Macmillan, London, 1920), reprinted in AFSL). As to how far the particular referent of a mental act is determined by some part of the essence intuited being applicable to it, and how far it is determined by the behavioural orientation of the psyche towards it, Santayana seems to have varied his opinion a good deal. The following note which I found in Santayana's hand on p. 177 of his copy of Russell's *Philosophical Essays* in the Houghton Library, Harvard, is of interest for its implied denial of the second factor, but though this is sometimes echoed in RT, I do not think it corresponds to his later view. 'If reality had no multiplicity, we should either have to describe it truly, or not to refer to it at all. What exposes us to error, is that we may conceive one element of reality [deleted: 'referring to it'] fixing it by some sign that determines it sufficiently, and then combine it with other elements (real or merely ideal) which are not conjoined with it in fact, e.g. [deleted: 'Julius'] Caesar was a Greek.'

34 Cf. 'Three Proofs of Realism' (as in note 33) and 'Literal and Symbolic Knowledge' (in OS). Also SAF, Chapter XVIII, RE, Chapters VIII and X, and RT *passim*. See also RB, p. 232; PGS, p. 518, etc.

35 Cf. RB, p. 456. In effect Santayana, like certain Idealists, though for different reasons, believed in *degrees* of truth.

36 Cf. RB, pp. 456ff. and 616.

VI The Material World

1 Cf. PGS pp. 9–10. But I cannot now trace the remark of which I am chiefly thinking.

2 Cf. J. J. C. Smart – *Philosophy and Scientific Realism* (Routledge & Kegan Paul, London, 1963); D. M. Armstrong – *A Materialist Theory of the Mind* (Routledge & Kegan Paul, London, 1968).

3 LRI, Chapter VII, especially final note. Santayana's use of the term 'concretion' may have derived from Berkeley. (Cf. *The Principles of Human Knowledge* (1710), §99.)

4 Cf. 'Some Observations on the Philosophy of George Santayana' by D. M. Cory in PGS, especially p. 96. See also PGS, p. 556.

5 LRI, pp. 77ff.

6 LRI, pp. 66–83.

7 See especially LRI, Chapter IV.

8 Cf. LRV, Chapter IV; RB, pp. 175–80, 197–8; PGS, p. 519.

9 Cf. Chapter II, no. 4; Chapter III, no. 3; Chapter IV, no. 7.

10 Cf. RM, Chapter II *passim* for all phrases quoted in this section.

11 Cf. RB, pp. 207–9.

12 F. H. Bradley made a similar point in *Appearance and Reality* (Allen & Unwin, London, 1893), Chapter XVIII. But while for Bradley the different time series would all 'come together' non-temporally as aspects of the Absolute Experience, for Santayana they would be utterly separate in existence, though in a certain sense belonging together in the Realm of Truth, a point which supports the feeling that Truth for Santayana performs some of the offices of the Absolute. (Cf. RB, p. 215.)

13 See Chapter IV, note 9.

14 Cf. AFSL, p. 22.

15 Cf. especially RB, pp. 200–1.

16 It should be read in conjunction with RB, pp. 149–52.

17 Cf. Russell – *Mysticism and Logic* (Allen & Unwin, London, 1917); Smythies – *An Analysis of Perception* (Routledge & Kegan Paul, London, 1956).

18 Cf. RB, pp. 240ff. Also POML, pp. 53–62 and 68–84.

19 Cf. RB, pp. 239–41.

20 Cf. Chapter II, no. 4 *ad fin.* of this present work; also Chapter IV, no. 7.

21 The subject receives an interesting treatment in A. E. Taylor's *The Elements of Metaphysics* (Methuen, London, 1903), Book III, Chapter IV.

22 Cf. RB, p. 244.

23 Cf. the epigraph from Spinoza to RS; also RB, pp. 132–3, 251–2, 470–2, 841. See also DL, III, and numerous passages throughout Santayana's writings.

24 See especially SAF, Chapter X *passim* and OS, pp. 94ff.

25 Cf. RB, pp. 135–7.

26 Cf. OS, p. 86; SAF, p. 82; RB, pp. 74; 125, 135, 157–9, 197–8; RT, Chapters VI and VII; RS, Chapter VI; DL, Chapters III and V.

27 Cf. RB, pp. 274–5.

28 Santayana likes to reserve the term 'actualization of an essence' for its exemplification in intuition (see, for example, OS, pp. 155–7), yet in spite of his own verbal preference it expresses his view exactly to say that each physical fact is an essence made actual or actualized.

29 Cf. *Process and Reality* by A. N. Whitehead (Cambridge University Press, 1929), pp. 39, 234, 438. For a comment by Santayana on vacuous actuality see *Santayana: The Later Years* by D. M. Cory, pp. 59–60.

30 See, for instance, RB, pp. 375ff.; also 'System'.

VII *Substance*

1 In his article 'Matter and Substance in the Philosophy of Santayana' (*Modern Schoolman*, November 1960) John Lachs suggests that, among the confusingly many uses of 'matter' and 'substance' in Santayana, the two which stand out as the most helpful are:

1   The use of 'matter' to mean something which is not itself an existent, but is 'a featureless, faceless force' which, by sweeping through the field of essences makes some of them, for the moment, into existents. In short, matter as opposed to substance is the unintelligible alloy which substance, here meaning the sum of physical things, or some part of that sum, involves in addition to whatever essences we may assign to it. (Cf. RM, p. 82; RB, p. 274.)

2   The use of 'substance' to mean either an individual natural object or the sum of all such objects, the physical cosmos.

I have not found that this has much basis in Santayana's own terminology. Apart from the fact that, grammatically, Santayana must speak of 'a substance' but not 'a matter', one could point to indications of precisely the converse contrast holding, for 'substance' is often described as the characterless something transmitted from natural moment to moment or, 'the dark principle of existence', the 'something not essence' which 'actualises or limits the manifestation of every essence that figures in nature or appears before the mind' (RB, p. 206), while the realm of matter is characterized rather as this world of ours in which we seek our food and flee our enemies.

More importantly, I think that the contrast between the two concepts, however named, is not required in quite this form. Although substance or matter is certainly something *more* (or *less*, as Santayana puts it) than *the form it takes on* at any moment, containing a mysterious potency in potential conflict with other such potencies, it is nonetheless true that it *does take on a form* at every moment. To say that 'matter can exist only in some form' (RB, p. 851) is not, as Lachs's discussion might be thought to imply, to say that it does not exist or have form. I would take my clue from such a passage as that below and say that matter or substance, that is a portion of the matter or substance of the world, becomes an individual thing or substance of some kind when, and for so long as, it takes on a suitable form, so that for the time being that portion of substance *is* that thing. Certainly one can consider this substance or matter in abstraction from any particular form and then one is thinking rather in terms of what Lachs calls matter, or one can think of it as having taken on a certain form, in which case one has an individual substance, but the difference is not really a difference in what is being referred to.

> The matter which by taking a particular form becomes a particular thing need never have worn that form before and may never wear it again. . . . Though at each moment it must be something specific, yet . . . we shall hardly be able to hold it down to any other *enduring* [my italics] characters than those involved in its distinctive function: which is to lend existence to certain essences in a certain order, and enable them to succeed and to confront one another in a competitive world. (RB, pp. 279–80)

Incidentally, Lachs invokes a principle in support of his interpretation, which, whatever its intrinsic merits as ontology, cannot be used for this purpose, since Santayana's ontology is in any case unambiguously inconsistent with it. The principle is that the constituents of distinct realms of being must not overlap, as the realm of matter and that of essence would do if essences are given a role in the realm of matter. As against this, it is sufficient to point out that the realm of truth is quite explicitly described as a 'tragic' segment of the realm of essence.

It is with no great confidence that I here disagree with so sensitive and distinguished a commentator on Santayana – though more on terminology than on any more fundamental point.

2 The most important material on substance and matter as discussed in this chapter is as follows, but relevant observations are to be found throughout RB and in many other places: SAF, Chs XIX–XXII; RE, Ch. IX; RM throughout, but especially Chs II, III, V, VI and IX. See also POML *passim*, especially pp. 68–84. See also 'The Secret of Aristotle' in DL.

3 Santayana seems somewhat vacillating in his treatment of potentiality (i.e. real potentiality, not mere logical possibility). Since counterfactuals have, for him, no genuine truth-value, one would expect him to take a rather dim view of 'unrealised potentialities', reducing them to what normally happens in circumstances such as one can imagine holding in this case also. This is evidently his official view, but his remarks at other times, especially regarding the expression by spirit of potentialities in the organism which may remain unrealized, seem to demand recognition of real potentialities as having a distinct ontological status. The position is complicated by his sometimes also identifying substance or matter with potentiality (in a manner complementary to the identification of essence with possibility). On the whole I take this to mean no more than that it is the substance, not the essence, of a fact which is available for transformation into other facts or, more obscurely, that its substance actually consists in its passage into other facts. Somewhat similar difficulties may be found in the notion of lateral tensions as actually consisting in mutual influence.

4 Cf. RB, p. 80.

5 For my recognition of this aspect of Santayana's philosophy I am especially indebted to Henry Wenkart's 'Santayana's Philosophy of

Matter and Mind' (unpublished Ph.D. dissertation presented to Harvard University, April 1970).

6 See Chapter IV, note 9.

7 Cf. SAF, pp. 201–3.

8 See SAF, p. 182, and compare RB, p. 226. See also Chapter III of the present book.

9 See especially RM, Chapter V, also Chapter II at RB, p. 203.

10 Cf. RB, p. 195; pp. 270–2; RM, Chapter IX. Also POML, Section IV, *passim*, and pp. 123–30.

11 RB, pp. 282–3.

12 Cf. Chapter IV, §2.

13 Cf. RB, pp. 287–8; POML, pp. 62–3; STTMP, p. 75.

14 *Process and Reality* by A. N. Whitehead (Cambridge University Press, 1929), e.g. at p. 84.

15 Cf. *The Idler and his Works*, pp. 129ff. and STTMP, III.

16 RB, pp. 280–1. Note that Santayana's use of 'event' here is not according to the definition he gives in discussing *tropes* and that the absence of change within a natural moment is an absence of real change compatible with the existence of a before and after of *specious* time. RM, Chapter V contains the main discussion of natural moments, but see also RB, pp. 323–5, and, for a somewhat different treatment, POML, pp. 68–84.

17 *Process and Reality* by A. N. Whitehead, Chapter III.

18 See, for instance, RB, p. 379.

19 *Essays on Truth and Reality* by F. H. Bradley (Oxford University Press, London, 1914), p. 159.

20 Cf. RB, pp. 284ff.

21 His doctoral dissertation on Lotze, especially the comparison of Lotze and Herbart, is of especial interest in this connection. It may be recalled that his teachers and colleagues Royce and James were both particularly involved in the rivalries of monism, monadism, pluralism, etc.

VIII   Truth

1 Cf. Letters, p. 104.

When not otherwise indicated the sources for the following account of Santayana's theory of truth are as follows: RT, Preface and Chapter V; 'Preface to Realms of Being' in RE; SAF, Chapter XXV; COUS, Chapter V (also pp. 73–4).

2 SAF, p. 268 (repeated in Preface to RT).

3 *Pragmatism* (1907) and *The Meaning of Truth* give James's Theory. For Santayana's views thereof see especially COUS, Chapters III and V. For Josiah Royce's theory in brief see *The Religious Aspect of Philosophy* (first published 1885) (Peter Smith, Gloucester, Mass., 1965) and for Santayana's view thereof see COUS, Chapter IV, especially pp. 100–5.

4 See, for example, RB, p. 447 (also RB, pp. 402 and 456ff.).

5 See, for instance, RB, p. 420. See also W. R. Dennes's comments in PGS, pp. 430–1.

6 Cf. RB, pp. 405–6.

7 Cf. my discussion in Chapter IV, no. 4.

8 For an account of the status of groups which I think would fit in with Santayana's ontology see my *Facts, Words and Beliefs* (Routlegde & Kegan Paul, London, 1970), Chapter V.

9 The liveliest expression of this attitude of Santayana's is his *Egotism in German Philosophy*, a book, however, which has a certain uncharacteristic cheapness of tone.

10 RB, pp. 448–9.

11 Cf. COUS, pp. 158ff. (also pp. 73–4). Santayana does not seem to distinguish between 'sign' and 'symbol' in any methodical way.

12 Actually Santayana talks rather of symbolic knowledge of the truth than of symbolic truth, but it is convenient to have a single term for the essences present to us in such knowledge. On the whole 'Symbolic and Literal Knowledge' in OS represents Santayana's clearest statement of this theme which is, however, pervasive in RB. (See especially RT, Chapter VII.)

13 Cf. RB, p. 452.

14 Cf. RB, pp. 260, 409, 437, 442–4, etc.

15 Cf. *Santayana: The Later Years* by D. M. Cory (Braziller, New York, 1963), p. 178. However, I am not charging Santayana with vagueness in the main themes of RT which are not those treated in this chapter, but with a certain vagueness in the definition given certain terms.

16 Cf. SAF, p. 267.

17 See, for example, RB, pp. 231–2 and pp. 486–8.

18 Cf. RB, p. 471.

19 Cf. 'Santayana, Then and Now' by Stirling P. Lamprecht in AFSL, pp. 313–16.

20 Cf. SAF, pp. 227–8; RB, p. 424 and pp. 445ff.

21 See LRV, footnote on pp. 30–1.

22 RB, pp. 424–5, though this seems to be confused with the view that the ontological categories in terms of which we think have an optional aspect.

23 RB, pp. 426.

24 Especially in RT, Chapter V.

25 Cf. RB, pp. 104–5.

IX *Truth and Time*

1 The main sources for this chapter are RM, Chapters IV and V; RT, Preface and Chapters IX and X; COUS, Chapter V. I have dealt more fully with some of the moral implications of Santayana's account of time and eternity in my article 'Ideal Immortality' in *Southern Journal of Philosophy*, Vol. 10, no. 2, Summer 1972 (special issue on Santayana).

2 See for example, 'Statements about the Past' in *Philosophical Essays* by A. J. Ayer (Macmillan, London, 1954); also 'Fatalism' in the same author's *The Concept of a Person* (Macmillan, London, 1963).

3 RB, pp. 500–1.

4 *Time and Modality* by A. N. Prior (Clarendon Press, Oxford, 1957) seems to suffer from this confusion in Chapters IX and X.

5 This view is advocated by C. J. Ducasse in his essay in *The Philosophy of C. D. Broad*, ed. P. A. Schilpp (Tudor Publishing, New York, 1959). It was advocated by Sir James Jeans among others – see his lecture *Scientific Progress* quoted in *The Natural Philosophy of Time* by G. J. Whitrow (Nelson, London, 1961), p. 256.

6 RB, p. 268.

7 Cf. note 18 in the last chapter and the discussion to which it is appended.

8 Theories roughly of this sort have been advocated by many philosophers, including Bertrand Russell, in *The Principles of Mathematics* (Allen & Unwin, London, 1903), §442; A. J. Ayer (op. cit, note 2); J. J. C. Smart, in *Philosophy and Scientific Realism*, and D. C. Williams, in 'The Myth of Passage' in *Principles of Empirical Realism*, reprinted in *The Philosophy of Time*, ed. R. M. Gale (Macmillan, London, 1968), an article in which Santayana is quoted in an oddly misleading way.

9 *The Nature of Existence* by J. M. E. McTaggart (2 vols, Cambridge University Press, 1921–7), Chapter 33. I doubt whether Santayana was familiar with McTaggart's argument, although he had enjoyed rather warm relations with him at one time.

10 There is an element of confusion in Santayana's presentation of his position stemming from his failure to distinguish clearly between a relational property (a property which simply consists in being in a certain relation to something else) and a relative quality, i.e. a quality which something assumes, or would assume, for a mind in a certain relation to it. (See next chapter at note 14.) Nonetheless the upshot of his position is reasonably clear and such as I expound below.

11 See Chapter II, no. 3 of the present book. Cf. RB, pp. 255 ff.

12 RM, Chapter IV.

13 *The Nature of Existence* by J. M. E. McTaggart, Vol. II, p. 16.

14 Evidently this view was argued for by G. H. Mead in *The Philosophy of the Present*. (See note 2 to D. C. Williams's essay referred to in my note 8.)

15 Cf. C. I. Lewis – *Mind and the World Order* (first published 1928. Dover Publications, New York, 1956), pp. 149–53. A. J. Ayer – *Language, Truth and Logic* (2nd edn, Gollancz, London, 1946), Chapter V *ad fin*.

Ayer soon abandoned the view, however, and Lewis presents it only in a hesitant manner; yet we find it implicit in various recent discussions of memory.

16 The most explicit statement of this theory with which I am familiar is Chapter II of C. D. Broad's *Scientific Thought* (Routledge, London, 1923). In *An Examination of McTaggart's Philosophy* (Cambridge University Press, 1938), Chapter XXXV, his position had evidently changed to one which puts past and future more upon a level, a less satisfactory position since either the past is treated as 'nothing at all' just as the future was in *Scientific Thought*, in which case there are no historical facts to which historical statements may correspond, or the future becomes a determinate reality awaiting its moment of present actuality, a view quite often supported (as, for example, by Richard Taylor in *Metaphysics* (Prentice-Hall, Englewood Cliffs, 1963) Chapter 6) but which retains every difficulty of absolute becoming (including those I press below) and none of its

advantages. (Broad may have thought that these problems were resolved by his insistence on the ultimacy of tenses as opposed to temporal predicates, but this does not explain, as did his previous theory, how historical propositions can correspond to facts.) Whitehead's theory of events as passing into an 'objective immortality' sometimes suggests a theory similar to that I discuss in the text, and open to the same objections; so does the outlook of all those for whom contingent statements about the future are not, like those about the past, true or false.

17 According to the Broad of *Scientific Thought* 'There is no such thing as *ceasing* to exist; what has become exists for ever. When we say that something has ceased to *exist* we only mean that it has ceased to be present. . . .' (p. 69) and elsewhere he speaks of all the events which exist at the moment when a judgement is made as including its predecessors but not its successors (since 'a present event is defined as one that is succeeded by nothing' (p. 68)). Surely it was unsatisfactory even in his own terms to think of earlier events as existing *at that moment*, and he should have said rather that I may always truly say '*This* event has predecessors, belonging of course each to its moment, but has no successors, belonging each to its moment.' For the tense of 'has' see below.

18 In *Scientific Thought* Broad says that events earlier than T do, and those later than T do not, exist at T. Surely he should have said, speaking at T, 'Events earlier than T exist, those later do not', a statement he would have to revise at the next moment, but which, all the same, would not be tensed in any ordinary sense. At a superficial level his treatment of tenses in *An Examination* is more coherent, but as it seems to leave no sense in which I can still say of past events that they *belong* to reality, it leaves the reference of historical statements mysterious. In both books Broad overlooks the distinction between 'I can still truly say that the Battle of Hastings is real' and 'I can truly say that the Battle of Hastings is still real'.

19 Broad seems oddly unaware of the apparent clash between Absolute Becoming and Relativity theory.

20 *Scientific Thought*, p. 66 (cf. note 17 above).

21 *An Analysis of Knowledge and Valuation* by C. I. Lewis (Open Court, La Salle, Ill., 1946), p. 19.

X Santayana's Ethical Theory

1 See *Santayana: The Later Years* by Daniel Cory (Braziller, New York, 1963), pp. 37–40.

2 Perhaps the most important sources for Santayana's ethical theory in its more abstract aspects are:

LRI   Introduction and Chapters VII–XII.
LRIV   Chapter XI.
LRV   Chapters VIII–X.
WD   Chapter IV, §IV
DL   Chapters VI and VII.
The Genteel Tradition at Bay.
RT   Chapter VIII.

PGS   pp. 554-73.
AFSL Section VII.
POML Section V.
PSL   *passim.*

3 See Russell's preliminary note added to 'The Elements of Ethics' as reprinted in *Readings in Ethical Theory*, eds W. Sellars and J. Hospers (Appleton-Century-Crofts, New York, 1952).

4 *Journal of Philosophy, Psychology and Scientific Method*, Vol. 8, no. 16, 3 August, 1911.

5 Cf. LRV, pp. 214-16, 240ff. and DL, Chapters VI and VII. Also RB, p. 100 and p. 480. This Socratic method is described under the heading of rational ethics, but so far as I can see its application is not limited thereto. Why could not one discover that a post-rational ideal represented one's deepest longing?

6 Chapter V, §4.

7 See, for example, LRI, pp. 259-60 and PSL, pp. 13-14.

8 The discussion of pain in POML, pp. 130-5 is intructive here. It seems to be implied that the aesthetic, sheerly qualitative, character of pain has no especial affinity to physical rejection but that with the essence of the detestable, under the aspect of which it is normally intuited, the case is otherwise.

9 Cf. especially WD, p. 154 and AFSL, pp. 350-1.

10 See, for example, LRV, pp. 58-9 and PGS, pp. 562 and 584.

11 Cf. POML, p. 132.

12 For his general attitude to moralities based upon *imperatives* rather than *ideals* see LRV, Chapter VIII especially pp. 226ff. See also the chapter on Kant in EGP. (See also *Letters*, p. 400 for a brief reference to W. D. Ross.)

13 Chapter IV, no. 8 towards the end.

14 Cf. Chapter IX, note 10, above.

15 Chapter IV, no. 8. For the assertion that good is somehow both relative to specific natures and also eternal see especially 'Ultimate Religion' in OS.

16 For two classic examples see A. J. Ayer, *Philosophical Essays*, Chapter 10 (Macmillan, London, 1954), especially pp. 247ff.; and Stevenson – *Facts and Values* (Yale University Press, New Haven, 1963), Chs V and VII.

17 See, for example, LRI, pp. 264ff. and LRV, pp. 256ff.

18 Royce makes a rather similar use of this principle in *The Religious Aspect of Philosophy* (first published 1885. Peter Smith, Gloucester, Mass., 1965) Chapter VI. Santayana may have been influenced here by his old teacher.

19 Cf. William James, *The Principles of Psychology* (first published by Henry Holt, New York, 1890. 2 vols, Dover Publications, New York, 1950), Chapter X; F. H. Bradley, *Appearance and Reality* (Allen & Unwin, London, 1893), Chapter XXI. One could also mention Royce again in this connection.

20 Santayana distinguished pre-rational morality, rational ethics, and post-rational morality. Something is said about these in the next chapter. It would take us too far afield were I to develop my own somewhat critical attitude to Santayana's complete account of pre-rational and post-rational morality.

21 See also the remainder of LRI, Chapter X and LRV, pp. 256–61 (and *passim* throughout LR).

22 Cf. my *Facts, Words and Beliefs* (Routledge & Kegan Paul, London, 1970), Chapter XII, §8, especially *ad fin.*

23 Santayana and 'Socrates' discuss this very issue in DL, pp. 115 *et ff.* with somewhat inconclusive results. The issue figures largely in Jan Narveson's *Morality and Utility* (Johns Hopkins Press, Baltimore, 1967), and is discussed in my 'Professor Narveson's Utilitarianism' in *Inquiry*, no. 3, Autumn 1968, Vol. II.

24 See, for example, LRI, pp. 257ff. The organization of individual impulses into a unitary ideal is compared to the organization of individual perceptions into a unitary conception of reality. Since, at least on his later theory, perceptions are themselves beliefs, it is only an extension of the same general idea in a direction suited to the later epistemology, if instead of perception we say belief.

25 On this, as on the whole question raised below of the extent to which a system of ideals may properly be developed *a priori* and independently of their practicability, the essay on Shelley in WD is of special interest.

26 Santayana appears to admit as much himself when he says: 'It is hardly too much to say, indeed, that prerational morality is morality proper' (LRI, p. 212.)

XI *Spiritual Life*

1 See his autobiography *passim*; SE (e.g. in 'Tipperary') and scattered observations throughout his writings.

2 Cf. LRV, Chapters VII–IX.

3 Gilbert Murray – *Five Stages of Greek Religion* (Clarendon Press, Oxford, 1925), Chapter IV.

4 Cf. the essays by M. K. Munitz and I. Edman in PGS.

5 Cf. RB, pp. 64–5, and PGS, p. 584.

6 Santayana's main account of the spiritual life is to be found in PSL and RS, Chapters VI–X. See also RE, Chapters I and IV; ICG, Part II; and 'A Change of Heart' in HW. *A General Confession* and the *Apologia* in PGS should be consulted for the way in which the old Santayana viewed its relation to the life of reason, also DP.

7 Cf. PSL, Section XX and RS *passim*. Schopenhauer should also be mentioned as a major influence in Santayana's conception of spirituality, though more in his treatment of the aesthetic experience in which as pure impersonal subject I confront Platonic ideas than in his treatment of the holy state in which the Will denies itself.

8 Cf. DP *passim*. See also RB, pp. 65 and 193.

9 E.g. at RB, pp. 714ff.

10 Cf. RB, pp. 811ff.

11 Cf. AFSL, pp. 79–80; PGS, p. 16; RB, pp xxxi–xxxii.

12 There is a sympathetic book on Santayana with this title, namely *Santayana: Saint of the Imagination* by M. M. Kirkwood (University of Toronto Press, 1961).

Index

Santayana's works are indexed under their titles; for other works, see authors' names.

Absolute becoming, 183–7, 237
Absolutism, 191, 193, 195
Abstraction, 77
Activism, idealistic, 15
Activity, 97–8; mental, 54–5, 61–2, 113, 117, 118–19, 122, 179; spiritual, 101, 103, 116, 143, 152
Adams, G. P., 12
'Aesthetic Soviet, An', 228
Aesthetics, 87–91, 228
Aims: harmonizing, 198–200, 204–6, 209; rational, 202–6 see also Desire; Intent; Purpose
Altruism, 200, 202–3
Analytical philosophy, 5
Animal faith, 47–8, 52–8, 62, 218; see also Belief
Animal Faith and Spiritual Life (AFSL), 227–8, 229, 231, 238, 239
Animation, belief in, 59–60
Anxiety, 117–18, 119–20
'Apologia, pro Mente Sua', 198
Apprehension, 39
Aquinas, St Thomas, 7
Aristotle, 9, 10, 102, 104, 148, 161, 176, 209, 212, 233
Armstrong, D. M., 52, 109–10, 231
Art, 16, 87–9
Attention, centre of, 139–40
Austin, J. L., 227
Avila, 21–2
Ayer, A. J., 8, 63, 235, 236, 238

Ballowe, J., 221
Beauty, 13–14; as liberator of essences, 86–92
Becoming, absolute, 183–7, 237
Behaviour: intuition and, 92, 115, 121–2; science of, 60, 97, 112
Behaviourism, 102–7, 112
Being, 78–9, 81, 85, 93, 145; pure, 75, 78–81; realms of, 95, 167, 233
Belief, 51–2, 64, 116; false existential, 122; in animation, 58–60; in existence, 203–4, in matter, 54–9, 61, 135–6; in nature, 59, 132–3; knowledge as, 52–3, 57, 63; moral, 196; origin of, 60, 63; reason and, 206–7; suspension of, 62; see also Animal faith
Bennett, J., 226
Bentham, Jeremy, 223
Berenson, Bernard, 28
Bergmann, Gustav, 227
Bergson, H., 228
Berkeley, G., 17–18, 23, 73, 231
Blue Sisters' Nursing Home, 28
Boston Latin School, 25
Boston School Regiment, 25
Bradley, F. H., 9, 42, 72, 78, 160, 161, 169, 201, 231
Bridges, Robert, 28
Broad, C. D., 151, 236–7
Buchler, J., 12
Butler, Bishop, 200

Cambridge University, 26
Causality, 110–14, 123
Change, 36–9, 48, 50–1, 150, 157; specious, 38, 40; time and, 178–81, 182–5
Character and Opinions in the United States (COUS), 234, 235; quoted, 18, 183
Christ, 216
Christianity, 14, 28–9, 210, 217
Coherence theory, 168, 206–7
Colour, 36–7, 40–1, 45–6
Conceptual analysis, 191
Concretions, 126–7
Conrad, J., 27
Consciousness, 59–62, 67, 97, 107, 109–13, 115–16, 123–4; essences and, 43, 65–7, 92–3, 120, 145–7; material existence and, 41–2, 43, 44, 59, 106; spirit as realm of, 211; stream of, 39
Contemplation, 14, 29, 118, 210, 212–14
Copernicus, N., 133
Correspondence theory, 168–9
Cory, Daniel M., 11, 13, 28, 224, 227, 232, 235, 237
Cosmos, 136–7, 170; Ptolemaic, 143; relative, 122
Critical Writings of George Santayana, 228

Dante, 7, 140
Death, 187
Democritus, 10, 133
Dennes, W. R., 234
Descartes, R., 10
Desire, 116, 117, 190, 191; *see also* Aims
Determinism, 149–50, 178
Dewey, John, 15–17 *passim*
Dialogues in Limbo (DL), 231, 233, 238, 239
Dimensions, 141–2, 180, 187
Discourse, 126, 132
Distance, 139–40, 144
Dizziness, 142
Dobrée, Bonamy, 224
Dogmatism, 30–1, 192, 196, 210
Dominations and Powers (DP), 239
Drake, Durant, 12
Dreams, 142, 168
Ducasse, C. J., 236

Duron, Jacques, 223

Egoism, 192, 200, 201, 203
Egotism in German Philosophy (EGP), 235, 238
Einstein, A., 133
Emotional essences, 72
Emotions, 108, 115, 117–20, 191–2; conflicting, 198–200, 202–3; morality and, 197–8; reason and, 198–203
Emotivists, 196
Empiricism, 43, 50, 54, 56, 76–7, 80, 153, 183, 192, 198
Epicureanism, 210
Epicurus, 7
Epiphenomenalism, 110, 112–13, 214–15, 219, 229
Epistemology, 4, 20, 30–1, 45, 62–4, 218
Essays in Critical Realism, 26, 230
Essences: absent, 117; actualized, 70, 134, 144–7, 158, 160, 166, 170–1, 175, 232; beauty and, 86–92; complex, 74–8, 82, 85–6, 160, 166–7; concretions and, 126; consciousness and, 43, 65–7, 92–3, 120, 145–7; definition of, 82, 115, 118; doctrine of, 10, 38, 42, 45, 65, 91, 92–4, 106, 219; elements of, 74–6, 79–80, 85–6; emotional, 72; exemplified, 69–72, 119, 144, 159, 174–5; existence and, 60–1, 130, 134, 136, 143–5; generic, 73–4, 76, 141; in nature, 71, 133–4, 143–5; indeterminate, 73–4, 77, 78–80; intuition of, 51–2, 65–9, 71, 73, 76–7, 80, 82, 84–5, 90, 92, 108, 113, 116–19, 121, 143–4, 146–7, 168; moral, 119, 144, 189, 191–2, 212; nature of, 81–2; non-existence of, 46, 51, 187; origin of, 99; primary, 76–7; realm of, 163–4, 233; relations between, 48–9, 74–6, 79, 82, 91, 115, 158–9, 173–5, internal and external, 82–6, 93, 171; sceptic's resting point, 42–4; spatial, 141–2, 144, 154–5; specific, 72–4, 77, 141; specious, 68, 144, 146, 158, 181, 182; spiritual, 108; sublimated, 141; temporal, 141, 144, 154–5, 180–1; truth and, 163–75; *see also* Tropes
Ethical hedonism, 195

Ethical judgements, 189–97, 198–9, 207–8, 213
Ethical naturalism, 189
Ethical relativism, 193–6, 204, 220
Ethics: analytical, 188–9; egoistic, 192; normative, 188–9, 191; rational, 209–10; reason in, 197–208, 209, 212–14; scope of Santayana's, 188–9; value qualities and, 189–99, 207–8, 213
Euclidean axioms, 141
Exemplification, 69–70, 72, 119
Existence, 44–5; concretions in, 126–7; essences and, 60–1, 85–6, 130, 134, 136, 143–5; material, 49–51, 67, 130–1, belief in, 54–8, 61, 135–6, doubted, 39–42, 45–6; occurrence and, 84; of mind, 32; pure Being and, 78, 85, 145; spirit and, 215; time and, 178–80, 185–6, 236–7; tropes as, 102; truth and, 172–5
Existential belief, 203–4; false, 122
Existential realms, 163
Existentialism, 85
Experiential flux, 48–50, 55–6, 130, 131, 172; doubt of existence of, 36–9

Facts: as essences, 170; as natural moments, 171; not truths, 170–1; mental, 138
Falsehood, 169
Fascism, 29
Fatalism, 16, 17, 214
Feigl, Herbert, 115
Fichte, 10, 50
Figures, 174–5
France, 4
Freedom, 149
Frege, G., 169
Future: reality of, 183–4; truth and, 177–80

Genteel Tradition at Bay, The, 237
'Genteel Tradition in American Philosophy, The,' 11–12
Given (the): consciousness and, 120; definition of, 66, 67–8, 118, 227; essences as, 65–9, 93; existence of, 58; significance of, 219
Goethe, J. W. von, 7
Good and evil, 189, 190–1, 193–4, 196, 207–8, 212

Goodness, 15, 17–19 passim, 105, 115, 189–90, 192, 194–5, 198–9, 213

Hallucination, 67
Happiness, 87
Harvard Monthly, 25
Harvard University, 25–7
Hedonism, 192, 195
Hegel, G. W. F., 17, 122, 173, 228
Henfrey, N., 228
Henze, D. F., 226
Herbart, J. F., 234
History, 9, 31
Hodgson, Shadsworth, 112
Holt, E. B., 26
Howgate, George, 221, 225
Hume, David, 10, 17–18, 50, 83, 150, 155, 192, 197, 198, 204–5
Husserl, E. G. A., 43, 128
Huxley, T. H., 112
'Hypostatic Ethics', 201
Hypostatic results, 109, 111

Idea of Christ in the Gospels, The (ICG), 239; quoted, 216
Idealism, 14, 19, 20, 53–4, 56, 128–9, 145, 153, 165
Idealistic monists, 161
Ideals, rationality and, 205–7
Identity across time, 102, 135, 150–1
Identity, virtual, of essences, 74–6, 90–1
Idler and His works, The, 234
Intelligence: artificial, 123, 219; pure, 212
Intelligible objects, 129–30
Intent, 68–9, 104–5; determination of objective, 121–4; intuition and, 116–21
Interpretations of Poetry and Religion (IPR), 14, 16, 225, 228
Intuition, 108–9, 113–16, 173; behaviour and, 92, 115, 121–2; intent and, 116–24; of essences, 51–2, 65–9, 71, 73, 76–7, 80, 82, 84–5, 90, 92, 108, 113, 116–19, 121, 143–4, 146–7, 168; of pictorial space, 140–2; of things, 67; pure, 210–12; spiritual life and, 210–12
Italy, 4

James, William, 5, 10, 14, 16–18 passim, 26, 104, 113, 125, 163, 201, 225, 234

Jeans, Sir James, 236
Johnson, W. E., 73

Kant, I., 7, 33, 68, 137, 141, 162
Kirkwood, M. M., 239
Knowledge, 16, 32–3, 47, 62, 104, 206; belief as, 52–3, 57, 63; definition of, 52, 85; symbolic, 143–4

Lachs, John, 10, 13, 232–3; and Shirley, 13, 221
Lamont, Corliss, 23
Lampoon, 25
Lamprecht, Stirling P., 235
Language, 89, 92, 102, 123, 220
Larrabee, H. A., 23
Last Puritan: A Memoir in the Form of a Novel, The, 12, 25, 27, quoted, 224
Lateral tension, 156, 161
Leibniz, G. W., 10, 161
Letters of George Santayana, The, 229, 234
Lewis, C. I., 236, 237
Life of Reason, The (LR), 5, 9, 13, 14, 20, 43, 125–32, 174, 188, 198, 205, 209–10, 225, 229; quoted, 128–9; *see also Reason in Art; Reason in Common Sense; Reason in Science*
'Literal and Symbolic Knowledge', 230
Location, 111
Locke, John, 10, 17–18, 23, 73, 76
Loeser, Charles, 26
Logic, 6
Lotze, R. H., 161
Lotze's System of Philosophy, 11, 26, 230
Lucretius, 7
Lyon, R. C., 221, 223

McTaggart, J. M. E., 180, 183, 236
Malcolm, N., 226
Materialism, 53, 110, 125, 219
Materialist philosophy, 4, 54, 125–32
Matter: essence characterizing, 80–1, 134; existence of, 49–51, 67, 130–1, belief in, 54–9, 61, 135–6, consciousness and, 41–2, 43, 44, 59, 106, doubted, 39–42, 45–6; habits of, 98–100; in *Life of Reason*, 125–32, 133; properties of, 134–8; realm of, 95–6, 151, 163, 179, 233; spirit's vision of, 143–7; spiritual attributes for, 150; substance and, 148, 151, 232–3

Mead, G. H., 236
Mechanistic theory, 105, 110, 112, 123, 219
Meinong, Alexius von, 45
Mental acts, 54–5, 61–2, 113, 117, 118–19, 122, 179
Mental development, 125–7
Mental facts, 138
Metaphor, 6
Metaphysics, 6, 8, 30, 135–6, 154, 159, 161
Mind: existence of, 32; nature of, 4, 95, 103–4, 107, 124; time and state of, 186
Moments: of spirit, 107, 111, 113–15, 117, 149, 150–1, 155, 159–60, 162, 179; of time, 177–8, natural, 154, 156–61, 171
Monadism, 162
Monism, 161–2, 172
Montague, W., 12
Moore, G. E., 27, 63, 72, 164, 169, 188–92, 194–5, 201, 224
Moral beliefs, 196
Moral essences, 119, 144, 189, 191–2, 212
Moral judgements, 190–3, 196–7, 198–9, 207–8
Moral philosophy, 188–91; *see also* Ethics
Moral relativism, 19, 201; *see also* Ethical relativism
Morality, 207; emotions and, 197–8; pre- and post-rational, 202, 209–10, 238; rational, 209–10; reason and, 197–208, 213; social norms and, 207–8
Munitz, M. K., 223
Munsterburg, Margaret, 225
Murray, Gilbert, 210
Mussolini, Benito, 29
My Host the World (HW), 239

Narveson, Jan, 239
Natural moments, 154, 156–61, 171
Natural philosophy, 133
Naturalism, 5, 15, 53, 59–60; ethical, 189
Nature: belief in, 59, 132–3; essences in, 71, 133–4, 143–5; knowledge of, 143–4; laws of, 96, 100–1, 149, 170
Nazism, 29

Nerve, failure of, 210
New Realism, The, 26
Newton, Sir Isaac, 133

Ontology, 4, 5, 6, 20, 30, 63, 128, 150, 219
Opinion, 85

Pain, 202–3, 238
Particularity, 93, 96, 126–7
Passmore, J., 221
'Penitent Art', 227, 228
Perception, 104, 131–2, 144
Persons and Places (PP), 21, 224, 229; quoted, 23–4
Pessimism, 17
Petrarch, 202–3
Phenomenology, 182
Philosophies of time, 182–6
Philosophy: analytical, 5; history of, 9; moral, 188–91, *see also* Ethics; natural, 133; political, 1, 2, 221
Philosophy, Santayana's: defects of, 220; importance of, 1–11, 220; nature and scope of, 7–9; revolution in, 6, 10
Philosophy of George Santayana, The (PGS), 198, 199, 222, 223, 227, 229–31 *passim,* 234, 238, 239; quoted, 109, 223
Physical facts: essences and, 144–7, 160; substance of, 149, 151–2
Physical Order and Moral Liberty (POML), 227–9 *passim,* 231, 233, 234, 238
Plato, 9, 10, 81, 99, 195, 209
Platonic realism, 27
Platonism, 4, 85, 87, 88, 129–30, 179, 192
Platonism and the Spiritual Life (PSL), 214, 228, 229, 238, 239
Pleasure, 194–5, 202–3
Poems, quoted, 8, 23
Poetic quietism, 15
Poetry, 7–8, 14, 16, 17
Political philosophy, 1, 2, 221
Popper, Karl, 226
Positivism, 183
Potentiality, 233
Pound, Ezra, 6
Pragmatism, 14, 16, 113, 128–9, 132, 169, 183, 184

Prior, A. N., 235
Progress, 17–19
Psyche, 95–101; definition of, 99–100, 106–7, 214; mechanistic theory of, 105, 110, 112, 123, 219; spirit and, 95–124, 219; tropes as, 96–8, 102–4
Psychology, 6, 60, 78, 103–4, 123, 127, 182, 219
Ptolemy, 133, 143
Pure Being, 75, 78–81
Puritanism, 16
Purpose, 104–6, 112, 115; *see also* Aims; Desire; Intent

Quietism, 15–16, 214
Quine, W. V. O., 123, 221

Rational aims, 202–6
Rational ethics, 209–10
Rationalists, 198
Rationality, 45, 126, 198–200, 202, 205–7; *see also* Reason
Realism, 20, 27, 145
Reality, 40, 44, 51, 70, 122, 129–30, 137, 149, 219, 230; past and future, 179, 183–5, 237
Realm of Essence, The (RE), xii, 78, 173, 226–8 *passim,* 230, 239; quoted, 222
Realm of Matter, The (RM), xii, 132, 136, 138, 177, 228, 229, 232–6 *passim;* quoted, 134, 135–6, 139–40, 142, 143
Realm of Spirit, The (RS), xii, 177, 214, 228, 229, 231, 239
Realm of Truth, The (RT), xii, 165, 170, 172, 177, 189, 228, 230, 231, 235, 237
Realms, 167
Realms of Being (RB), 5, 9, 12, 96, 136, 138, 145, 153, 155, 174, 227–36 *passim,* 239; quoted, 75, 86–7, 103, 134, 135–6, 139–40, 142, 143, 154, 176–7, 180, 181, 186, 187, 189, 230, 233
Reason, 16, 19–20, 109, 130; beliefs and, 206–7; cognitive and practical, 205–6; definitions of, 15, 198–9, 201, 207; emotions and, 198–203; ethics and, 197–208, 209–10, 212–14, 238; life of, 189, 205, 209, 211–12, 214; morality and, 197–208, 213; spirit and, 209–13
Reason in Art (LRIV), 228, 237

Reason in Common Sense (LRI), 20, 60, 129, 223, 229, 231, 237–9 *passim*; quoted, 127, 131–2, 200, 202–3
Reason in Science (LRV), 20, 231, 235, 237–9 *passim*; quoted, 200–1
Reductionism, 218
Relations: between essences, 48–9, 74–6, 79, 82, 91, 93, 115, 158–9, 171, 173–5; contrastive, 83, 86, 154, 173, 174; external, 40, 42, 45–6, 58, 71, 116, 137, 158–9, 161, 236, and internal, 82–6, 93, 113–15, 171, 219; holistic, 83–6, 142, 154; temporal, 42, 49, 137, 152–4
Relativism, ethical, 19, 193–6, 201, 204, 220
Relativity, 237
Religion, 14, 24–5, 28, 217; *see also* Christianity
Revolution, 6, 10
Richards, I. A., 17
Rome, 28
Ross, J. J., 227
Ross, W. D., 193, 210
Royce, Josiah, 5, 26, 161, 163, 225, 234, 238
Russell, Bertrand, 5, 6, 10, 20, 27, 45, 63, 72, 84, 141, 166, 169, 189–91 *passim*, 221–2, 224, 236
Russell, Lord (J. F. Stanley), 27
Ryle, Gilbert, 103–4, 109–10

Saint of imagination, 215
Sanborn, Thomas Parker, 25
Sanity, 15, 223
Santayana, Augustin (George's father), 21–4
Santayana, George: biography of, 21–9; family of, 21–5; works: bibliography, 222, chronology, 11–13; *see also* individual titles
Saunders, J. T., 226
Scepticism, 30–46, 62–3, 218; absolute, 63; return from, 47–52
Scepticism and Animal Faith (SAF), 5, 9, 30–1, 35–6, 44, 47–50, 132, 206, 222, 226, 228–31 *passim*, 233–5 *passim*; quoted, 32–4, 37–41, 51–2, 55–6, 57, 164
Schlick, M., 150
Schilpp, P. A., 12
Schopenhauer, A., 9, 10, 88, 136, 239

Schwartz, B., 12
Science, 145, 146, 206, 219
Sculpture, 89
Self, 49–51, 56; and psyche, 101–2, 107
Self-determination, 149
Self-existence, isolated, 46
Selfishness and spirituality, 214–15
Sense of Beauty, The (SB), 5, 13–14, 16, 87, 90, 228
Sense-data, 73, 131, 227
Sets, 167, 235
Shelley, P. B., 224
Shock, 49, 51
Smart, J. J. C., 231, 236
Smythies, 231
Social norms, morality and, 207–8
Socrates, 239
Socratic method, 191
Soliloquies in England and Later Soliloquies (SE), 239
Solipsism, 32, 62; of the present moment, 34–6, 38, 45, 218; romantic, 33–4, 201
'Some Meanings of the Word "Is"', 228
Some Turns of Thought in Modern Philosophy: Five Essays (STTMP), 229, 234
Soul, 99
Space: centre of, 139–40, 142–3; location in, 111; pictorial, 138–42; private and public, 140–1; real, 138, 140, 142, 152, 155–7; time and, 70–2, 138, 148–9, 152 156–7
Spatial essences, 141–2, 144, 154–5
Spinoza, B., 9, 136, 161, 192, 228, 231
Spirit, 17, 99; acts of, 101, 103, 116, 143, 152; essence of, 108; existence and, 215; importance of, 10, 112–13; impotence of, 109–12, 214–15; intuition and, 210–12; matter and, 143–7, 150, 219; moments of, 107, 111, 113–15, 117, 149, 150–1, 155, 159–60, 162, 179; psyche and, 95–124, 219; realm of, 95–6, 104, 106–8, 163, 211; reason and, 209–13; time and, 153
Spiritual life, 189, 209–17
Spirituality, 219; Christian, 217; definition of, 215–16; selfishness and, 214–15

Sprigge, T. L. S., 235, 239
Stanley, John Francis (Lord Russell), 27
Stanley of Alderney, Lady, 22–3
Stevenson, C. L., 205, 238
Stoicism, 8, 210
Strawson, P. F., 123
Strong, Charles, 26
Sturgis, Susana, 22, 24–5
Sturgis family, 21–2
Style, Santayana's, 2, 6–7, 23, 138, 218, 220, 221
Substance, 54–9, 148–62; definitions of, 145, 150–1; matter and, 148, 151, 232–3; properties of, 134–8, 149; through time, 152–6, 159–62
Sullivan, Celestine J., Jnr, 222
Superstition, 138
'Symbolic and Literal Knowledge', 235
'Synthesis and Memory, On', 227
'System in Lectures', 20, 115

Taylor, A. E., 231
Taylor, Charles, 105
Taylor, Richard, 182
Teleology, 104–5
Thales, 133
Thought, 146–7, 201, 220; verbal, 123
Three Philosophical Poets (TPP), quoted, 7–8
'Three Proofs of Realism', 226, 230
Time: change and, 178–81, 182–5; essences and, 93, 141, 144, 154–5, 180–1; existence and, 178–80, 185–6, 236–7; identity across, 102, 135, 150–1; moments of, 177–8, natural, 154, 156–61, 179; philosophies of, 182–6; real, 138, 152, 156, 182; reality and, 179, 183–5, 237; relations through, 42, 49, 137, 152–4; sentimental, 144, 180, 181; space and, 70–2, 138, 148–9, 152, 156–7; specious, 180, 181, 186; spirit and, 153; substance through, 152–6,

159–62; truth and, 176–87; see also Truth, eternal
Tolerance, 193, 195–6
Tropes, 96–8, 101–5
Truth: contingent, 172, 173–4; conventional, 170; depsychologizing of, 163, 169; dramatic, 170, 180; empirical, 183; essences and, 163–75; eternal, 163, 165, 176–7, 179, 187; existence and, 172–5; facts not, 170–1; literal, 132, 167–8, 169, 180; moments of spirit and, 114; realm of, 95, 163, 166, 171, 233; symbolic, 132, 168–70 passim, 180; theories of, 168, 206; time and, 176–87

'Ultimate Religion', 238
United States of America: hostility to Santayana in, 28; philosophy in, 4–5
Unity, 75, 77, 161
Universalizability, 194–5
Universals, 72–3, 81, 96, 127, 169
Universe, 161, 166
'Unknowable, The', 12

Value: absolute, 190; qualities, 189–97, 213, 220, reason in, 197–208

Walker Fellowship, 26
Watling, J., 52
Watson, John B., 103
Wenkart, Henny, 233–4
Whitehead, A. N., 5, 9, 115, 145, 150–1, 156, 157, 159, 162, 185, 219, 237
Williams, D. C., 236
Wilson, Douglas L., 221
Winds of Doctrine (WD), 20, 189, 224, 237–9 passim; quoted, 160
Wisdom, J., 226
Wittgenstein, L., 33, 61, 86, 173, 183